31/10/05

The Predicament of Postmodern Theology

B

THE PREDICAMENT OF POSTMODERN THEOLOGY

Radical Orthodoxy or Nihilist Textualism?

Gavin Hyman

Westminster John Knox Press
LOUISVILLE • LONDON

All rights reserved. No part of this book may be reproduced or transmitted in any form or by any means, electronic or mechanical, including photocopying, recording, or by any information storage or retrieval system, without permission in writing from the publisher. For information, address Westminster John Knox Press, 100 Witherspoon Street, Louisville, Kentucky 40202-1396.

Cover design by Mark Abrams
Interior design by Sharon Adams

First edition
Published by Westminster John Knox Press
Louisville, Kentucky

This book is printed on acid-free paper that meets the American National Standards Institute Z39.48 standard. ∞

PRINTED IN THE UNITED STATES OF AMERICA

02 03 04 05 06 07 08 09 10 — 10 9 8 7 6 5 4 3 2

Library of Congress Cataloging-in-Publication Data is on file at the Library of Congress, Washington, D.C.

ISBN 0-664-22366-4

For my parents

Contents

Acknowledgments

My intellectual debts are manifold, but my chief indebtedness is to Graham Ward, who supervised the writing of this work in its earlier incarnation as a doctoral dissertation. His supervisions were always challenging and stimulating, and my work has been immeasurably improved as a result of them. I am grateful for his intellectual generosity in the midst of disagreement. For his constant encouragement, I am also deeply grateful to Don Cupitt, who gave generously of his retirement time and offered countless criticisms and suggestions. I am further indebted to Gerard Loughlin and George Pattison, who examined this work in its doctoral form and made numerous helpful comments.

I should also like to thank my fellow graduate students at Peterhouse, Cambridge, for numerous philosophical and theological conversations that have left their imprint on these pages. I especially thank John N. Clarke, Guy Collins, Laurence Hemming, Michael Mack, and Biagio Mazzi. I am also grateful to Jeffrey Hensley for numerous conversations on radical orthodoxy, conducted both in person and electronically. I must further thank John D. Caputo and Carl

Raschke for making copies of unpublished papers available to me. Thanks are also due to Philip Law of Westminster John Knox Press, for guiding me through the publication process.

I thank the following for permission to reproduce material previously published elsewhere: Fergus Kerr, O.P. editor of *New Blackfriars,* for parts of chapter 3 published in "Hick and Loughlin on Disputes and Frameworks," *New Blackfriars* 79 (1998): 391–405; and Oxford University Press, for sections of chapter 5, published as "John Milbank and Nihilism: A Metaphysical (Mis)Reading?" in *Literature and Theology* 14 (2000): 430–43.

I am most grateful to the Humanities Research Board of the British Academy for awarding me a research studentship, without which the research for this book would not have been possible. I am also grateful to the Department of Religious Studies at the University of Lancaster, for appointing me to a lectureship, and to all my colleagues there for their support and friendship.

Finally, but most important, I should like to thank my parents, Graham and Barbara Hyman. I am deeply grateful to them for their ceaseless love and support. My debts to them extend far beyond the bounds of this book, which I nevertheless dedicate to them.

Introduction

At the "beginning" of a new millennium, we seem to have arrived at the "end" of time. This end of time would perhaps be more accurately characterized as a time of endings. More than ever before, we live at the end of the world, or at least at the end of the world as we have known it. The end of the world brings with it the end of ideology and dogma; the end of art; the end of the planned system, of Marxism, socialism, and the welfare state.[1] It brings with it also the closure of the book, the end of history, the disappearance of the self, and the death of God.[2] With the death of God comes the end of "Beginnings" as well as the end of "Ends." Without a beginning and without an end, everything is collapsed into the "superabundant virtual present."[3] Nothing is hidden and nothing is to come; everything is both spatially and temporally *present.* When all is presence and everything is present, then everything is realized. Or so it would appear.

But to claim that everything is present is to repress that which is absent. And to proclaim the end of the (old) world is simultaneously to inaugurate the beginning of a (new) world. In this new world, the time of endings seems itself to end, as that which is repressed returns, that which was thought dead is resurrected, and that which was thought to have ended begins all over again. But in this strange new world, that which returns, that which is resurrected, and that which begins again is not merely a return of what went before. On the contrary, that which returns, returns *differently*, is resurrected *differently*, and begins *differently*, for at the end of the world things can never be the same again. This strange new world is constitutive of our contemporary condition: the condition of postmodernity.[4]

Nowhere is this strange condition more evident than in religion.[5] For if religion was thought to have ended, there is a sense in which it has also returned. And yet it is evident that if religion is returning, it is returning *differently*. The religion that returns is not quite the same as the religion that prevailed before. This paradox has been discussed by Gianni Vattimo. He says that today, "religion comes to be experienced as a *return*. In religion, something that we had thought irrevocably forgotten is made present again, a dormant trace is reawakened, a wound re-opened, the repressed returns."[6] The reasons for this return are many and various. Vattimo identifies two in particular: first, the sense of new and unprecedented impending global threats (such as fear of atomic war, prolifera-tion of atomic and other weapons, risks to the ecology of the planet, genetic engi-neering); and second, the fear of losing the meaning of existence, and fear of the "profound boredom which seems inevitably to accompany consumerism."[7]

But if these are two principal motivations for the return of religion (and doubt-less there are many others), then this return is itself made possible by the "end" of the modern prohibition of religion. The situation is rendered even more complex, however, when it is realized that the end of the prohibition of religion coincides with the end of the very thing that many seek in their return to religion, namely, a secure foundation or fundamentalism. Out of this situation arises a contradic-tion that Vattimo characterizes as follows: "The breakdown of the philosophical prohibition of religion . . . coincides with the dissolution of the great systems that accompanied the development of science, technology and modern social organi-zation, but thereby also with the breakdown of all fundamentalism—that is, of what, so it seems, popular consciousness is looking for in its return to religion."[8] In other words, if the return to religion is made possible by the end of founda-tionalism, is it not the case that religion is itself foundational?

In Anglo-American Christian theology, there have been two primary responses to this contradiction or paradox that is intrinsic to our contemporary condition. The first response claims that the "end" of foundationalism brings with it also the "end" of theology, whereas the second response, on the contrary, claims that the "end" of foundationalism actually opens the way for the "return" of theology.[9] The former response originates from the 1980s and was developed primarily by Don Cupitt in Great Britain and by Mark C. Taylor in the United States. Their respective projects are quite distinct, although they share some "family resemblances" in that they both write within the post-Nietzschean space of the death of God and the postmodern space of the end of metanarratives. With the death of God, all foundations dissolve, and all-encompassing grand narratives subside. Taylor says that God functions within a semiotic system as the secure base on which everything else rests: "When this foundation crumbles or becomes inaccessible, signs are left to float freely on a sea that has no shores."[10] Reality becomes radically linguistic, with the result that all meaning gets its sense within language, there being no access to any extralinguistic reality.

In this new linguistic reality, Christian theology, as traditionally understood, also comes to an end. Hence, Taylor has described his work as "a/theology," and Cupitt has recently described his work as "post-Christian." For both, theology must become postecclesiastical, post-Christian, and posttheological. Both remain concerned, however, with questions that may vaguely be described as "religious." Taylor says, "Even when appearing resolutely secular, twentieth-century culture is haunted by religion. . . . Religion often is most effective where it is least obvious."[11] And Cupitt continues to champion a post-Christian form of religious practice.[12] But if there is a return of religion for Cupitt and Taylor, it is a very "weak" return, and if, as we have said, religion returns differently, Cupitt and Taylor emphazise the difference. Gerard Loughlin has referred to this version of postmodern a/theology as "textualist but finally nihilist."[13] In this context, he uses the term *nihilism* pejoratively, whereas both Cupitt and Taylor have affirmed it as an apposite term for their respective projects.[14] In what follows, therefore, I follow Loughlin in describing this form of postmodern a/theology as "nihilist textualism."

The other principal way in which the return of religion has manifested itself in our contemporary condition is to be found in the recuperation of an orthodox Christian theology, a recuperation that is nonetheless profoundly informed by the insights of postmodern thought. The genealogy for this version of postmodern theology may be traced back through such figures as Rowan Williams, George Lindbeck, Nicholas Lash, Hans Frei, and Donald Mackinnon. Nevertheless, it was given its most influential and significant expression during the 1990s, particularly in the work of the British theologian John Milbank and also in the work of Graham Ward, Catherine Pickstock, and Gerard Loughlin. For these thinkers, the end of modernity does not merely give rise to the textualist free-for-all of postmodern nihilism. They maintain that such a move is insufficiently radical because this form of postmodernism is merely the logical culmination or apotheosis of modernity.[15] Instead, they seek to recover premodern modes of thought, in particular premodern modes of *theological* thought. For only theology can guard against nihilism, which they claim is a form of necrophilia—a philosophy of death.[16]

Here, too, however, theology "returns differently." For although they seek a recovery of premodern orthodox theology, these thinkers recognize that this must be a recovery of something *different* in our contemporary condition. On the one hand, they embrace the antifoundationalism, the narrativism, and what Milbank calls the "linguistic idealism" of postmodernism.[17] On the other hand, they return to theology in a much stronger sense than the nihilist textualists, for they attempt to recover the medieval paradigm whereby theology absorbs and makes possible all other discourses. In other words, theology returns as a metanarrative which (to use Milbank's word) "positions" all other narratives, discourses, and disciplines completely and without reserve. This version of postmodern theology has been variously named—"postmodern Augustinianism," "conservative postmodern theology." and "postmodern orthodoxy," to cite but a few. In what follows, however, I refer to it as "radical orthodoxy," the term by which it has generally come to be known over the last few years. This baptism or "naming" was publicly confirmed with the publication in 1999 of a collection of essays titled *Radical Orthodoxy: A New Theology*.[18]

It may be said that radical orthodoxy and nihilist textualism provide two radically antithetical theological responses to our postmodern predicament. What is particularly striking, however, is that these two responses have largely failed to confront and engage each other. In particular, radical orthodoxy makes serious and challenging criticisms of postmodern nihilism to which the nihilist textualist writers have manifestly failed to respond. Indeed, not only nihilist textualism but also other forms of modern and liberal theology have failed to take up Milbank's gauntlet. Although many theologians have been quick to distance themselves from the radical orthodox enterprise, an extended and thorough critique of the project has yet to appear.

It is the primary aim of this book to disrupt this absence by providing a rigorous critique of radical orthodoxy from a postmodern perspective. This perspective has something in common with the nihilist textualism of Cupitt and especially Taylor. It will become clear, however, that the process of "out-narration" is not unidirectional, and that radical orthodoxy itself allows one to perceive many deficiencies in the projects of nihilist textualism. In particular, it will be seen that nihilist textualism is, in many respects, insufficiently *post*modern. I therefore point toward a third postmodern disposition, a "fictional nihilism" that is *neither* the radical orthodoxy of John Milbank *nor* the nihilist textualism of Don Cupitt. A subsidiary, though equally necessary, aim of this book is to provide an analysis of the relationship of these two versions of postmodern theology to each other, to the postmodern condition out of which they both, in different ways, emerge, and to the philosophical epoch of modernity against which they both, in different ways, react. It is only out of such an analysis that a properly informed evaluation can emerge.

In chapter 1, I provide an account of the cultural and philosophical condition of postmodernity, drawing in particular on the work of Fredric Jameson, Perry Anderson, and Jean-François Lyotard. I then discuss and summarize the two main theological responses to such a condition, taking Don Cupitt as a paradigm of nihilist textualism and John Milbank as a paradigm of radical orthodoxy. I show that whereas Cupitt is much more willing to embrace this cultural condition, together with its implications for theology, Milbank embraces it only insofar as it allows for the return of theology. Once theology has returned, Milbank then provides a theological critique of the very postmodernism that made his theology possible. Milbank's attitude to postmodernism is therefore much more ambivalent than Cupitt's. I suggest that the differing evaluations of postmodernism on the parts of Cupitt and Milbank cannot be understood apart from their respective evaluations of modernity, a discussion I turn to in chapter 2.

Whereas it is often thought that modernity began somewhere around the sixteenth century, particularly with the philosophy of René Descartes, I consider the work of Hans Urs von Balthasar and other, more recent scholars (including those of radical orthodoxy) to show how many aspects of Cartesian philosophy are inconceivable without certain theological innovations in the thirteenth and fourteenth centuries on the part of such theologians as John Duns Scotus. If the logic of Scotist thought was manifested in Descartes's philosophy, then it reached its culmination in the philosophy of Immanuel Kant. I show how this "modernist" philosophical tradition is given contemporary expression in the work of liberal theologians such as John Hick. Furthermore, I show how Cupitt's postmodernism emerged organically and progressively out of a similar liberal theology that he previously espoused. In this way, it can be seen that nihilist textualism essentially stands in a relationship of *continuity* with modernity, even if it is shown that the logic of modernity must ultimately subvert itself. In contrast, radical orthodoxy is emphatically *dis*continuous with modernity, insisting that the project of modernity is itself a logical outworking of the fundamentally secular and hence "heretical" moves of Duns Scotus. Insofar as postmodernism is a (continuous) exacerbation of modernity, it, too, is fundamentally secular and heretical, and both modernity and postmodernity must be left behind in favor of theology. But insofar as postmodernism interrogates and criticizes modernity, this aspect may be embraced by Milbank as an ally for his cause. Thus, the respective stances of Cupitt and Milbank toward postmodernism can be understood only in terms of these thinkers' antithetical evaluations of modernity.

In chapter 3, I consider the question of why Cupitt has failed to confront the challenge presented to his work by radical orthodoxy. I argue that he is ultimately unable to address the challenge because his project is located within a realist/anti-realist framework that is a manifestation of the dualism of modernity. This means that any viewpoint or narrative that lies outside this framework is reduced to nothing or is distorted by being subsumed into a framework it refuses. I show how Cupitt follows the latter strategy, insisting that radical orthodox theologians are "non-realists in disguise." The "otherness" of radical orthodoxy as an-"other" theology is thereby destroyed, and the essence of its viewpoint is severely distorted, for Cupitt insists on interpreting radical orthodoxy in terms of a framework that radical orthodoxy itself refuses. The result is that Cupitt is unable to identify and confront the true essence of its challenge. I argue, therefore, that if a critique of radical orthodoxy is to be effective, it must move beyond and leave behind the realist/anti-realist framework altogether.

I undertake such a critique in chapter 4, where I again take John Milbank's work as a paradigm of radical orthodox theology. My criticisms here are of two main types. First, I argue that Milbank's absolute conception of the theological metanarrative is itself undesirable in its inevitable effects. I show how it gives rise to a dualistic opposition between theology and nihilism, and that this, in turn, gives rise to a whole series of derivative dualisms. I show how the initial dualism gives rise to a violent warfare between theology and nihilism as well as to violent readings and treatments of of all other, subsidiary narratives. I also suggest that Milbank's metanarrative resists the "mastery" of modernist metanarratives only with difficulty. These characteristics are particularly problematic because much of Milbank's rhetoric depends on his contention that (his) theology is the only metanarrative that can resist dualism, violence, and mastery.

Second, I argue that Milbank's absolute metanarrative is, in any case, inherently unstable, and that it repeatedly deconstructs itself from within. I suggest that Milbank can resist mastery only by invoking a fictionalist (or nihilist?) supplement that cannot be derived solely from the theological metanarrative itself. The very existence of such a supplement undermines the status of Milbank's metanarrative *as* an absolute metanarrative. I demonstrate that in Milbank's project, the Christian (meta)narrative is itself "positioned" by Milbank's own (meta)narrative, which is again distinct from the Christian narrative. Furthermore, when Milbank provides an account of the way in which his (meta)narrative "out-narrates" other (meta)narratives, he thereby invokes a "meta-metanarrative" that converges remarkably with the metanarrative of nihilism he is so concerned to reject. In this way, Milbank's absolute metanarrative appears to deconstruct itself from within, for when every metanarrative is positioned by a higher level of metanarrative, the very concept of metanarrative is itself destabilized. It seems that, in postmodernism, a metanarrative is as impossible as it is unavoidable.

Having criticized radical orthodoxy from a postmodern perspective, I reverse the direction of confrontation in chapter 5. Here, I defend postmodern nihilism from Milbank's virulent attacks and (mis)interpretations. I distinguish between a metaphysical nihilism and a fictional nihilism and argue that Milbank's "out-narration" of nihilism is directed solely at a metaphysical form of nihilism. This form of nihilism espouses a metaphysics of the nothing, the nothing that *is*. As such, it is, as Milbank claims, a disguised form of positivism and consequently refuses all nihilistic implications. I claim that nihilism is properly accomplished only with a weakening of its own ontological status: when it is recognized that nihilism is no more than a fiction. The fictionalism that nihilism ascribes to everything else must ultimately be ascribed even to itself. Furthermore, I argue that Nietzsche himself would be better interpreted as a fictional nihilist, and that any attempt to read him in a metaphysical fashion does undue violence to his texts. I argue that it is precisely such a fictional nihilism that Milbank fails to confront. Insofar as postmodern nihilists are themselves fictional nihilists, the metaphysical nihilism that Milbank out-narrates is, in effect, a straw man. In the face of a properly accomplished fictional nihilism, Milbank's criticisms would appear to subside.

Finally, in chapter 6, I consider what a writing of fictional nihilism might look like. First, I argue that Cupitt's nihilism is insufficiently fictional. The difficulty here is that Cupitt espouses what is essentially a *modern* postmodernism, in which the "other" is repressed. When the "other" is eradicated, everything is present and nothing is hidden. This is the modern utopia of the presence of the present. Without an "other," a "principle of travel," Cupitt's narrative becomes static, stable, and insufficiently reflexive. Cupitt wants to "overcome" reflexivity rather than embrace it. The result of this is that he appears to lapse into what he himself describes as an "obsolete metaphysics." Mark C. Taylor rectifies Cupitt's neglect in this regard. Constantly aware of the "other" that always returns, Taylor is sent on an endless voyage of exile; for the "other" ruptures every system, dislocates every location, and refuses every habitation. Taylor therefore passes over every location and is consequently exiled to the nonplace of nowhere—the desert.

It is my suggestion, however, that such a movement is insufficiently embodied. Refusing and passing over every location, Taylor exiles himself to literally nowhere. I suggest that although we should follow Taylor in his movement of perpetual departure, we should *move through* locations, traditions, and habitations rather than merely *pass over* them. I suggest that such a movement is exemplified in the writings of Michel de Certeau. For although de Certeau departs on an "endless exodus of discourse," he nevertheless *moves through* the finite, through narratives, particularities, bodies, and locations. Although all discourses must ultimately be left behind in the name of the "other," they can be properly left behind only if they have first been inhabited. I also resist the attempts of some theologians to "domesticate" de Certeau's writings in favor of a more orthodox theological reading. For although theology, as a heterological discourse par excellence, is a narrative that de Certeau wants to wander through, his heterological concern for the "other" means that theology itself must also, ultimately, be left behind.

I suggest, therefore, that Michel de Certeau shows us not so much the way forward as the way to "get lost" in our postmodern condition. He narrates an endless exodus of discourse that may serve as a paradigm for a writing of fictional nihilism. His writings exemplify the a/logic of the neither/nor that rejects the either/or of both radical orthodoxy and nihilist textualism. In the conclusion, I point toward a third territory for postmodern theology, in which theology repeatedly "returns" to haunt the movement of perpetual departure. In this sense, we can never be done with theology. But this return cannot be absolute, and the movement of perpetual departure can no longer be anchored in a theological origin. To be anchored in this way is to return to theology as metanarrative, a return that is as undesirable as it is impossible. Understood in this sense, theology must always also "depart."

Having now completed the prelude or introduction to these particular wanderings, we must now attempt the impossible: that is, we must now attempt to begin at the beginning.

Chapter 1
(A/) Theology and the Postmodern Condition

... As it was in the beginning.... But how was it in the beginning? What was the beginning? What does it mean to speak of the beginning? Can we go back to the beginning? *Can we ever begin at the beginning?*

In our contemporary condition, the concept of the beginning has become inherently problematic. People no longer know where to begin. In a world in which linear time has collapsed and history has "ended," the traditional narrative structure of "beginning," "middle," and "end" has become destabilized. The beginning, middle, and end, or the past, present, and future, have been collapsed into a "superabundant present." The past is no longer simply that which has passed but that which is with us still, as the present sensibility embraces nostalgia, pastiche, and *bricolage* and thereby unites the present with the (present) past. Similarly, the future is no longer simply that which is to come but that which has already arrived and which is with us now. The present condition cannot imagine anything that is beyond itself and so unites the present with the (present) future.[1]

Without foundations, there is no primary origin, no absolute beginning;

everything has already started; everything is mutually founded by something else. The world is understood in terms of dependent co-origination, as Gautama Buddha would say (for now the distinction between East and West has also been destabilized),[2] and as Jean-François Lyotard would say, no phrase is the first.[3] For some, this "superabundant present" embodies the fulfillment of a long-held desire. For others, the present condition becomes merely present again, as they look, with hope, for a better future that is "other" than the present and that is yet to come. But whether one wants to embrace or to reject the present condition, that irrepressible question returns to haunt us: where to begin? The concept of the beginning has become inherently problematic. People no longer know where to begin.

Ludwig Wittgenstein encapsulated this difficulty with characteristic brevity when he said, "It is so difficult to find the *beginning*. Or, better: it is difficult to begin at the beginning."[4] Commenting on this, Gerard Loughlin has said that Wittgenstein "did not mean that it is difficult to begin at the beginning and not *further on*; he meant it is difficult to begin at the beginning and not try to go *further back*."[5] In other words, to try to go further back to an unfounded beginning that founds and is the beginning of everything else is an illusion. The beginning can only be where we already are: in the middle. As Jacques Derrida puts it, "what is put into question is precisely the quest for a rightful beginning, an absolute point of departure, a principal responsibility."[6] In which case, "We must begin *wherever we are* . . . in a text where we already believe ourselves to be."[7] To begin where we are, then, is to begin at the beginning. But this, of course, is to raise the question of where we are now, or where we believe ourselves to be. I reply to this question not with an argument or with a demonstration, however, but simply with a declaration of belief, namely, that the cultural condition within which we now find ourselves would best be characterized as "postmodern."

In this chapter, I want to begin at the beginning with a discussion of where we are—in the middle—in the postmodern. I discuss where, when, and how postmodernism "began," what it means for our cultural condition to be postmodern, and some of the implications postmodernism has for philosophy. I then turn to the question of what it means for theology to be postmodern, looking at the two major theological responses to our postmodern condition: postmodern "nihilist textualist" theology and postmodern "radical orthodox" theology. We shall see that whereas nihilist textualist theology embraces and celebrates our postmodern condition as simultaneously a consummation and a radical questioning of theology, the response of radical orthodoxy to postmodernism is more ambivalent. Initially embracing the postmodern as providing a clearing for the recovery of a credal and patristic theology that, it claims, was lost sight of after the late Middle Ages, it then "begins" with this theology as a standpoint from which it radically questions and criticizes the very postmodernism that cleared the way for its own return. This ambivalence means that radical orthodoxy begins to move away from the postmodern toward the postsecular, even if this moving away is never quite completed, so that it becomes both postmodern and not postmodern simultaneously. But now, let me begin with a political gesture that declares my own hand. Let me begin at the beginning; where we already are; in our present condition; in the postmodern.[8]

Postmodernism: A Cultural
and Philosophical (Hi)Story

What is the "postmodern"? Perhaps the most obvious (and slightly banal) answer is that it is literally *post*-modern; it is something that succeeds, rejects, overthrows, or transcends the modern. *Postmodernism* is thus a negative and parasitic term that depends on the negation of something else for its self-definition. This negativity and parasitism empty the term of any weight or substance. It is the *post*-script to something else and has no content or definition of its own. As such, it is less "real" than that which preceded it. In Margaret Atwood's novel *Cat's Eye* (1990), Elaine Risley bemoans the prevalence of "post this, post that. Everything is post these day, as if we're all just a footnote to something earlier that was real enough to have a name of its own."[9] Postmodernism, then, "begins" with the modern and cannot be understood in isolation from it.

Fredric Jameson says that most varieties of postmodernism "emerge as specific reactions against the established forms of high modernism, against this or that dominant high modernism which conquered the university, the museum, the art gallery network and the foundations."[10] One result of this is that there will be at least as many postmodernisms as there were modernisms, as the former emerge only as specific reactions against the latter: "That obviously does not make the job of describing postmodernism as a coherent thing any easier, since the unity of the impulse—if it has one—is given not in itself but in the very modernism it seeks to displace."[11] If this is the case, then we are called to consider the nature of the relationship between postmodernism and modernity. In what way does the postmodern succeed, reject, overthrow, or transcend the modern? This, in turn, leads us to inquire into the meaning of the "modern."

A more comprehensive answer to this question is deferred until chapter 2, where I identify some of the chief characteristics of the modern, particularly as they relate to theology. For the moment, however, I provisionally (and inevitably inadequately) characterize the modern as the desire for an all-encompassing mastery of reality by rational and/or scientific means. It may be said that this desire was most fully incarnated in the speculative metasystem of G. W. F. Hegel. Ben Quash, for instance, has spoken of Hegel's system as "the epitome of modernity's quest for absolute knowledge" and as "the icon of modernity's titanic aspirations."[12] But Hegel's was not the only manifestation of the quest for mastery. This modern desire was an infectious one that was disseminated across numerous cultures and disciplines and articulated by diverse thinkers. But in whatever guise this desire was manifested, it was always marked by the trace of an exclusion. This is because in order for this mastery to be accomplished, the system itself had to exclude, expel, or negate that which was deemed to fall outside it, namely (more often than not), the nonrational or nonscientific. This was the great paradox of the modern desire for mastery: that in its quest for universal and totalizing comprehension, its system was obliged to *exclude* or *repress* that which lay outside it, thereby calling its universal and total comprehensiveness into question. This paradox instituted an inherent instability into the modern project itself, not only because the quest for mastery appeared to undermine itself in the very process of its own articulation but also because that which was excluded or repressed was always liable to return to destabilize the system. At the heart of modernity, therefore, lies an irrepressible question: "Does the repressed return to subvert the System?"[13]

One of Sigmund Freud's fundamental psychological notions was that of the repressed. The "repressed" is that which the psyche desires to expel or eradicate in order to avoid "unpleasure." But for Freud, the important point was that the repressed is not actually eradicated but is banished to the realm of the unconscious, whence it is liable to reappear or "return" in, for instance, dreams or hysterical symptoms.[14] Similarly, it may be said that modernity's "other," that which it attempts to negate, is not finally abolished but only repressed and is liable to return to call the "presence" of modernity into question. In this sense, we may provisionally characterize the postmodern as the return of the "other" that modernity sought to repress. As such, postmodernism cracks modernity's mirror of identity, rationality, and mastery. It inhabits the borders and margins of the modern, continually haunting, questioning, and disrupting it. Thus, it may be said that the postmodern is not something that comes *after* the writing of modernity but is rather *always already* hiding in between its lines. This further indicates that the postmodern cannot be isolated or separated from the modern, on which it is parasitically dependent. For postmodernism does not so much "react against" the modern as bring to light the paradoxes and fissures within modernity itself, which the latter attempts to conceal. This goes some way to explaining why, as we have already observed, postmodernism has never acquired a distinctive name of its own but has always been named merely in terms of that which it is not.

Furthermore, it is for this reason that commentators have often resisted speaking of postmodernism "replacing" the modern, as if the two terms were the names of distinct periods of time. Rather, commentators have often preferred to speak of the modern and the postmodern as two contrasting "sensibilities" that may, and perhaps necessarily, coexist. Lyotard, for instance, refers to modernity as a "tradition," insisting that "modernity is not an era in thought, but rather a mode (this is the Latin origin of the word) of thought, of utterances, of sensibility."[15] The corollary of this is that we are never entirely finished with the modern. Even in the midst of our postmodern condition, within which the "end of modernity" is frequently proclaimed, modernity never comes to a final end; for in interrogating the modern, postmodernism remains indebted to it, in and through that very act of interrogation. This is why Derrida has always insisted on distinguishing between the "end" and the "closure." For although he writes of the closure of metaphysics and of logocentrism, he has always been careful *not* to say that they have ended. For instance, in the context of a discussion of "metaphysico-theological" notions, he says that "it is not a question of 'rejecting' these notions; they are necessary and, at least at present, nothing is conceivable for us without them. . . . The age of the sign is essentially theological. Perhaps it will never *end.* Its historical *closure* is, however, outlined."[16] It may be said, therefore, that post-modernism performs the "closure" of a modernity that never "ends."

I shall now identify some of the various and diverse manifestations of this "per-formance," as they have surfaced in contemporary culture in recent years. To this end, I particularly draw on Perry Anderson's book *The Origins of Postmodernity* (1998).[17] In it, Anderson provides what David Bromwich calls "the best short account that has yet appeared of the uses of the word 'Post-Modern' and the pro-grammes the idea has served."[18] Anderson traces the first use of the word back to the 1930s, when it was used as an aesthetic category in the world of Hispanic lit-erary criticism. The term *postmodernismo* was coined by Federico de Onís to describe a conservative "reflux" within modernism itself. He maintained that this transitional pattern would itself be succeeded by an *ultramodernism* that would intensify the radical impulses of modernism to a new pitch.[19] Although Anderson discusses various appearances and derivations of the word over the next forty years, he says that its first appearance as a concept that is of more than just "circum-stantial significance" may be traced back to 1972, with the appearance of the review *boundary 2: Journal of Post-Modern Literature and Culture.*

One of the most significant contributors to this review was Ihab Hassan, who had published *The Dismemberment of Orpheus: Toward a Postmodern Literature* (1971). In this book, Hassan advanced a new reading of literary history, saying, "A different line has emerged *within* the tradition of the modern. It leads more directly, through the present, to a literature to come. Its authors sing on a lyre without strings."[20] In an article published later that year, however, Hassan broad-ened out his detection of a postmodern sensibility from the literary to the con-temporary culture at large. Anticipating our understanding of postmodernism as the repressed "other" of modernity, Hassan said that "postmodernism may be a response, direct or oblique, to the Unimaginable which Modernism glimpsed only in its most prophetic moments."[21] Like all good postmodernists to come, Hassan resisted providing a definition of the postmodern and resorted instead to a series of "elisions" to make or qualify his point.[22] But he was unequivocal in his exhortation: "It is time for everyone to open up alternatives to the Unimagin-able."[23] One such alternative to the Unimaginable was soon to be opened up in a very prominent way in the field of architecture, to which Hassan had given scant consideration in his own analyses of postmodernism. As Anderson says, "Ironically, it was the art to which [Hassan] gave least attention that finally pro-jected the term into the public domain at large."[24]

In 1966, the architect Robert Venturi published *Complexity and Contradic-tion in Architecture*, which Mark C. Taylor describes as "the nonoriginal begin-ning of postmodern architecture," even though *postmodernism* was not a term privileged by Venturi himself.[25] This was followed by *Learning from Las Vegas* (1972), which quickly established itself as the statement par excellence of postmodern architecture. Reacting against the "ugly and ordinary architecture" of modernity, Venturi called for a turn to decoration, image, and spectacle. We may say that Venturi was calling for a return of that which modern architecture had repressed. He says that modern architects abandoned or repressed a tradition of iconology in which "painting, sculpture, and graphics were combined with architecture."[26] Instead, they pursued an architectural form, the creation of which was to be "a logical process, free from images of past experience, determined solely by program and structure."[27] This is contrasted with the Las Vegas Strip, which is constituted by images, signs, and symbols in abundance. In effect, the Strip stands as the antithesis of modern architecture, insofar as that which modern architecture repressed is here allowed to run riot. Venturi says that the Strip shows the value of symbolism and allusion: "Allusion and comment, on the past or present or on our great commonplaces or old clichés, and inclusion of the everyday in the environment, sacred and profane—these are what are lacking in present-day Modern architecture. We can learn about them from Las Vegas as have other artists from their own profane and stylistic sources."[28]

But the architectural critic who explicitly used the term *postmodernism* and thrust it into the public eye was Charles Jencks, who published his *Language of Post-Modern Architecture* in 1977. In his introduction to the revised edition, Jencks said that when he first started using the term in 1975, he considered it a temporary label, but that he had now become convinced of its merit. This was primarily because the term "describes the duality of the present situation quite well."[29] In other words, Jencks wanted to draw attention to what we have already identified as a characteristic of postmodernism, namely, that it simultaneously moves beyond and yet remains indebted to the modern. Speaking of postmodern architects "of the moment," Jencks says that they have "not yet arrived at a new synthetic goal, nor have they given up entirely their Modernist sensibility, but rather they are at a half-way house, half Modern, half Post."[30]

Jencks says that postmodern architecture moves beyond modernism by leaving behind its elitism. This is done not by dropping that elitism but rather by "extending the language of architecture in many different ways—into the vernacular, towards tradition and the commercial slang of the street. Hence the double-coding, the architecture which speaks to the elite and the man on the street."[31] For Jencks, it was this "double-coding," above all, that defined a postmodern building. He said, "The buildings most characteristic of Post-Modernism show a marked duality, conscious schizophrenia."[32] It was thus a marriage of the historical and the traditional, the ancient and the contemporary, the quality and the popular. As Anderson says, "It was this liberating mixture of new and old, high and low, which defined postmodernism as a movement, and assured it the future."[33]

If postmodernism was now defined as a movement, it was yet to be articulated philosophically. Two years after Jencks published his groundbreaking book, however, this philosophical articulation of the postmodern appeared with the publication of Jean-François Lyotard's book *La Condition postmoderne: Rapport sur le savoir* (1979). It was initially written as a report for the government of Quebec, which had requested that Lyotard produce a report on the condition of "contemporary knowledge." At the time, he was surprisingly unaware of the appropriation of *postmodernism* by the architectural critics; it seems he had acquired the term directly from Ihab Hassan.[34]

For Lyotard, the most remarkable feature of knowledge in our postmodern condition was its inextricable link with *narrative*. He said that narratives "determine criteria of competence and/or illustrate how they are to be applied. They thus define what has the right to be said and done in the culture in question, and since they are themselves a part of that culture, they are legitimated by the simple fact that they do what they do."[35] This repudiation of external legitimation constituted a rejection of foundationalism, the dominant philosophical framework of modernity.[36] Lyotard distinguished between narrative and scientific knowledge. He said that whereas narrative knowledge does not give priority to the question of its own legitimation, the opposite is the case with regard to scientific knowledge. The result is that whereas narrative knowledge approaches scientific discourse as a variant in the family of narrative cultures, scientific knowledge questions and dismisses the validity of narrative statements altogether, as they are never legitimated by argumentation or proof. Lyotard said that this unequal relationship is an intrinsic effect of the rules specific to each game: "It is important to recognise its special tenor, which sets it apart from all other forms of imperialism: it is governed by the demand for legitimation."[37]

According to Lyotard, scientific knowledge was experiencing a crisis, signs of which had been accumulating since the end of the nineteenth century. But this crisis was not the result of a "chance proliferation of sciences." Rather, it represented "an internal erosion of the legitimacy principle of knowledge. There is erosion at work inside the speculative game, and by loosening the weave of the encyclopedic net in which each science was to find its place, it eventually sets them free."[38] So the chief characteristic of the postmodern condition was a move away from scientific knowledge toward narrative knowledge. Or, alternatively, postmodernism was characterized by the return of the narrative mode that modernity had repressed. I return to the primacy of the narrative mode in postmodernism in due course. But we should note the other defining characteristic of the postmodern condition for Lyotard, which was the loss of appeal and credibility of the "grand narrative," which is a "metanarrative" or "master story."

A metanarrative or grand narrative was defined by Lyotard as "precisely narrations with a legitimating function."[39] A grand narrative, therefore, was the arbiter from which all little narratives would derive their legitimation. It operated as an "ultimate organising logic" that "positions" all little narratives and explains how they all relate to one another.[40] We have already observed that the modern sensibility is characterized by the desire for the mastery of reality, usually by rational and/or scientific means. We may now say that the grand narrative was the means by which this desire was realized. As Lyotard pointed out, grand narratives are "those that have marked modernity," a time in which they proliferated. They included emancipatory metanarratives, whether of reason, freedom, or labor; metanarratives of enrichment through the progress of capitalist technoscience; and even, he said, "the salvation of creatures through the conversion of souls to the Christian narrative of martyred love. Hegel's philosophy totalizes all of these narratives and, in this sense, is itself a distillation of speculative modernity."[41]

It is precisely such grand narratives that Lyotard maintained have become untenable: "The grand narrative has lost its credibility, regardless of what mode of unification it uses, regardless of whether it is a speculative narrative or a narrative of emancipation."[42] So there is no longer any unifying explanation or narrative that posits an absolute beginning and an absolute end. Indeed, the beginning and end, as we have seen, are collapsed into the present. So we dwell solely in the *ici et maintenant,* within which the narratives we tell are solely little narratives, without alpha and without omega. Lyotard said, "We no longer have recourse to the grand narratives—we can resort neither to the dialectic of Spirit nor even to the emancipation of humanity as a validation for postmodern scientific discourse. But . . . the little narrative [*petit récit*] remains the quintessential form of imaginative invention, most particularly in science."[43]

Although one of the most celebrated and cited of Lyotard's works, *The Postmodern Condition* was by no means his most intellectually accomplished, as he himself later admitted.[44] Nevertheless, as Anderson points out, the significance of the volume lay in the fact that it was "the first book to treat postmodernity as a general change of human circumstance."[45] Whereas previous uses of the term had been restricted to specific trends or dispositions within particular disciplines, whether literature and poetry (Hassan) or architecture (Venturi and Jencks), Lyotard for the first time used the term to denote a cultural condition in which we all dwell. Postmodernists were no longer merely artists, writers, and architects, but now, according to Lyotard, we are all postmoderns. We are all dwelling in the cultural milieu of postmodernism. Needless to say, not everyone was happy with Lyotard's characterization of our present condition. Most notably, Jürgen Habermas delivered his address "Modernity—An Incomplete Project" in Frankfurt just a year after Lyotard published *The Postmodern Condition.* Yet, though Habermas provided a robust defense of modernity and the Enlightenment heritage against the postmodern attack, even he had to admit that the spirit of the times was changing, and that the project of modernity, incomplete or not, was giving way to something else.[46] Thus, Anderson says, "If the emergence of an intellectual terrain typically requires a negative pole for its productive tension, it was Habermas who supplied it."[47] Even critics of postmodernism, therefore, were beginning to concede, albeit regretfully, that our present condition is postmodern.

It is at this point that Perry Anderson's account of the history of postmodernism as an intellectual concept reaches its almost Hegelian (or perhaps, more appropriately, Marxist) apex in the work of Fredric Jameson. Undoubtedly, Jameson's contribution was to provide "one great vision" to command the field. His writings on the postmodern began in 1982, and after they had cumulatively grown over the following decade, they were collected to form the now-classic *Postmodernism, or, the Cultural Logic of Late Capitalism* (1991). This book exemplifies the peculiarly *un*postmodern encyclopedic nature of his analysis, as it ranges over culture, ideology, architecture, space, economics, video, and film. In the first chapter, Jameson identifies a number of defining characteristics of the "new systematic cultural norm" that he identifies as "postmodernism." It is worth recounting these, as they go some way toward answering our initial question: what is postmodernism?

The first characteristic is a new depthlessness, "a new kind of superficiality in the most literal sense, perhaps the supreme formal feature of all the post-modernisms."[48] This is evident in the pop art of Andy Warhol, the literally depthless architecture embodied in the free-standing wall of Wells Fargo Court, the theme of the "death" of the subject itself (which Jameson says is one of the more fashionable themes in contemporary theory), and the preoccupation with image and simulacrum. Without foundationalism, then, substance and heaviness disappear in favor of lightness and depthlessness. The second feature is a weakening sense of the historical, as history itself becomes "a vast collection of images, a multitudinous photographic simulacrum."[49] This is evident in the architectural plundering of random historical forms to produce an "overstimulating" simulacrum, in nostalgia films that "restructure the whole issue of pastiche and project it onto a collective and social level" and in contemporary historical novels that "represent" not the historical past but only our "ideas and stereotypes about that past."[50] When the subject loses its capacity to organize its past and future into coherent experience, the result is "a practice of the randomly heterogeneous and fragmentary and the aleatory." The temporal gives way to a culture "increasingly dominated by space and spatial logic."[51]

Another feature is that of a new emotional tone, which Jameson thinks is best expressed in terms of "something like a camp or 'hysterical' sublime."[52] This contemporary and fashionable conception nonetheless owes much to the works of Edmund Burke and Immanuel Kant and is linked particularly to a crisis of representation. Finally, Jameson considers the relationship of all these characteristics to a whole new technology. He does not wish to imply that this technology is the "ultimately determining instance" of contemporary social life or of our cultural production. Rather, he suggests that our representations of contemporary technology are but the surface manifestations of something latent, deeper and more sinister, namely, the global system of multinational capitalism. Thus, he says that contemporary technology is "mesmerizing and fascinating not so much in its own right but because it seems to offer some privileged representational shorthand for grasping a network of power and control even more difficult for our minds and imagination to grasp: the whole new decentered global network of the third stage of global capitalism itself."[53]

One distinctive feature of Jameson's analysis, of course, is that, like Anderson's, it is informed by a commitment to Marxism. Jameson's contention is that the popular culture of postmodernism is inextricably bound up with the economic system of late capitalism.[54] What distinguishes the present time from previous ones is the fact that the cultural and the economic have become conflated; they have become as "one." Jameson criticizes this culture for failing to see anything beyond itself, that is, for conflating the future with the present. He says, "It seems to be easier for us today to imagine the thoroughgoing deterioration of the earth and of nature than the breakdown of late capitalism; perhaps that is due to some weakness in our imaginations."[55]

Jameson's more fertile imagination is informed by the Marxist heritage. He urges us to follow Marx in attempting to think the impossible, "namely, to think this development positively *and* negatively all at once; to achieve, in other words, a type of thinking that would be capable of grasping the demonstrably baleful features of capitalism along with its extraordinary and liberating dynamism simultaneously within a single thought, and without attenuating any of the force of either judgment."[56] He says that the urgency of the subject demands that we at least attempt to think about the cultural evolution of late capitalism dialectically, as both catastrophe and progress at once. Thus, for Jameson, the new political art (insofar as it is possible at all) "will have to hold to the truth of postmodernism, that is to say, to its fundamental object—the world space of multinational capital—at the same time at which it achieves a breakthrough to some as yet unimaginable new mode of representing this last, in which we may again begin to grasp our positioning as individual and collective subjects and regain our capacity to act and struggle which is at present neutralized by our spacial as well as our social confusion."[57] So, for Jameson, postmodernism is both affirmed and rejected.

Bromwich says that postmodernism has sometimes seemed to fascinate Marxists such as Anderson and Jameson because it provides abundant examples with which to illustrate the decadence of late capitalism. These specimens should be sampled, as they show us how "a new culture, engendered by bourgeois society itself, is hollowing out and destroying the bourgeois life-form and making way for something different. . . . It seems on balance more a Hegelian than a Marxist stance, in which sheer wonder predominates, wonder that the most arid and stifling of present-day tendencies are working nevertheless to furnish a future for someone."[58] To the extent that Jameson's narrative "positions" postmodernism, insofar as he sees the postmodern epoch as part of a greater whole, it would seem that Jameson employs a (Marxist) grand narrative that is "other" than the postmodern. He speaks of postmodernism from "above," as it were, rather than from "within."[59] Jameson's analyses, then, are both postmodern and not postmodern. Postmodernism is something of which he is critical but that he nonetheless regards as necessary. And Jameson has always emphasized how it is not possible, either intellectually or politically, simply to celebrate postmodernism or to "disavow" it.[60] We shall see below that, in this sense, there are some parallels (although there are also important differences) between Jameson's evaluation of post-modernism and that of John Milbank. For both Jameson and Milbank, post-modernism is something to be embraced in the hope that it will itself give way to something infinitely better, whether a Marxist utopia or the kingdom of God.

Postmodernism and (a Narrative of) Narrative

I now turn to a specific defining characteristic of our postmodern condition, namely, the primacy of the narrative mode in postmodern accounts of knowledge such as that of Lyotard. I suggest that, for obvious reasons, this is the character-istic that will be of most relevance when we turn to discuss the interface between postmodernism and theology. Although Jameson does not explicitly discuss this in the survey we have just been considering, it is clear that this narrative primacy constitutes a tacit assumption in all his writings. This can be seen, for instance, when he says, "I trust we are by now far enough along in our consciousness of the narrative structure of historicity that we can forget about hoary old chestnuts about the evils of totalization or teleology."[61] The narrative structure of historic-ity and, indeed, of all our knowing is, it seems, taken for granted. But how did this primacy of the narrative mode arise?

We have already seen that the first writer to make an explict connection between postmodernism and the narrative mode was Lyotard. But although the novelty of Lyotard's thought lay in this specific connection, it has to be said that there was no novelty in Lyotard's emphasis on the narrative mode itself. Indeed, this is a theme that would already have been familiar to French philosophers and theorists through the work of such writers as Michel Foucault, Michel de Certeau, and Paul Ricoeur in the 1960s and 1970s. And indeed, a much older pedigree may be traced back through Sigmund Freud to Friedrich Nietzsche. I now turn to a brief consideration of this genealogy.[62]

As I have already intimated, and as I explicate more fully in chapter 2, the nar-rative mode of discourse was one that modernity tended to repress, as "rational" and "scientific" modes of knowledge were in the ascendant. Indeed, Amos Funkenstein has argued that the primary characteristic of modern knowledge was its conflation of the "theological" and the "scientific." The profoundly narrative structure of theology was denied, as theological knowledge was distorted into a form of scientific knowledge.[63] There were voices of protest from within moder-nity itself, on the part of such thinkers as Robert Lowth, Johann Georg Hamann, George Berkeley, Giambattista Vico, Johann Gottfried Herder, and Søren Kierkegaard.[64] But these still, small voices were generally drowned and engulfed by the waves of their episteme. Some years later, however, these waves were quelled somewhat by the louder and angrier voice of Friedrich Nietzsche.

Nietzsche's fundamental contention was that "truth is a fiction whose fictive status has been forgotten."[65] This insight was consequent on Nietzsche's declara-tion of the "death of God," a declaration that was not a metaphysical claim about

the (non)existence of God but rather a declaration that eradicated the foundations of a whole mode of thought. In this way, what distinguished Nietzsche from
previous voices of protest was that whereas they had protested in the name of theology, it was precisely this theology against which Nietzsche directed his vitriolic
attacks. Repudiating the scientific or positivist mode of knowledge, which
claimed to establish facts "in themselves," Nietzsche insisted that "facts is precisely what there is not, only interpretations."[66] As I argue in chapter 5, this committed Nietzsche to a radical fictionalism or perspectivism, which in turn led him
to recover the narrative mode of discourse that modernity had repressed. It was
perhaps this recovery of narrative, more than anything else, that became Nietzsche's chief legacy to his poststructuralist and postmodernist successors.

One such successor was Sigmund Freud. Although Freud rarely used the word
narrative, the words he used to designate other discourses, and also to designate
his own designating discourse, were all terms that pertained to narrativity.[67] The
significance of Freud's writings for an understanding of narrative lies not so much
in the content of his writings as in his estimation of the character of those writings. For instance, in *Moses and Monotheism* (1939), he referred to his own discourse by the use of *Darstellung* (exposition), *Konstruktion, Dekonstruktion,* and
Aufbau (edifice), while he spoke of religious discourse in terms of *Sage, Mythus*
(myth), *Tradition, Dichtung* (poetry) or *fromme Dichtung* (pious poetry), and
Erfindung (invention). The terms *Darstellung* and *Konstruktion* are used to refer
both to his own discourse and to religious discourse, thus destabilizing the literary distinction between the discourse being designated and the discourse that is
designating.[68] For Freud, the narrative character of all our knowing is inescapable.
He referred to his own case studies as "short stories" that lacked the "serious
stamp of science."[69] Furthermore, he said that his own descriptions of the oper-
ations of the psychical apparatus were "fictions" or "theoretical fictions."[70] Thus,
as James J. DiCenso says, we do best to "understand Freud's hypotheses in *narrative* and even *mythical* terms. His histories represent an intertwining of literary,
speculative and scientific imagination."[71]

Similarly, the narrative significance of the writings of Michel Foucault lies not
so much in the subjects of his archeological and genealogical historiography as in
his understanding of the character of his own discourse. Against those who maintain that he is constructing yet another panoptical analysis of the very sort that
he is analyzing, Foucault has always insisted that his own writing is itself part of
a "game of truth." He says, "I am fully aware that I have never written anything
other than fictions. For all that, I would not want to say that they were outside
truth. . . . One 'fictions' history starting from a political reality that renders it
true, one 'fictions' a politics that does not yet exist starting from a historical
truth."[72] Destabilizing the distinction between subject and object, Foucault
therefore regards his writings as stories, fictions, narratives.

Another French thinker who regards his writings of history as the creation of
fables is Michel de Certeau. De Certeau was concerned to elucidate the narrative
character of all our knowing. His book *The Writing of History* (1975), which was

a pioneering work in the field of historiography, destabilized the distinction between history and fiction. It was the study of writing as historical practice. The past, said de Certeau, is the fiction of the present. He said that historiography "cannot be thought of in terms of an opposition or adequacy between a subject and an object; that is nothing more than the play of the fiction it constructs."[73] For de Certeau, the primacy of the narrative mode arises from the destabilization between the real and the fictitious, a destabilization that he traces back to the "literary fantastic" of the nineteenth century: "That literature presupposed, between *real* and *fictitious*, the break brought about by an epistemology of objectivity. By playing one of these two terms against the other . . . it progressively muddled the opposition on which the positivist affirmation of reality rests. In place of the localizations that distinguish between the objective and the subjective, it substituted the disquieting insecurity of these determinations and therefore of the real itself. This work (novelistic or pictorial) of destabilization attacked the scientific dichotomy of the nineteenth century from behind the lines."[74] With this destabilization comes an alchemical conversion from a "chart of knowledge" to a "garden of delights," from a "referential" function of language to a "poetic" one, from a "scientific" mode of knowledge to "narrative."[75] According to de Certeau, contemporary society has witnessed the completion of this alchemical conversion: "Our society has become a recited society, in three senses: it is defined by *stories* (*récits*, the fables constituted by our advertising and informational media), by *citations* of stories, and by the interminable *recitation* of stories."[76] So modernity's scientific mode of knowledge has finally passed away. Ours is now a *recited* society, a society that is *narrated*.

We see, therefore, that the transformative shift from metaphysics to fiction, from a scientific to a narrative mode of knowledge—inaugurated by Nietzsche—finally reached its consummation in the postmodern sensibility. Before Lyotard had made the explicit connection between "postmodernism" and "narrative," the primacy of the narrative mode had already been established. In a narrated line running from Nietzsche to Freud to Foucault, de Certeau, and Lyotard, Nietzsche's narrative vision was gradually realized. (It should also be noted that this is not the only possible narration of this genealogy, nor does it claim to be exhaustive.) It may be said, therefore, that one of the (many) defining characteristics of the postmodern condition is succinctly encapsulated by the slogan "Narrative is all, and all is narrative."

It is at this point that we turn to consider the implications of this transformative shift or alchemical conversion for theology. They are by no means unambiguous; on the contrary, they appear to be profoundly ambivalent. On the one hand, it is a shift that was inaugurated by Nietzsche's proclamation of the "death of God" and his relentless efforts to eradicate the "shadows" of the dead God. This was followed by Freud's psychological explanations of religion, de Certeau's repeated references to the "weakness of believing" (*faiblesse de croire*) and the apparent need to leave Christianity behind in the name of the "other," and Lyotard's proclamation of the end of all metanarratives, including

that of Christian redemption. Ironically, on the other hand, Nietzsche's opposition to the "scientific" discourse of modernity in favor of the "narrative" discourse that modernity repressed actually created a clearing for that most
narrativist of all discourses—theology. In this sense, Nietzsche's proclamation
of the *death* of God actually prepared the way for the *return* of God; for it has
been said that the God against whom Nietzsche set himself was merely an idolatrous God of metaphysics, whose death opened the way for the return of the
God of faith.[77] Paradoxically, therefore, our present condition seems to announce
both the end *and* the beginning of theology. Indeed, both impulses have found
theological expression, giving rise to both a postmodern a/theology *and* a postmodern theology. Departure *and* return . . . nihilism *and* God . . . end *and*
beginning . . . a/theology *and* theology. Such is the paradox of our postmodern
condition.

I now turn to these two diverging postmodern theological impulses. For both
versions, the various forms of "both/and" we have been considering are displaced
by various forms of "either/or": departure *or* return . . . nihilism *or* God . . . end
or beginning . . . a/theology *or* theology. Each version defines itself in terms of
which side of these antinomies it embraces, and which it represses. Thus, nihilist
textualist theology embraces the death of God, the advent of nihilism, the end of
theology, and the birth of a/theology, whereas radical orthodox theology embraces the return of God, the overcoming of nihilism and secular reason, and the
rebirth of theology. These antithetical impulses are reflected in their respective
relationships to postmodernism. We shall see that nihilist textualism embraces
and celebrates the postmodern condition and its various defining characteristics
as I have been discussing them in this chapter. Radical orthodoxy, in contrast,
initially welcomes certain aspects of the postmodern, but as a means of creating
a new theological space from which to call that very postmodernism into question. In a manner slightly analogous to Jameson, therefore, radical orthodoxy
deconstructs the very postmodernism that makes its theology possible. I now discuss each of these diverging postmodern theologies in turn, looking first at the
project of nihilist textualism, then at the project of radical orthodoxy.[78]

Postmodernism and Theology:
Nihilist Textualism

We observed in the introduction that nihilist textualist theology is usually associated with the work of Mark C. Taylor and Don Cupitt. We also saw that to
name both thinkers "once" with the same name, however, is a misleadingly unifying gesture, for their respective projects are diverse, in style and in content.
What does unite them is the fact that, for both, postmodernism, as I have been
portraying it in this chapter, is both unavoidable—it is "what we have"—and
welcome—it frees us from the tyranny of both foundationalist philosophy and
dogmatic theology. For both Taylor and Cupitt, theology does not and cannot

challenge postmodern culture; rather, it must adapt itself to it. Both thinkers may be described as "narrativist" theologians, although the narrative mode is most explicitly evident in Don Cupitt's work. It is for this reason that I concentrate on Cupitt's project in this chapter, as I attempt to explicate the connections between postmodern theology and the postmodern narrativism I have been discussing above.[79]

Don Cupitt's theological project has constantly evolved during his thirty or so years as a professional philosopher of religion. Until around 1979, he was a quintessential modernist liberal theologian, a "latitudinarian."[80] With the publication of *Taking Leave of God* (1980), he began to articulate his "non-realist" interpretation of the Christian faith, but it was not until the publication of *Life Lines* (1986) that continental and postmodern thought began to make an imprint on Cupitt's work. It was at this point that Cupitt began to describe his work as "postmodern," although this, too, later developed into an "expressionist" project with the publication of *Creation Out of Nothing* (1990), and the movement has continued throughout the 1990s. In the next chapter, I discuss the story of his move from liberalism to non-realism during the years 1979–1981. In this chapter, however, I discuss his postmodern expressionism, as articulated particularly in *What Is a Story?* (1991), *After All* (1994), *The Last Philosophy* (1995), and *Solar Ethics* (1995).

For Cupitt, postmodernism begins theologically with the death of God and philosophically with the end of foundationalism.[81] In the wake of these losses, Cupitt maintains that theology and philosophy must make a new start. He is quite clear that this new start must be with language, because it is our most solid foundation. He says that philosophy has always started with what it has perceived as being most solid. In the past, this has been Being, matter, a priori truths of reason, or experience. But now, he says, "perhaps the true universal stuff, in which and of which everything else is constructed, is the sign and communication. For every aspect of what we call 'reality' is established in and by language."[82] And if we ask what there *must* be, even on a "most thoroughgoing constructivist" account, the first thing, the very least thing that there must be, is language: "for language is something, one of the very, very few things whose existence cannot self-consistently be denied, denial being in itself a linguistic act. And language is now moving, for this sentence is being read. So the world is at least a communications network, with messages of many kinds flying around, along (no doubt) various channels."[83] And this in itself, he says, must mean that there is temporality and a discharge and scattering of energies. The procedure here is clearly Cartesian, with Cupitt doubting everything until he arrives at that which cannot be doubted—language. Language, then, becomes the "foundation" for his subsequent "system." Like Lyotard's philosophy of phrases, this seems to be a "sort of Cartesianism without the subject."[84]

Language for Cupitt is not only the foundation or starting point of his new philosophy, but it is also the philosophical beginning of the world. He says that we do best to picture this world as "a beginningless, endless and outsideless stream of language-formed events that continually pours forth and passes away."[85] This stream of events becomes real to us, is formed by us, in and through language. He says that philosophy has always been concerned with what makes things real enough to be thinkable. For Plato, it was the Forms; for Kant, it was concepts. In this place, Cupitt puts language, "with the advantage that as I insist that our world is already formed by our language, so I'm also claiming that our world is thereby constituted as a flowing temporal world, a *life*-world. So it is that we enact the unity of life and language, the flesh and the word, life-time and world-time."[86] Thus, words are signs, and in the unity of flesh and the word, the old distinction between the signifier and what is signified breaks down. There can be no talk of any extralinguistic reality or extralinguistic meaning, for language creates reality and language is meaning.

If this is the case, however, then language can no longer be regarded as a "secondary" representation of something "primary." Indeed, Cupitt maintains that the primary is abolished altogether, with the result that "everything is secondary." We thus dwell within a postmodern condition of secondariness: "There is no pure datum, no primary substance, no 'absolute,' nothing that is always ontologically prior. Nothing is always real, from every point of view. We are always in secondariness, moving around as a sniper does, trying different angles."[87] But if the primary is abolished and all we have is secondariness, then the world of language and the world of consciousness "are all made of just the same stuff and indeed are all merely different ways of reading the one continuous flowing process."[88] There is a clear debt to Spinoza here; the philosophical outlook that Cupitt has in mind is monistic, with everything being created out of and within the one continuous flowing process.[89]

Another defining characteristic of postmodernism that Cupitt embraces, and which is consequent on his view of the radical linguisticality of reality, is the primacy of narrative. He says, "Our human world is everywhere and outsidelessly temporal, language-formed and *therefore* a flux of narratives."[90] So if our human world is everywhere a flux of narratives, there is a sense in which fiction is prior. Thus, Cupitt maintains that "fiction comes first. First the world has got to be fictioned into existence from nothing by some kind of story—religious, cosmological, evolutionary, historical or whatever and only then can we find a place for talk of truth and falsity, relative to the world as thus produced within the story. Fiction logically precedes factuality, and then after fiction, and relative to the world it has established, come along theories, evidences, arguments, points of view, alliances and oppositions."[91] So if language comes first and is the most basic category, then more particularly, narrative is the prior and most basic category of language.

Just as de Certeau claimed that we now live in a recited society, so Cupitt claims that our contemporary culture is profoundly fictionalist. He says that our whole life is lived in and by stories. Like Paul Ricoeur, he says that stories give us a timescale and our roles to play. They evoke our desires and show us how to fulfill them. In short, stories give us our *place* in life.[92] In this sense, stories are also edifying in that they are community-building. Communal stories can be collectively drawn on to construct a meaningful public life in which we can all share and participate.[93] For Cupitt, there is no way out of these stories, although he maintains that there is some value in retaining the illusory attempts to do so, because "when they fail, as they must, our dreams of escape and transcendence will at least have the beneficial side-effect of renewing our understanding of how and why it is that this, here and now—as, for example, this particular chain of signs that you are now scanning—is all there is for us, and all there could be."[94]

If this is the case, then it has to be said that religion is also only a set of stories. For Cupitt, however, this is not to devalue religion. As a story, religion is no less justified and no less important than any other story. Indeed, in many ways, it is more important than any other story: "Every society needs a religion, in the sense of a collection of communally-possessed life-guiding stories. But such an account of religion explains and naturalizes it, and we recognize that there is nothing to stop us from inventing fresh stories, or even redesigning religion altogether."[95] Again, for Cupitt, this can only be a good thing because it frees us from the tyranny of theological realism and philosophical foundationalism. As we have already observed, Cupitt embraces postmodernism precisely because it overcomes these twin tyrannies. He says that religion "needs to be held at the level of a game, kept light, fictional and symbolically rich. Self-mocking, even, because religion that is not reflectively aware of its own fictionality quickly becomes too serious, and therefore clumsy, violent and oppressive."[96] For this reason, then, postmodern theology and religious belief will have to be "cheerfully fictionalist" and avoid the tyranny of a master narrative.[97]

Religion will be one of many narratives we appropriate and make our own and by which we live our lives. But it cannot be regarded as the uniquely privileged narrative that organizes and unifies all the other narratives by which we live. Cupitt says, "We cannot now expect to be able to unify our lives under a single master-story, because we do not see how just one story, while still being truly a story, could be uniquely privileged and different in kind from all other stories."[98] This, of course, is to give credence to Lyotard's proclamation of the end of grand narratives. Perhaps one of the most common criticisms of this position, the force of which is recognized by Lyotard himself, is that to proclaim the end of grand narratives is itself to reinstate yet another grand narrative.[99] I discuss this criticism in more detail in chapter 4. But Cupitt also recognizes the paradox here, when he says that "we can perhaps finally admit that we have after all presented a new master-narrative. It could not be avoided. We found we had lost all the old master-narratives and were now continuously improvising, retelling, embroidering, making it up as we go along. But in relating all this we found that not to have a master-narrative is also still to have one."[100] So, like Lyotard, Cupitt embraces a metanarrative that proclaims the end of metanarratives, and this may be viewed as another instance of Cupitt's "enjoyable and ambiguous dance between affirmation and negation."[101]

We have seen, then, that postmodern nihilist textualist theology embraces many of the defining characteristics identified by Jameson. With its emphasis on the fictiveness, lightness, and nonseriousness of narratives; the overcoming of the distinction between signifier and signified; and the consequent emphasis on surface and secondariness, nihilist textualist theology embraces the postmodern characteristics of depthlessness and superficiality. Second, its insistence that historical, traditional, and particularly religious narratives can be reappropriated, repackaged, and redesigned for the present reveals a typically postmodern weakening of historicity. Third, its concern with the "crisis of representation" and its insistence that we can gain no access to an extralinguistic reality is much indebted to postmodern notions of the sublime, even though Cupitt's immanent monism suggests a parallel indebtedness to the modernist tradition. And in light of this wholehearted embrace of the postmodern cultural condition, it is not at all surprising to find that Cupitt is equally at ease with its economic correlate of late capitalism.[102] In short, for nihilist textualist theology, postmodernism "is so good because it is so material."[103]

Postmodernism and Theology: Radical Orthodoxy

The relationship of radical orthodox theology to postmodernism is rather more ambivalent and complex. Furthermore, it should be emphasized that radical orthodoxy is by no means a monolithic, homogeneous theology.[104] In particular, there are differences among radical orthodox theologians themselves with regard to their respective evaluations of postmodernism. Graham Ward and Gerard Loughlin, for instance, are rather more enthusiastic about the opportunities for theology offered by postmodern thought than are John Milbank and Catherine Pickstock. Loughlin suggests that there is "not so much an opposition as a differential relation" between thinkers like himself and Ward on the one hand and Milbank and Pickstock on the other.[105] To a certain extent, this is indeed the case. All four are opposed to what they consider to be the secular humanism of modernity, and in this sense, they are all literally *post*-modern. Furthermore, Milbank's opposition to what he considers to be the nihilistic postmodernism of Nietzsche's philosophical successors—Heidegger, Deleuze, Lyotard, and Foucault—is shared by Ward and Loughlin.

There are, however, also some very real and substantial divergences among these theologians, the most prominent of which is perhaps the contrasting readings of the work of Jacques Derrida provided by Pickstock and Ward.[106] Whereas Pickstock charges Derrida with sophistry and accuses him of providing a "deathly" account of language, "instituting the very things he abhors at the centre of his philosophy," Ward provides a much more theologically positive reading, insisting that Derrida allows for "an alterity that may be other than the *nihil*," and which faith can name as God.[107] Thus, whereas Ward and Loughlin continue to speak of their projects as versions of "postmodern" theology, Milbank and Pickstock prefer to speak of a "post-postmodern agenda" and a theology that is more "postsecular" than postmodern.[108] In this and sub-sequent chapters, however, I concentrate on the work of John Milbank, who has emerged as the unofficial leader of this group of theologians, and whose book *Theology and Social Theory* (1990) is generally regarded as having founded a new way of doing theology that has subsequently come to be known as rad-ical orthodoxy.

John Milbank welcomes the advent of postmodernism insofar as it entails the end of modernity: "The end of modernity, which is not accomplished, yet con-tinues to arrive, means the end of a single system of truth based on universal rea-son."[109] With this ending comes the end of the modernist idea of a "naked truth," free of assumptions that can be expressed unproblematically in language. This was the dream of Spinoza, for example, who wanted his philosophical sys-tem to "shine forth like a jewel" in its self-evident truth, quite apart from its author and context. Postmodernism, however, rejects such a notion of truth, maintaining that meanings of words are always shifting and always dependent on the perceptions, presuppositions, and assumptions of both speaker and hearer and on the context in which the speaker and hearer are situated. All "truths" have a history, and this history is the history of their construction. A "naked" truth, pure and simple, always exceeds our grasp and, as such, is never attainable. The notion of a static, fixed, and stable truth, apprehensible by means of rational enquiry, has ended and is ending. Recognizing this, Milbank asks, "Why should truth just 'show' itself to the person without assumptions? All our 'truths' are only 'assumptions' or takings up from previous linguistic arrangements."[110] This means that truth claims get their sense and are intelligible only within particular *narratives*.

The narrative mode therefore comes to the fore as the most basic category. In this sense, too, Milbank embraces the postmodern. He says, "In post-modernity there are infinitely many possible versions of truth, inseparable from particular narratives. Objects and subjects are, as they are narrated in a story. Outside a plot, which has its own unique, unfounded reasons, one cannot con-ceive how subjects and objects would be, nor even that they would be at all."[111] In other words, all knowledge is narrative knowledge. All is narrative, and nar-rative is all. Unlike the categories of explanation (i.e., natural science) and understanding (i.e., human sciences), narrative "does not assume punctiliar facts or discrete meanings. Neither is it concerned with universal laws, nor universal truths of the spirit. Yet it is not arbitrary in the sense that one can repeat a text in just any fashion, although one can indeed do so in any number of fashions."[112] We cannot repeat a text in just any fashion because the text forms a "loose and complex knot of resistance" that may be registered in any number of ways but can never be undone altogether. Neither can we precisely place it "for it belongs, ultimately, to a whole wider network of resistances and counter-resistances, which we ourselves, by our intervention, are further adjusting and altering."[113] So, for Milbank, as for the other postmodern thinkers I have considered in this chapter, narration "is the final mode of comprehension of human society. To understand or to explain a social phenomenon is simply to narrate it, although this remains an inherently questionable activity."[114] Already, however, we begin to register a certain difference between Milbank and other postmodern thinkers, for his point that a text cannot be read "in just any fashion" seems to protest against the "indeterminacy of meaning" promoted by textualists such as Cupitt and Taylor.

For Milbank, postmodernism is also to be welcomed because it entails the end of the master narrative of secular reason. This means that narratives no longer have to "measure up to accepted secular standards of scientific truth or normative rationality."[115] For Milbank, however (unlike Lyotard and Cupitt), the end of the master narrative of secular reason does not mean that we abandon ourselves to the proliferation of little narratives. On the contrary, he insists that all our claims, all our narratives, are subject to an "ultimate organising logic." This is as true of Lyotard's philosophy as of any other, for, as Lyotard half suspects, to narrate the end of the grand narratives is itself to reinstate another grand narrative. Similarly, to insist on the arbitrariness of one's narrative is itself to make a claim about the "way things are," namely, arbitrary; and so one again finds oneself reinstating a metanarrative. According to Milbank, this paradox can never be escaped, so instead of a rhetoric proclaiming the end of metanarratives, one should promote a rhetoric of the inescapability of metanarratives. For Milbank, the important point about the end of the modernist master narrative of secular reason is not the end of master narratives generally but the end of the *particular* master narrative of *secular reason*. For the end of this particular master narrative allows for the return of a different master narrative, an-"other" master narrative, a master narrative of the "other," namely, the master narrative of *Christian theology*.

We may say, therefore, that Milbank is a postmodernist insofar as he rejects the notion of a static, fixed, "naked" truth; accepts the ubiquity and inescapability of language; recognizes the primacy of narrative in all claims to knowledge; and celebrates the end of the master narrative of secular reason. In all these respects, Milbank shares common ground with the postmodern philosophers and the nihilist textualist theologians we have been considering in this chapter. But we have also registered a significant difference, which renders his relationship to postmodernism more complex. For Milbank, postmodernism is to be welcomed because it means the end of the particular metanarrative of secular reason and thereby opens the clearing for the return of a different (theological) metanarrative. This theological metanarrative, he claims, is the best story for us to live by. This is not because it can be shown to be more rational or more justified than any other, for with the end of secular reason, notions of foundational justification collapse, and all discourses are "on a level." Rather, speaking from within a theological narrative, Milbank identifies two main "reasons" that Christianity is not quite "on a level" with other discourses, and why it is therefore the best story to live by.

First, Milbank argues that Christianity can become "internally postmodern" in a way that may not be possible for every other narrative. What he means by this is that "it is possible to construe Christianity as suspicious of notions of fixed 'essences' in its approach to human beings, to nature, to community and to God, even if it has never fully escaped the grasp of a 'totalising' metaphysics."[116] He says that the doctrine of creation out of nothing affirms temporality, becoming, and emergence, and that a reality suspended between nothing and infinity is a reality of flux, without substance, made only of relational differences and ceaseless alterations.[117]

Second, Christianity tells a story of the priority of harmony and peace, as opposed to the story of nihilism, which prioritizes difference and violence. It is at this point that Milbank equates postmodernism and nihilism: "Postmodernism seems to imply nihilism, albeit of a 'positive' kind, embracing contingency and arbitrariness as the real natural good."[118] For Milbank, the nihilist narrative is the only serious rival to the Christian narrative because all other ideologies, whether of secular reason, scientific truth, or Enlightenment humanism, are "masked" or "disguised" versions of nihilism. For any ideology that attempts to exclude God must ultimately be nihilistic.[119] Faced with this either/or, nihilism or theology, Milbank claims that only Christianity can harmoniously embrace difference. This is because whereas nihilist postmodernism embraces a rhetoric of violence, where a plurality of discourses violently conflict and compete with one another,[120] Christianity "pursued from the outset a universalism which tried to subsume rather than merely abolish difference: Christians could remain in their many different cities, languages and cultures, yet still belong to one eternal city ruled by Christ in whom all 'humanity' was fulfilled."[121] At this point, Milbank appeals to the "musical" ontology of Augustine in *De musica:* "In music there must be continuous endings and displacements, yet this is no necessary violence, because only in the recall of what has been displaced does the created product consist." So, for Christianity, true community is to be found in the freedom of peoples and groups to be different while refusing indifference, in a consensus "that is only in and through the inter-relations of community itself, and a consensus that moves and 'changes': *a concentus musicus.*"[122]

Thus, positioning himself within the Christian metanarrative, which embraces and "positions" all other narratives, Milbank seeks to "outwit" or "out-narrate" nihilistic postmodernism: *not*, he insists, by seeking to reinstate reason but by offering an unfounded and radical alternative, the persuasiveness of which will speak for itself. Having welcomed postmodernism insofar as it creates a space for the return of theology, Milbank then seeks theologically to "out-narrate" or "overcome" the very postmodernism that made his theology possible. His theology is therefore postmodern and not postmodern. Like Jameson, Milbank regards postmodernism as both good and bad, something to be embraced but only because it will give way to something infinitely better. But unlike Jameson, for Milbank this "something else" will not be ushered in by means of a Marxist dialectic, but only by proclaiming the Christian gospel.

Interlude

In this chapter, I have provided an account of the cultural and philosophical rise of postmodernism and discussed some of its defining characteristics. In particular, I identified the primacy of the narrative mode of discourse in postmodernism as being of particular relevance for the emergence of the two forms of postmodern theology we have been considering. We saw that whereas nihilist textualist theology embraced the philosophical nihilism of postmodernism, radical orthodox theology embraced postmodernism only insofar as it allowed for the return of the metanarrative of theology. Situated within this theology, radical orthodoxy then rejects the nihilism of postmodernism as being incorrigibly secular and violent. I now suggest that this fundamental divergence may be understood in terms of an antithetical evaluation of modernity itself. For Cupitt celebrates postmodernism as a logical extension of modernity and traces a continuity between his own, postmodern vision and the thought of Spinoza, Hegel, Marx, Feuerbach, and Nietzsche.[123] In contrast, Milbank opposes postmodernism insofar as it is an exacerbation or the apotheosis of modernity, and he embraces postmodernism insofar as it overcomes and acts as the scourge of modernity. This opposition to modernity is essentially a *theological* opposition, and it is one not shared by the nihilist textualists. In the next chapter, therefore, I discuss the philosophical sensibility of modernity, which, we shall see, is crucial for a proper understanding of our contemporary predicament of postmodern theology.

Chapter 2
(A/)Theology and Modernity

In the previous chapter, we saw that our postmodern condition gives rise to two antithetical theological impulses. I shall now show how these impulses arise from two divergent evaluations of the *modern* epoch. This is crucial for a proper understanding of the ways in which these two theologies may be described as *postmodern*, and also for a proper understanding of why nihilist textualism has failed to confront the radical orthodox challenge. We shall see that nihilist textualism regards modernity as a necessary "transitional period" between what is considered to be the objective rationalism of the classical period and our own postmodern condition. Radical orthodoxy, in contrast, considers modernity to have taken a fundamentally wrong turn, the logical culmination of which is the nihilism of contemporary postmodernism. The modern turn was fundamentally wrong because it was a turn away from the sacred to the secular, from theology to nihilism.

We shall see, however, that these divergent evaluations of modernity conceal a certain convergence. For both nihilist textualism and radical orthodoxy regard modern philosophy and its corollaries of secular humanism and liberal theology to be inherently unstable and untenable; they contain *within themselves* the seeds for their own destruction. According to their own internal logics, they must ultimately subvert themselves and unmask themselves as nihilism and postmodernism. Without a teleology and without a theology of history, however, nihilist textualism has no criteria with which to *evaluate* the modern turn, and so it just moves *further on*. Radical orthodoxy, in contrast, theologically evaluates the modern turn as a secular one and consequently rejects it, together with its postmodern exacerbation. In this sense, postmodernism is embraced insofar as it overcomes modernity but is rejected insofar as it exacerbates modernity.

In this chapter, I proceed in four parts. First, I discuss the work of Hans Urs von Balthasar and more recent scholars to show how the foundations for the modern turn in philosophy, typically associated with René Descartes, were actually laid down by certain developments within theology itself during the fourteenth century. In the thought of Duns Scotus, and subsequently Cardinal Cajetan and Francisco Suárez, earlier modes of theological thought, particularly those of St. Thomas Aquinas, were abandoned. The primary movements here were the emergence of a prior and univocal concept of "being," the consequent dissolution of God's ontological transcendence, and the subsequent breakdown of Aquinas's doctrine of analogy. We shall see that it was these movements that prepared the way for the Cartesian "revolution" in modern philosophy, and which reached their culmination in the thought of Immanuel Kant. Second, I show how these movements are given contemporary expression in the liberal theology of John Hick. In Hick's theology, we can detect an implicit indebtedness to Duns Scotus and an explicit reliance on Kant. In spite of his commitment to "realism," we shall see that Hick resists a slide into "non-realism" only with difficulty.

Third, I analyze Don Cupitt's transition from a liberal theological framework (similar to that of Hick's) to his later non-realism and subsequent postmodernism. I argue that this transition was prompted not by external pressures but by a logical outworking of certain characteristics of the modern liberal framework itself. Finally, and in contrast, we shall see that far from intensifying or exacerbating these modernist characteristics, John Milbank's postmodern theology confrontationally reacts against them. Like Cupitt, he argues that modernity must culminate in nihilism, but unlike Cupitt, he argues that theology must overcome nihilism, together with the modernity that gave it birth. Thus, we shall see that whereas nihilist textualism may be regarded as the *apotheosis* of modernity, radical orthodoxy may be regarded as the *scourge* of modernity.

The Birth Pangs of Modernity

Ever since the "modern" has come to denote an epoch or a sensibility that is past and historical (though not completely past and not entirely historical), as opposed to what is present and contemporary (*modo*—"just now"), debates have raged over where and when the modern actually begins.[1] "Beginnings" have ranged from the establishment of the printing press by Gutenberg in 1436 to the rise of Protestantism beginning with Luther's excommunication in 1520, the end of the Thirty Years War in 1648, and the American and French Revolutions of 1776 and 1789.[2] Philosophically, Descartes's *Meditations* has been regarded as a fundamental turning point, although Richard Rorty has identified philosophical modernity with foundationalism and claims that this was only fully realized with Kant.[3] Stephen Toulmin's subtle and more complex account has suggested that modernity actually had two beginnings—the humanistic and literary beginning in the 1500s, a century before the philosophical and scientific.[4]

These "beginnings" have all been radically questioned, however, by the Swiss theologian Hans Urs von Balthasar and more recently by Éric Alliez, Catherine Pickstock, and William C. Placher, among others. They have convincingly shown how these various "beginnings" of modernity may all be regarded as manifestations of a much more fundamental shift that took place within theology itself during the fourteenth century. This shift revolved around ontology, and more particularly, a taking leave of the ontology of St. Thomas Aquinas. It is this shift that I shall explore in this part of the chapter.[5] The resulting genealogy is one that is adopted by the theologians of radical orthodoxy in order to identify the founding moment of modernity as a fundamentally "heretical" wrong turn within theology itself. In this way, they are able to diagnose modernity as a secular error that can be rectified only by and within theology. As Graham Ward puts it, such a genealogy "extend[s] the historicism of modernity/postmodernity theologically, in terms of the ecclesial tradition (which is central to any understanding of a theology of history)."[6]

It should also be said, however, that one need not share radical orthodoxy's "diagnosis" or its prescribed "cure" to be persuaded of the general validity of its genealogy. One can recognize that these fourteenth-century theological innovations prepared the way for the modernity that followed without necessarily regarding them as a "wrong turn" and without necessarily maintaining that they should or can be "rectified." This is not to say that these innovations constituted an enlightened "correction" of earlier errors. Rather, it is simply to say that without a theological (or radical orthodox) benchmark with which to evaluate them, one may regard them simply as a contingent intellectual rupture that (for better or worse) "happened," and in the wake of it, one must simply move *further on*. Indeed, I suggest that this is the spirit in which Michel de Certeau, for instance, narrates his own theological genealogy of modernity, and it is in the same spirit that I now turn to consider the genealogy in question.[7]

Hans Urs von Balthasar says that in Aquinas's ontology, "being (*esse*), with which he is concerned and to which he attributes the modalities of the One, the True, the Good and the Beautiful, is the unlimited abundance of reality which is beyond all comprehension, as it, in its emergence from God, attains subsistence and self-possession within the finite entities."[8] The crucial point here is that "being" only "is" in its emergence from God, thus enshrining the priority of God.

If this were not the case, the result would be that God and creatures share a common genus, which is what Aquinas vehemently denies. He says that "God is not a measure that is proportionate to what is measured; so it does not follow that he and his creatures belong to the same order."[9] One result of this is that all language predicated of God is used *analogically*: "This way of using words lies somewhere between pure equivocation and simple univocity, for the word is neither used in the same sense, as with univocal usage, nor in totally different senses, as with equivocation."[10] Rather, in analogical language, a word predicated of God is related to the way in which it is predicated of creatures, but what the word actually means when applied to God in God's self, we cannot know. Thus, although God is not of a genus with creatures, and although God is ontologically transcendent, some knowledge of God, however imperfect, is attainable by means of analogical participation. Aquinas, therefore, refuses to compromise the priority of God, with the result that God's ontological transcendence is preserved. It was this ontological transcendence that came to be destroyed during the fourteenth century.

Balthasar claims that the turning point came with the rise of Averroism in the 1250s, which claimed to be the only serious interpretation of the sole "scientific" philosopher, Aristotle. It attempted to discover how far human reason could go in the inquiry into the ultimate grounds of Being, without any revelatory knowledge. It placed philosophy above theology as the sole comprehensive science that could identify reality, rationality, and necessity.[11] With Duns Scotus, Averroism was adopted by theology. Duns Scotus was a Franciscan priest and was the first major Christian theologian to conceive of "being" as a concept. His fundamental contention was that "being is univocal to the created and uncreated."[12] Balthasar says that this decision arose out of Duns Scotus's concern for the formal object of philosophy in the face of Christian theology. Reason now grasps being alone as its first unlimited concept, and reason thereby transcends the distinction between finite and infinite Being: "The concept has not only logical (expressive) universality, but also metaphysical universality, for it captures Being in its objective and all-comprehending ('catholic') generality, so that *it can be univocally applied to infinite and to finite Being*, that is to God and the world, to substance and accidents, to act and potentiality."[13]

The result of this move was that the concept of "being" had become prior to God. Being was now something in which God and humanity shared, even though God shared in it to an infinitely greater degree than humanity. As Duns Scotus puts it, "Whatever pertains to 'being', then, in so far as it remains indifferent to finite and infinite, or as proper to the Infinite Being, does not belong to it as determined to a genus, but prior to any such determination, and therefore as transcendental and outside any genus."[14] The result of this was that God's ontological transcendence was destroyed. But with the destruction of this ontological distinction, God's transcendence now had to be articulated on a single level of ontology. God infinitely transcends humanity only in "intensity of being." And without an ontological difference, the possibility of analogical participation in the divine was destroyed. So although there was an ontological continuity between God and humanity, there was an infinite metaphysical distance between them. In other words, God's *ontological* transcendence became an *epistemological* transcendence.[15] As Éric Alliez says, "In effect, once the *primary mover of conti-nuity* (the Aristotelo-Thomist principle of universal analogy) has been aban-doned to a universal conception of being giving no means to creatures to distinguish themselves ontologically from God by analogically drawing near to him, the distance between finite and infinite becomes infinite."[16] Paradoxically, therefore, Duns Scotus's univocal concept of Being simultaneously brings God closer to creatures *and* moves him further away. He is brought closer to creatures insofar as he "exists" in the same way as them (though with greater intensity), but he is also moved further away insofar as there is an infinite abyss between them that analogical language is no longer able to bridge. As Catherine Pickstock puts it, "the 'same' becomes the radically disparate and unknowable."[17]

But the story does not end with Duns Scotus. Although Balthasar does not discuss Thomas de Vio, Cardinal Cajetan, there can be no doubt that he is a lead-ing character in this plot, as William C. Placher has recently made clear.[18] His crucial contribution was his development of the doctrine of analogy as articu-lated in his treatise on *The Analogy of Names* (1498). It is clear that Cajetan him-self thought his account of analogy to be faithful to that of Aquinas, and that he was merely "systematizing and developing" it.[19] For centuries, subsequent com-mentators took him at his word, but in recent years this has increasingly been called into question. It has been claimed that Aquinas's account of analogy was deliberately and necessarily unsystematic, and that Cajetan's very attempt to sys-tematize it constituted a betrayal.[20]

Cajetan distinguished between three apparent forms of analogy: the analogy of inequality, the analogy of attribution, and the analogy of proportionality. But, for Cajetan, "according to the true sense of the term . . . only the last mode consti-tutes analogy, and the first one is entirely foreign to analogy."[21] He says that this is because, whereas the so-called analogy of inequality is, in fact, a form of univoc-ity, the analogy of attribution is, on the contrary, merely equivocation.[22] But the important point here is to consider why Cajetan regards the analogy of attribu-tion as equivocal. He defines it as those things "which have a common name, and the notion signified by this name is the same with respect to the term but differ-ent as regards the relationships to this term."[23] He follows Aquinas in citing the example of *healthy,* which is used of an animal as a *subject* of health, of urine as a *sign* of health, and of medicine as a *cause* of health. He says that in this example "it is perfectly clear that the notion of health is not entirely the same nor entirely different, but to a certain extent the same and to a certain extent different. For there is a diversity of relationships, but the term of those relationships is one and the same."[24] Cajetan says that the logician calls analogous names of this kind "equivocal," and he is inclined to agree. This is because a name analogous in this way has no "definite meaning" that is common to all its analogates, and the diverse relationships expressed by the latter are implied in an "indeterminate and confused way."[25] It is because of this indeterminacy that Cajetan regards the analogy of attribution as merely a form of equivocation and therefore not a genuine variant of analogy at all.

In contrast, Cajetan embraces the analogy of proportionality as "analogy in the proper sense" and defines it by saying that "those things are called analogous by proportionality which have a common name, and the notion expressed by this name is similar according to a proportion."[26] Furthermore, he says that the analogy of proportionality may be divided into two occurrences—"metaphorical" and "proper." In the former, one formal meaning is realized in one of the analogates, which is then predicated of the other by metaphor, and Cajetan says that scripture abounds with this form of analogy when teaching of God by means of metaphor. But he says that the analogy of proportionality occurs in the *proper* sense when "the common name is predicated of both analogates without the use of metaphors. For instance, *principle* can be predicated of the heart with respect to an animal and of a foundation with respect to a house."[27] For Cajetan, this is preferable to other forms of analogy because it predicates perfections that are "inherent in each analogate," whereas the other forms of analogy arise from "extrinsic denominations"; thus, he says that "metaphysical speculations without knowledge of this analogy must be said to be unskilled."[28] So Cajetan prefers the analogy of proportionality over the analogy of attribution because the latter is too imprecise and too equivocal. Within the analogy of proportionality itself, he prefers "proper" over "metaphorical" occurrences for precisely the same reason. With each move, therefore, he develops an account of analogy that is increasingly precise and specific and decreasingly equivocal.

So, although Cajetan evidently thinks that his account of analogy is in accord with that of Aquinas,[29] it is clear there has been a fundamental shift here toward univocity. Indeed, Cajetan himself says that the analogy of proportionality is "in a certain sense midway between what is analogous by attribution and what is univocal."[30] Cajetan's theory of analogy is a prime example of the way in which, after Duns Scotus, it was thought that God could be referred to with "clear and distinct" ideas, without "confusion." As Placher observes, "Cajetan had moved a long way from Aquinas. Unsystematic references have become a systematic theory. . . . Far from offering a series of reminders concerning how we cannot understand what we mean when we speak of God, analogy now functioned as a way of explaining just what we do mean."[31]

Francisco Suárez, a Spanish Jesuit, further intensified this "univocist drift"[32] in the theory of analogy, particularly in his *Disputationes metaphysicae* (1597). Balthasar makes it clear that Suárez "has recourse to the Scotist notion of 'univocal being,' the *ens ut sic*, which as the simplest and most universal concept (*conceptus simplicissimus*) is the precise object of metaphysical enquiry."[33] He goes on to say that if this univocal, all-embracing notion were relinquished for the sake of an *analogia entis*, then all the clarity and certainty of metaphysics would be threatened. Thus, Suárez says that "we ought not to deny the unity of the concept in order to defend the analogy; rather, if we had to relinquish one or other of them, then this would be analogy, which is uncertain, and not the unity of the concept, which is based on *certain and demonstrable grounds.*"[34] Thus, analogy is downgraded because it is "uncertain," whereas the metaphysics of being is preferable because it is based on "certain and demonstrable grounds."

We can see here the priority of certainty that was to obsess Descartes and that would characterize the modern philosophical doctrine of foundationalism. As Balthasar points out, for Suárez, a metaphysics that has knowledge of Being as a whole "includes God in the sphere of its object"[35] and can develop a priori the dimensions of Being without direct reference to God and the world. And yet, as the purest realization of "real Being," God is the precise object of metaphysics, its *objectum primarium ac principale.*[36] Thus, Balthasar says that this collapses the distinction between theology and metaphysics and thereby prepares the way for the metaphysics that was to follow. He says that "once freed from the external theological discipline of faith and of the schools, what Suárez pursues with the complete naivety of the schoolman, becomes . . . the direct foundation for modern metaphysics from Descartes, Spinoza and Leibniz to Kant and Hegel."[37]

The implications of this fundamental shift occasioned by Duns Scotus and his successors were wide and far-reaching. For one thing, the dissolution of God's ontological transcendence and the establishment of a univocal concept of Being resulted in a "desymbolization" of the universe.[38] For not only was God said to "exist" univocally, but God was also said to be "good" and "true" univocally. Thus, God came to be spoken of in terms of "clear and distinct" ideas. This, in turn, resulted in an increased emphasis on representation, for if we know what it means to say that God "exists," and if we can use "clear and distinct" ideas to refer to God, then it appears that God can be referred to in much the same way as other "things." Thus, liturgical performance, narrative, and analogy give way to reference, science, and representation.

It is to Duns Scotus, then, that the modern repression of the narrative mode referred to in the previous chapter may be traced. And this emphasis on representation was not limited to theology. As Alliez says, "Politically, economically, from a public as well as a private point of view, *representation has become absolute.*"[39] Furthermore, this emphasis on representation gave rise to a corresponding emphasis on the distinction between subject and object. For if *ens* is, as Duns Scotus says, "the first natural object of our understanding," then this object has to be perceived and represented by a subject. Here is the appearance of the distinction between subject and object *prior to any theological considera-tion.*[40] In all these ways, therefore (and doubtless in many others[41]), it may not be too much of an exaggeration to regard Duns Scotus as the "founder" of modernity.[42] Alliez, for instance, says, "What can be seen to be constituted . . . is a thought whose moving edges end up leading to that scientific revolution destined to make an 'epoch' of our modernity."[43]

In particular, Alliez calls Kant the "last Scotist"[44] and suggests that Duns Scotus's philosophy is doubly implicated in Kant's critical revolution. First, we have seen that Duns Scotus's dissolution of the ontological transcendence of God resulted in an infinite abyss between the finite and infinite. This abyss reaches its culmination in Kant, where knowledge of God is deemed to be beyond the reach of metaphysics; it "ends up delivering the transcendental a priori of a God already so inaccessible to reason that the revelation functions as an object (*supplet vicem objecti*), a pure object of faith, a 'thing in itself' and not one for us."[45] Second, Alliez says that Kant extends and completes the break with Aristotelianism. Kant marks the temporal and brilliant end of this revolution, "when the categorical diverting of the divine to which the dynamics of transcendence lent its voice is no longer anything but time, empty form, . . . no longer existing 'in itself' except within the relation between being and cognition, within the a priori foundation of the object of prefigured being."[46]

This line of continuity running between Duns Scotus and Kant is significant because we shall see that the Kantian heritage is accorded a pivotal role not only in certain strands of the modern, liberal theological tradition but also in the process of the subversion of that tradition into a subsequent postmodernism. As Bernard Reardon says, "Immanuel Kant is a Janus-figure. One face looks back across the century which produced him, while the other is turned toward that which succeeded it, of which his doctrines are in important ways the herald."[47] Thus, insofar as Kant was the "last Scotist," it may be said that the contemporary tradition of modern liberal theology (together with that of liberal secular humanism), as well as the postmodernism that emerged out of it, is derived from certain philosophical movements that took place within theology beginning in the fourteenth century.

John Hick: Modernity Incarnate

It is time now to look at how Duns Scotus's legacy is manifested in contemporary theological thought. To this end, I shall discuss the modern liberal theology of John Hick. This is not to suggest that Hick explicitly acknowledges his intellectual indebtedness to Duns Scotus, but we shall see that the implications of the Scotist innovations we have been discussing are fully explicated in Hick's thought. Furthermore, Hick's explicit indebtedness to Kant firmly places him in a "modernist" philosophical tradition, the origins of which, we have seen, may be traced back to Duns Scotus. Indeed, in his doctoral dissertation and in a spray of articles, Gerard Loughlin has comprehensively explicated the ways in which John Hick is indebted to a specifically "modernist" philosophical tradition.[48] Any number of contemporary theologians are illustrative of this indebtedness to modernity, but John Hick is perhaps one of the most provocative, influential, and prolific in both the United States and Great Britain and has been described by Don Cupitt as the "platonic ideal of the liberal theologian."[49]

Let us begin with a brief identification of the intellectual and philosophical climate within which Hick's work arose. When Hick embarked on his academic career in the mid-1950s, the philosophical climate was still much dominated by the logical positivism championed by A. J. Ayer. As Adrian Hastings observes, "With the fading away of British Hegelianism, the ruling school was that of 'Linguistic Analysis', whose most influential exposition was to be found in A. J. Ayer's *Language, Truth and Logic* (1936). At that point 'Linguistic Analysis' had been synonymous with 'Logical Positivism,' according to which all metaphysics, all theology, and all statements of religious belief were but meaningless nonsense."[50] For Ayer, all meaningful statements had to be capable of verification. But by the mid-1950s, this orthodoxy was increasingly called into question by religious apologists and others. One such effort could be found in the symposium *New Essays in Philosophical Theology* (1955), edited by Antony Flew and Alasdair MacIntyre,[51] referred to by Hastings as "a pretty weak theistic defence against a prevailing agnostic confidence that linguistic philosophy had finally demonstrated the meaninglessness of religion."[52] Another such effort was R. B. Braithwaite's essay "An Empiricist's View of the Nature of Religious Belief" (1955).[53] Yet another was John Hick's first book, *Faith and Knowledge*, published two years later in 1957. What was significant about all these contributions was that their respective (and very different) defenses of the legitimacy of religious language did not constitute challenges to the logical positivist framework itself; rather, it was claimed that religious language could be defended *within* such a framework.

This is evident in John Hick's book when he acknowledges that "verifiability is a valid criterion of factual meaning. Accordingly, in order to be either veridical or illusory the mode of experiencing that we call religious faith must be such that the theological statements which express it are either verifiable or falsifiable."[54] It is in response to this challenge that Hick develops his notion of "eschatological verification." He says that the possibility of experiential confirmation is "built into the Christian concept of God; and the notion of eschatological verification seeks to relate this fact to the problem of theological meaning."[55] Hick's point is that religious statements are not akin to R. M. Hare's *bliks*,[56] nor should they be understood in terms of the "conative" utterances of R. B. Braithwaite, for at death, either the theist or the atheist will be vindicated. Thus, theism is not just an attitude to life but a statement about reality that will one day be verified or falsified.

Hick points out that the notion of "eschatological verification" has not been developed as part of an apologetic for religious belief or to confirm the religious believer in his faith, "but that the philosopher—whether believer or not—wants to know what aspects of Christian belief bring that system of belief within the accepted criteria of meaningfulness."[57] He is therefore taking up the gauntlet thrown down by the logical positivists and accepting their ground rules, insofar as they claim that meaningful religious statements stand in need of verification.[58] Indeed, these ground rules formed the parameters of Hick's philosophical framework throughout his career. In this sense, therefore, the epistemology set out in *Faith and Knowledge* remains fundamental to all his subsequent writings. In his own words, "my own subsequent writings in the philosophy of religion have proceeded in a natural trajectory from the epistemology of *Faith and Knowledge*."[59]

Although the theology became progressively more liberal, the underlying epistemological structure remained relatively constant.

I shall now consider how God is conceived within this "positivist" framework.
It is significant that, for Hick, knowledge of God is attained in much the same
way as we attain knowledge of the natural and human spheres. It would appear
that God is a "thing," albeit an infinite and unique "thing," and can be known
to us in the same sort of way as other things.[60] In *Faith and Knowledge*, Hick is
concerned to show that "while the object of religious knowledge is unique, its
basic epistemological pattern is that of all our knowing."[61] He distinguishes
among three main orders of situational significance: the natural, the human, and
the divine. In each of these realms, a basic act of interpretation discloses to us the
existence of the sphere in question, thus providing the ground for our many and
diverse interpretations within that sphere. Thus, as Hick explains, his purpose
has been to "bring out the similarity of epistemological structure and status
between man's basic convictions in relation to the world, moral responsibility and
divine existence."[62] There is therefore an epistemological continuity between
human knowledge of God and of the world. We have already seen that such a
continuity was made possible by the innovations of Duns Scotus and the subsequent dissolution of Aquinas's understanding of analogy.

This epistemological continuity between religious experience and sense experience inevitably has implications for how Hick understands God's transcendence. The tendency of post-Scotist thought to make God epistemologically
rather than ontologically transcendent, as observed above, is equally explicit in
Hick's writings, as in his discussion of man's freedom in relation to God: "The
kind of distance between god and man that would make room for a degree of
human autonomy is *epistemic distance*."[63] His argument is that God's reality and
presence cannot be self-evident and unambiguously manifest in the natural environment, since this would compromise humankind's freedom in relation to the
Divine. It is for this reason that God must be epistemologically transcendent:
"God must be a hidden deity, veiled by his creation. He must be knowable, but
only by a mode of knowledge that involves a free personal response on man's part,
this response consisting in an uncompelled interpretative activity whereby we
experience the world as mediating divine presence."[64] So Hick writes of God
being hidden and transcendent exclusively in epistemological terms. Ontologically, God appears to be as one with the rest of the world, our knowledge of God
corresponding to our knowledge of the natural and human spheres.[65]

Hick's conception of God's ontological "oneness" with the world has
inevitable implications for the way in which he understands language to refer to
God. We have seen that whereas Aquinas emphasized that God's ontological
transcendence meant that *nothing* could be said of God univocally, Hick is not
content with such mystery. For although he wants to speak of "metaphor" in religious language, this is merely an emotive way of conveying something that can
be translated into "literal" language. In other words, it is a distinctively "modern"
understanding of metaphor.[66] For example, Hick argues that faith in eternal life

must necessarily be pictured in quasi-earthly terms if it is to have any meaning. He says that unless this is the case, it is in danger of falling into meaninglessness. He asks, "Is it a responsible use of language to speak of eternal life, immortality, the life to come, heaven and hell, and then to add that this language carries no implications whatever regarding the continuation or otherwise of human personality beyond the grave?"[67]

Once again, it is evident that Hick is caught in a modern antinomy between language referring in an unequivocal sense and language carrying "no implications whatever." The possibility of a linguistic theory that transcends this antinomy is not considered.[68] The result is that Hick finds it necessary to "spell out" in an unambiguous and unequivocal way, in terms of "clear and distinct" ideas, what is meant by various theological statements and doctrines. Thus, he says, "a doctrine which can mean anything means nothing. So long, then, as we refrain from spelling out our faith it must remain empty."[69] The inevitable result of such spelling out, however, is that Hick's understanding of theological doctrines tends toward anthropomorphism, which is precisely what Aquinas wanted to avoid in his insistence on the ontological transcendence of God. Thus, for Hick, eternal life, for instance, is merely a continuation of this life, with all its cognitive limitations, but on a higher level.[70]

Paradoxically, however, although Hick wants to speak of God and Christian doctrines in terms of clear and distinct ideas and in unambiguous and unequivocal language, God eventually becomes so epistemologically transcendent that God becomes dogmatically unknowable and almost disappears altogether. We have already observed this paradox in the first section of this chapter, where we saw that Duns Scotus's dissolution of the ontological difference between God and humanity resulted in an epistemic distance that gave rise to an infinite abyss between them. The inexorable consequence of this is that God becomes strictly and substantively unknowable, as in the philosophy of Immanuel Kant. This emphasis on the unknowability of God is most evident in Hick's philosophy of religious pluralism, which dates from *God and the Universe of Faiths* (1973), and which was given its most comprehensive expression in *An Interpretation of Religion* (1989). It is also in his philosophy of religious pluralism that his indebtedness to Kant is most explicit. As Gerard Loughlin says, "The character of Hick's unknowing, like that of his fellow mythographer Don Cupitt, is Kantian. If his hermeneutic is Kant's categorical, his *apophasis* is Kant's noumenal. It is not the disclosure of a revelation, but the display of an epistemology. . . . Hick's epistemology is merely the affirmation of human ignorance."[71]

Indeed, in Hick's pluralist hypothesis, God has become so epistemologically distant as to be displaced by the "Real," about which we can have no substantive knowledge, although "God" is retained as a particular and mythological expression of the "Real." The pluralistic hypothesis is best summarized in Hick's own words, when he says that "the great world faiths embody different perceptions and conceptions of, and correspondingly different responses to, the Real from within the major variant ways of being human; and that within each of them the transformation of human existence from self-centredness to Reality-centredness is taking place. These traditions are accordingly to be regarded as alternative soteriological 'spaces' within which, or 'ways' along which, men and women can find salvation/liberation/ultimate fulfilment."[72]

This proposal is founded on the centrality of religious experience, which is, for Hick, the sole grounds on which the religious believer may justify her beliefs. He says that "it is totally reasonable and rational for the religious person, looking at the whole continuum of religious experience and participating in one's own small way in that continuum, to proceed to live and to form beliefs on the basis of it."[73] But this also leads Hick to take seriously the experience of religious believers in the other world religious traditions. He can perceive no grounds for denying the validity of these experiences as well and so concludes that they must be equally valid as grounds for belief for the respective experiencers. But because the contents of these experiences, as well as the contents of the belief systems they are purported to uphold, are blatantly contradictory, this leaves Hick open to the charge that these experiences and the traditions within which they occur are all illusory, or at least works of human construction. It is in order to guard against this charge that Hick asserts that there is a divine Real behind all these various experiences of it. Thus, Hick says that these experiences, together with the divine *personae* and *impersonae* to which they give rise, "are not illusory but are empirically, that is experientially, real as authentic manifestations of the Real."[74]

To articulate the distinction between the Real in itself and the Real as humanly experienced, Hick invokes the Kantian distinction between noumenon and phenomenon. In the *Critique of Pure Reason*, Kant points out that since the properties of the object as experienced by the subject "depend upon the mode of intuition of the subject, this object as *appearance* is to be distinguished from itself as object *in itself*."[75] Thus, he distinguishes between noumenon and phenomenon, or between the *Ding an sich* (the thing in itself) and that thing as it appears through the interpretation of consciousness. Hick says that Kant uses the term *noumenon* not in the positive sense of "that which is knowable by some faculty of non-sensible intuition (for we have no such faculty)"[76] but in the negative sense of "a thing in so far as it is *not an object of our sensible intuition*."[77]

Hick, however, invokes this Kantian epistemology with two qualifications. First, Kant was concerned with the construction of the physical world in sense perception, whereas Hick applies this theory to the realm of religious experience. While recognizing that Kant himself does not make this move, Hick says that this "does not bar others, inspired by his basic insights, from seeing religious and sense experience as continuous in kind, thereby extending Kant's analysis of the one, in an appropriately adapted form, to the other."[78] Second, for Kant, the noumenal world, together with the human mind, produces the phenomenal world of our experience through the "filter" of what Kant calls the *categories* of understanding (quantity, quality, relation, modality, and their subdivisions), which are a priori and hence universal and invariable. Hick, however, maintains that these categories (of religious experience) "are not universal and invariable but are on the contrary culture-relative. It is possible to live without employing them; and when they are employed they tend to change and develop through time as different historical influences affect the development of human consciousness."[79]

This latter modification is highly significant. For Kant clearly distinguished between judgments of perception and judgments of experience; the former are only subjectively valid, whereas the latter have objective validity. It is only when judgments of perception have been filtered through the a priori categories that they are able to become judgments of experience and thereby become objectively valid. In other words, for Kant, it is the a priori categories that secure and preserve the objectivity of knowledge; without them, knowledge would be mere subjectivity. As Kant puts it, these categories determine empirical judgments "thereby procuring them universal validity, and by means of them, making judgments of experience in general possible."[80] In dispensing with the a priori character of these categories and in making them culture relative, Hick precludes the objectivity of knowledge that is so fundamental to Kant's system (and on which his refutation of Humean skepticism rested). This, in turn, means that Hick's residual (and now groundless) objectivism (i.e., the Real) becomes increasingly empty and superfluous. In other words, Hick's Real is now giving way to the nonreal. As Paul Eddy puts it, Hick's proposal "represents an intensification of Kantian subjectivity—transposed to the religious realm—and thus threatens any realist core with immanent collapse."[81]

Following J. William Forgie, Eddy observes that, for Kant, the categories "shape" the experience, but they do not provide the *content* of the experience. For Hick, in contrast, the categories do contribute to the actual phenomenological content of the experience. He says that Hick's qualification "forces the conclusion that the human subject's religious category-analogues, schematized by their religio-cultural systems, *can* account for both the form and content of religious experience. And thus one is forced to ask what, in fact, differentiates Hick's neo-Kantian constructivism from the essentially identical reductionist anti-realist models?"[82] This question is a pertinent one, for this slide toward non-realism is one that Hick resists only with difficulty. It would appear to be the inexorable outcome of his qualified Kantian epistemology.[83] We shall see below how Don Cupitt takes an almost identical epistemology to its logical conclusion.

But what is particularly significant here is that the infinite abyss between the Divine and the human, instituted by Duns Scotus, now reaches its apotheosis. Through Hick's invocation of Kant, the "last Scotist," the word of Scotus has become incarnate in the theology of Hick. For now the Divine has become so epistemologically distant that even the word *God* can no longer apply to it. The Real is utterly mysterious and completely hidden, something "outside the scope of our cognitive capacities."[84] The Real appears to have become so distant that it has almost disappeared from the epistemological horizon altogether. In a line that we shall see to be continuous, this disappearance is finally realized in the nonrealism and subsequent postmodernism of Don Cupitt.

Nihilist Textualism:
The Apotheosis of Modernity

I shall now discuss the ways in which our two versions of postmodern theology are related to the "modernist" tradition we have thus far been considering, and I suggest that they are related to it in quite antithetical ways. I begin by looking at the postmodern nihilist textualist theology, showing that it initially accepts the modern liberal framework and then presses its premises so thoroughly and consistently that they eventually subvert themselves. To illustrate this, I look again at the work of Don Cupitt, to show how his move from realism to non-realism, and subsequently from modernism to postmodernism, was prompted by a prior acceptance of the modern liberal framework. I identify three factors in particular: first, a Kantian-inspired epistemology; second, a distinctively modernist understanding of the *via negativa*; and third, an ethical emphasis on the concept of disinterestedness. So I argue that Cupitt's postmodernism emerged organically and logically out of the modern liberal theology he had formerly professed.[85] It is in this sense, therefore, that I suggest that nihilist textualist theology should be regarded as the *apotheosis* of modernity.

I begin by examining the nature of the modern liberal theology that Cupitt formerly espoused. He subsequently described it as "a moderate version of British Empiricism"[86] that emerged out of the same philosophical and cultural milieu as that of Hick, as outlined above. Much of his work was devoted to the early-nineteenth-century Anglican theologian Henry Mansel,[87] whom Bernard Reardon has referred to as a striking example of "Kantian agnosticism."[88] This is significant because, although Cupitt was as firmly committed to a Kantian epistemology as was Hick, his interest in Mansel is indicative of those strands of Kant's thought that Cupitt was pressing into service, namely, the idealist and agnostic strands. For although Kant did not explicitly espouse either idealism or agnosticism, these are certainly modes of thought for which "Kant's philosophy might be called in aid."[89]

During the 1970s, however, Cupitt remained committed to realism and objectivism. Thus, he was as one with Hick in his insistence on the cognitive nature of religious statements and in rejecting the sort of non-realism he was later to profess. He said, "Faith may enable a man to apprehend an object which otherwise he could not have apprehended, but it does not create that which it apprehends. On the contrary, it is in the last analysis receptive."[90] If religious language is receptive, however, one is led to inquire into the nature of this reception. How does religious language "connect" with that about which it purports to speak?

Cupitt addresses this question in *The Leap of Reason* (1976). He suggests that the subject's religious quest begins with an affirmation of the *possibility* of an objective, transcendent realm on the basis of the subject's "own heightened consciousness": the leap of reason. This transcendent realm is an absolute perspective "from which human world-views can be compared, and which provides the Archimedean point by which we can make the transition from one of them to another."[91] A great communal effort "projects human and this-worldly features upon the unknowable face of the transcendent." This results in all the "myth, doctrine, morals, rituals, symbols, and visible institutions." Such a religion is true insofar as its fruits are intellectually, morally, and aesthetically satisfying. There must, however, be an iconoclastic negation of such a religious system, in recognition that "I am obliged to recognize the limitations of even the noblest religious system that can be devised."[92] Cupitt acknowledges that such a negation gives rise to a built-in agnosticism, and to guard against this, he advocates that religion live in a constant flux and reflux between the affirmation and negation of all religious symbols. He says that this is central to any monotheistic religion: "It is this fiery dance between the affirmation of images and their negation, between rapturous piety and the cry of dereliction, which is the heart of religion."[93]

We may say, therefore, that the religious philosophy of the early Cupitt embodied a number of quintessentially modern and liberal characteristics. He begins with the individual's "heightened consciousness" and prelinguistic religious experience; he regards religious traditions as local mythical expressions of a single underlying reality; and he exercises subjective rationality as a means of expressing a universal human condition. I shall now look at the philosophical processes by which Cupitt subverted this tradition, showing how the subversion was prompted by an explication of what was already implicit in this modern liberal framework itself.

Rowan Williams has observed that the foremost figures of influence in Cupitt's subversion of liberalism into non-realism were Kant and the Buddha. Whereas the Buddha is the authoritative precedent for Cupitt's religious vision, Kant provides that vision with much of its philosophical underpinning.[94] Like Hick, therefore, Cupitt embraced a Kantian epistemology, and with much the same qualifications. First, Cupitt rejected Kant's universal categories in favor of cultural-relative ones. Kant, he said, "recognized that our empirical knowledge is relative to intellectual programming, but thought he could vindicate the objectivity of knowledge by proving *a priori* that there is and can be only one programme. But we know empirically that there is an endless variety of different programmes."[95] Like Hick, therefore, Cupitt intensified Kant's subjectivist tendencies by insisting on the relativity of his categories. He thereby moved away from Kant's universalism to a much more subjectivist relativism. Although at this point he still resisted thoroughgoing relativism by invoking a transcendent realm "which alone is able to relativize and so overcome relativism itself,"[96] as with Hick's Real, this came to appear increasingly empty and superfluous. It was therefore a small step to abandoning the noumena in favor of nothing but phenomena, to abandoning the Real in favor of the non-real.

Thus, when Cupitt criticized the "thinness" of Hick's theism, he was as much criticizing his own transcendent cipher of four years earlier: "the more Hick realizes how varied and how human religion is, the thinner his God must surely become. When everything said of God is seen as highly variable, symbolic and culturally conditioned, then religious language ceases actually to describe God.

It becomes cultural expression, not metaphysical description."[97] For Cupitt, once this is realized, religion becomes noncognitive, expressive, regulative, and non-realist. He urges Hick to "take just one more step and say that religion is wholly human and that religious practices and values must be chosen and followed for their own sakes, disinterestedly. . . . Like painting and music, religion is not obliged to be about anything other than itself."[98] And it is evident that it is precisely Cupitt's appropriation and development of a Kantian epistemology that tended him toward this subjectivism and non-realism.

Let us now turn to the second decisive internal pressure that prompted the turn from liberalism to non-realism. Stephen Ross White asks what it was that prompted Cupitt to take this turn in 1980 and answers, "It was, I believe, a fusion of his previous ideas about the *via negativa*—now worked out more fully and in a more organized fashion—with a new realization of the implications of that negative way if followed to its own logical conclusion."[99] The *via negativa* had always been an important concept for Cupitt, because of its importance for divine transcendence, which he had always striven to preserve. If God is indeed utterly transcendent, then God cannot be contained by or equated with the divine images found in the various religious traditions or programs. But the harder the concept of (epistemological rather than ontological) transcendence is pressed, the less knowable, and therefore the less *real,* God becomes.

As we saw in our discussion of Duns Scotus, without an ontological difference between God and humanity, divine transcendence can be preserved only by making God epistemologically more and more distant until God eventually disappears altogether. As Cupitt says (in a mode that is more Spinozist that Kantian), "Over the years I have tried to combine belief in God with spiritual freedom by pressing the themes of the 'negative theology' and the divine transcendence ever harder. . . . God had to become objectively thinner and thinner in order to allow subjective religiousness to expand. It is only one step further to the objectively atheous position here propounded."[100]

The Christian tradition of negative theology is, of course, an ancient one. It has been suggested, however, that Cupitt's appropriation of it is distinctively modern, and that it is framed by philosophical presuppositions that are inherently anti-incarnational. Denys Turner, for instance, has pointed out that Cupitt's *via negativa* has little in common with classical mystical apophaticism.[101] In fact, this was something that Cupitt freely admitted: "The old negative way belonged with and was intelligible in terms of a certain view of the universe which has now passed away."[102] Cupitt says that this universe was one that was comprised of a hierarchy of powers or energies, in which the doctrine of "degrees of being" made sense. It was thus a "descending power-hierarchy" emanating from above. The old negative way belonged to this ancient universe, and now that it has passed away, the old negative theology must give way to a modern one. "The modern negative theology, after Kant, has to endure objective uncertainty about the existence of God. There are many ways of trying to cope with this but, however one copes with it, it is a new situation."[103]

So Cupitt posits a clear distinction between the classical negative theology of Aquinas and his own "modern" negative theology after Kant. Aquinas's apophaticism may have been intelligible in a medieval universe, but in our universe, claims Cupitt, such formulas appear utterly vacuous. This is perhaps to be expected of an epistemology that is ultimately derived from Aquinas's archrival, Duns Scotus. But it is for this reason that Cupitt instead espoused a modern Kantian understanding of the *via negativa*, maintaining that Kant's fundamental innovation in this respect was to insist that it is God's *existence* rather than God's *nature* that is unknowable.[104] Cupitt says, "For Kant the proofs of God's existence fail, and the old doctrine is in any case empty and morally objectionable. In his view, acceptance of a positive revelation of supra-rational truth would subject us to an odious *despotism of mystery*. The Ideal of Reason is an available God who is intellectually and morally acceptable, and we must preserve strict agnosticism about the real God."[105] Cupitt therefore makes a distinction between two conceptions of God: an "available God" and a "real God." It is the latter that guarantees objectivity of knowledge and a metaphysical realism, and yet it is this conception that a fully developed negative theology must leave behind. In other words, the constitutive, transcendent God must give way to the regulative "working God" of practical religion. With this move, truth becomes subjective and realism gives way to non-realism.

A third internal pressure that induced the turn to non-realism was an ethical emphasis on the concept of disinterestedness. Cupitt says that "religion is a requirement of absolute disinterestedness, and that one should be thus absolutely disinterested is not a thing that can be determined *ab extra* by any metaphysical fact whatsoever."[106] Indeed, Cupitt claims that metaphysical facts can only destroy disinterestedness, or at the very least lead to intolerable paradoxes. How, Cupitt asks, is disinterested love of God possible when, according to the canons of the Council of Trent, for instance, "it was perfectly correct for the Christian to be motivated by the thought of heavenly rewards and hellish punishments"?[107] For Cupitt, the presence of such *motives* destroys disinterestedness, and the only way for religious doctrines to be purged of such eudaemonism is for them to operate "in an informal and mythological fashion. . . . The doctrines work not as rational motives but merely as picturesque reinforcements of the autonomous religious requirement."[108] So, when pressed to its extreme conclusion, the concept of disinterestedness pushed Cupitt toward a non-realist interpretation of theological doctrines. Once again, however, Cupitt's concept of disinterestedness is one that is deeply indebted to Kant. For Kant, the moral person "stands in need neither of the idea of another Being over him, for him to apprehend his duty, nor an incentive other than the law itself, for him to do his duty."[109] Indeed, morality "is perfectly able to ignore all ends, and it ought to do so."[110] For an act to be properly moral, it must be performed regardless of any incentive or end.

The concept of disinterestedness does stand in some continuity with the ancient Christian tradition, and Balthasar traces a line from Meister Eckhart (to whom Cupitt also appeals) and Tauler to Ignatius and Fénelon. He says that, just as for these thinkers, "the detachment and indifference of *amour pur* becomes perfect as love solely for the Beloved, in the same way Kant demands the performance of good for the sake of the good, without primary consideration of happiness or goal or reward."[111] But in contrast to premodern thinkers, Kant was following in the wake of the early moderns, who took the concept of disinterestedness to new extremes. They emphasized the idea of loving God for God's own sake, quite apart from *any* considerations of reciprocity, whether of one's own eschatological destiny or of God's regard for oneself.[112] As Kenneth Kirk has pointed out, the protest against motives for ethical action attained its greatest volume in the seventeenth century and, indeed, reached the heights of controversy in the dispute between Bossuet and Fénelon.[113]

John Milbank says that the earlier tradition resisted such an extreme interpretation for two main reasons. First, following Balthasar, he says that to claim to acknowledge God in abstraction from our own hopes and fears may appear to constitute a self-obliteration in the face of otherness, but it also indicates a paradoxical identification with this otherness and an impossible crossing of the creator/creature divide—in which case, the relationship between creator and creature becomes "strikingly depersonalized." Second, Milbank says that to love anything quite apart from any consideration of its influence on oneself means not loving that thing in its specificity but merely for its possession of an abstract quality of "being" that it shares with everything else. In the case of God, it turns out to mean "not only to over-identify with him, but also to over-identify with a mere cipher, or at best a hovering will. Hence the mystical discourse on indifference tended to determine the essence of the unknown as empty freedom or even, incipiently, the void."[114] In other words, an extreme (or modernist) emphasis on the doctrine of disinterestedness correspondingly leads to a construal of the Divine as a void or, in Cupitt's terms, as a "real" God about which we must remain agnostic.

Furthermore, Milbank says that "extreme 'disinterest' in one's activity, though it can only be exercised by a subject, tends also to a suicidally sacrificial will against oneself. That is to say, it ends ineradicably to depersonalize or devolve into a will to be a fully usable object."[115] So, for Milbank, such a concept of disinterestedness ultimately leads to the annihilation not only of the Divine but also of the self. Once again, therefore, it appears that Cupitt's appeal to disinterestedness is another distinctively modern appropriation of another apparently ancient concept, a modernist appropriation that ultimately leads to an embrace of the nihilistic "void." Again, Cupitt's eventual postmodernism may be regarded as the apotheosis or logical culmination of the modern and liberal theological tradition he had formerly occupied.

To a certain extent, Cupitt concurs with such an analysis. This is clear when he describes postmodern religion as *ecstatic liberalism*.[116] But for Cupitt, postmodernism is not only the culmination but also the subversion of liberalism. Hence, he says that when one has made the postmodern turn, "then Enlightenment *passes* completion and begins to turn back upon itself and devour itself."[117] Radical orthodox theologians agree that such nihilistic postmodernism is the culmination of liberalism but deny that there is any real subversion of the tradition. Graham Ward, for instance, suggests that nihilism "is not the deconstruction of the liberal tradition (however much [nihilist postmodernists] employ the term 'deconstruction'), it is the apotheosis of the liberal tradition."[118] Thus, far from being a subversion of liberalism, Cupitt's postmodernism is viewed as a form of "cosmic liberalism." Let us therefore turn to examine the relationship of radical orthodoxy to the modernist philosophical tradition we have thus far been examining.

Radical Orthodoxy: The Scourge of Modernity

For postmodern radical orthodox theologians, the whole project of "modernity," inaugurated by Duns Scotus, is considered to be a "wrong turn," and it is considered as such on theological grounds; for in placing God in a predefined arena of being, Duns Scotus was denying the primacy, ultimacy, and absoluteness of God. Insofar as this innovation denied the priority of God, it entailed a turning away from God and, as such, was a fundamentally "heretical," idolatrous, and secular move. Milbank says that Duns Scotus's innovation eventually "encourages the thought that God is not so much *esse* as meekly ontic, 'a Supreme Being', or 'first cause'. Already with Cajetan, God is considered to fall under the category of 'individual', where for Aquinas, he was neither individual nor universal. Hence the transcendentality of Unity is lost, and monotheism lapses into idolatry."[119]

For Milbank, because the whole project of modernity (philosophical, cultural, economic) is founded on this Scotist move, modernity itself cannot be other than heretical, idolatrous, and secular. And because, as we saw in the previous chapter and in our discussion of Cupitt above, postmodernism is, in many ways, an "exacerbation" of modernity, it, too, is equally heretical, idolatrous, and secular. Thus, insofar as "secular" postmodernism is the culmination or apotheosis of modernity, it is a postmodernism that Milbank wants to overcome, whereas insofar as postmodernism genuinely *overcomes* modernity, it is a postmodernism that Milbank wants to embrace. But he maintains that the only postmodernism that can genuinely overcome modernity is theology. This is because modernity is itself founded in the antitheological moment of Duns Scotus, and so an overcoming of that modernity can reside only in the reversal of Duns Scotus's antitheology, a reversal into theology. In this sense, only theology can be a genuine *post*-modernism; only theology can overcome metaphysics; and only theology can overcome modernity.[120] It is clear, then, that in contrast to postmodern nihilist textualist theology, radical orthodoxy *overcomes* rather than *develops* the modernity it succeeds. In this act, it stands as the *scourge* of modernity.

Thus far in this chapter, we have considered a genealogy of modernity in which Duns Scotus stands at one end and Immanuel Kant at the other. We saw that Éric Alliez described Kant as the last Scotist, and that Kant was the dominating presence in Hick's epistemology, as well as in Cupitt's "hyperbolical subversion" of it. We also saw that Alliez emphasized Duns Scotus's implication in Kant's critical revolution. Conversely, Milbank has suggested that, with hindsight, we may view Kant as being implicated in Duns Scotus's revolution, and that the latter's metaphysics has a "proto-transcendentalist" character.[121] It would appear, then, that Duns Scotus and Kant are equally implicated in the metaphysics of modernity, and that each is implicated in the metaphysics of the other. Thus, if Milbank stands as the scourge of the univocity of Duns Scotus, he equally stands as the scourge of the transcendentalism of Kant.

We have seen that one of the major factors of influence in Cupitt's transition from a modern liberal framework toward (if not into) his subsequent postmodernism was a conflation of a Kantian epistemology with the *via negativa*. It is precisely such a conflation that Milbank is concerned to reject. Like Cupitt, he distinguishes between the negative way of Aquinas and the negative way of Kant, but unlike Cupitt, he maintains that Aquinas's way is the only theologically viable option. He says that, whereas Kant is totally agnostic concerning "God-in-himself," but in a way dogmatic with regard to God's relationship with finite beings, Aquinas completely reverses this situation: that is, Aquinas is less agnostic concerning "God-in-himself" but more agnostic with regard to the conditions of our relationship to God. According to Milbank, "It is only Aquinas's agnosticism which really exemplifies the principle that there is no *ratio* between finite and infinite, and upholds the ontological difference."[122]

Milbank suggests that Kant's "metaphysics of the sublime," as articulated in the *Critique of Judgement*, is crucial here, and indeed, that Kant's entire philosophy is in a sense an aesthetic of the sublime. This is because, for Kant, it is possible to stand at the *boundary* of reason and understanding, of noumenon and phenomenon. Unlike a limit, which is primarily negative, a boundary has a positive aspect—to grasp it, one must, in a way, stand outside it, even if this standing outside is very minimal, as it was for Kant. For Kant knew absolutely that there was an "other" beyond this boundary but did not know the content of this "other" or the "things in themselves." What Kant did know, however, was that our finite categories could not apply to the "other."[123] Thus, Milbank says that "one will recognize that far from being (like Aquinas) agnostically cautious about the extrapolation of categories from our material, finite, temporal existence, Kant was *metaphysically dogmatic* in affirming that they *do not at all* apply, precisely because he believed (unlike Aquinas) that he had direct cognitive access in practical reason to what the immaterial and atemporal is like."[124] Milbank goes on to say that from this vantage point, Kant supposedly "saw" that categories such as "cause" and "substance," though not derived from sensation, can be applied only to the deliverances of sensation. But when this happens, the nihilistic and postmodern turn becomes inevitable: "Once the notion of a pre-established harmony and a noumenal exceeding of the categories of the mere 'understanding' are abandoned, one will realize that such categories simply belong to our linguistic being-in-the-world, and the question, 'Can they be extrapolated?' pertains to the question 'Is there a "beyond", a transcendent at all?'"[125] In other words, a conflation of the *via negativa* with Kant's agnosticism inexorably leads one to abandon the transcendent (as indeed Cupitt did), and such abandonment is ultimately nihilistic and, as such, the antithesis of Christianity.

Thus, Milbank would claim that Cupitt's error is not to have extrapolated the nihilistic tendencies in Kantian metaphysics (an extrapolation with which he concurs) but rather to have accepted the Kantian epistemology in the first place. Milbank suggests that the nihilistic tendencies in Kantian metaphysics were recognized as long ago as the late eighteenth century by the "radical pietists" Johann Georg Hamann and Franz Heinrich Jacobi. He says that Jacobi in particular was able to show how Kant's critical turn did not disturb Spinoza's requirement that the real only be recognized by a court of "irresistible rational necessity," with the result that "the Spinozistic void re-appears as the things-in-themselves which are epistemologically nothing, and therefore beyond Kant (as Fichte soon agreed with Jacobi) might as well *be* nothing. And again, what we truly know are only appearances—so, in effect, once more: nothing."[126] This is a tendency we saw manifested in Hick's work and fully realized in Cupitt's. We saw that Hick's "Real" became so epistemologically transcendent as almost to disappear altogether, and that for Cupitt, Kant's "things-in-themselves" or Hick's "Real" does indeed become "epistemologically nothing."

Milbank says that Kant's limitation of perception to a supposed legal constitution of the finite is actually a false modesty that turns dialectically into Promethean hubris, because "if the finite does not convey some inkling of the infinite, it might as well be a finitude our subjectivity has somehow constructed and the infinite might as well be the trans-subjective abyss our subjectivity emerges from and again negatively projects—as Fichte, Hegel and Schelling all in the last analysis concluded."[127] So Milbank argues that without God, "nothing" becomes as real as actuality itself. He says that, paradoxically, this is the irrational conclusion to which reason must necessarily be led.[128] If this is the case, then all forms of thought that are not theologically grounded (that is, all forms of thought that trace their lineages back to Duns Scotus) are disguised forms of nihilism. Postmodern nihilism removes this disguise and reveals itself for what it is.

This means that, for Milbank, the ultimate and unavoidable choice lies between theology and nihilism. He says that to be human means, primarily, that we must reckon with an immense depth behind things, and that there are only two possible attitudes to this depth. The first follows Kant in distinguishing between what is clear and what is hidden; "but then the depth is an abyss, and what appears, as only apparent, will equally induce vertigo."[129] This is why critical philosophy or pure reason is ultimately the stance of nihilism, and postmodernism simply adds that appearances themselves are in ceaseless flux. The second possible attitude is that "we trust the depth, and appearance as the gift of depth, and history as the restoration of the loss of this depth in Christ. By comparison with *this reason*—Christianity—we can see easily the secret identity of all impersonal religions which celebrate fate or the void with the nihilism of modernity."[130] So Hick's "liberal enclave" is an illusion, for modern liberalism contains within itself the seeds for its own destruction. And Cupitt's journey from his own liberal enclave to his subsequent non-realism and postmodernism vividly illustrates the way in which these internal seeds grow to devour themselves. Thus it is that Milbank presents us with a choice of either nihilism or theology and says that it is indeed an "either/or." He says that there is "no liberal enclave in which one can shelter from 'mystical nihilism.' The real cultural issue lies between this nihilism and theology."[131] For Milbank, as we have seen, the only resolution of this cultural issue must be the out-narration of nihilism by theology. Thus, far from being the apotheosis of modernity, the postmodernism of radical orthodox theology stands as the scourge of modernity.

Interlude

If it is generally the case that postmodernism—in whatever context—is inexplicable apart from the modernity with which it is bound up, then this chapter provides a particular and vivid illustration of that generality. For we have seen that the two radically divergent theological responses to postmodernism on the part of Cupitt and Milbank are explicable only in terms of their antithetical evaluations of modernity. For Cupitt, modernity is to be embraced as a necessary transitional period between the tyranny of dogmatism and the salvific freedom of our postmodern condition. For Milbank, in contrast, modernity was a disastrous "wrong turn" that took Christendom away from perfect freedom in the service of Christ to the nightmare of a secular tyranny that is drained of value. And yet, this radical divergence conceals a certain convergence, namely, that both Cupitt and Milbank maintain that modernity is inherently unstable, that it must deconstruct itself according to its own premises, and that it must ultimately culminate in nihilism.

The divergence lies in their respective evaluations of this culmination. Nihilist textualist theology embraces postmodernism because it is the explicit culmination of modernity, whereas radical orthodox theology rejects it on the same grounds and embraces postmodernism only insofar as it is the overcoming of modernity. Given the centrality and inescapability of this postfoundational divide, it is perhaps to be expected that Milbank should devote so much attention to out-narrating nihilism. What is surprising, however, is that Cupitt (and, indeed, Taylor and the other nihilist textualist theologians) devotes so little attention to addressing the challenge of radical orthodoxy. Why has this been the case? It is to this question that I turn in the next chapter. I shall show that it is Cupitt's residual modernism that precludes him from acknowledging the challenge of radical orthodoxy as an "other" framework and that gives rise to his appropriation of it for his own non-realist cause.

Chapter 3

Disputes and Frameworks

Why is it that Don Cupitt (and other nihilist textualist theologians) has failed to identify, confront, and address the very real challenge presented to his thought by the radical orthodox theology of John Milbank? One of the principal aims of this book is to rectify Cupitt's neglect in this regard, and so it is of crucial importance to understand why such a neglect has prevailed. In this chapter, I suggest an answer that derives from a Wittgensteinian understanding of the nature of disputes within and between frameworks. It also derives from my analysis of Cupitt's relationship to modernity, as detailed in chapter 2.

I argue that Cupitt treats his dispute with Milbank as one *within* a single framework rather than *between* two different frameworks. Cupitt's failure to identify radical orthodoxy as occupying an "other" framework results in his distorting Milbank's theology and thereby in Cupitt's failing to locate the true essence of Milbank's challenge, precluding the possibility of any genuine engagement and "combat." I delineate this argument by proceeding in four parts. First, I discuss Wittgenstein's analysis of disputes within and between frameworks. We shall see that whereas disputes within a common framework proceed by means of reasoned arguments, disputes between frameworks proceed quite differently, namely, by methods of persuasion motivated by considerations of "charm." Second, I show that Cupitt shares a common philosophical framework with modern liberals such as Hick. Although they stand at opposite ends of the spectrum, they nonetheless occupy a single framework that allows only for a realist or an anti-realist understanding of language; there is no possibility of a linguistic analysis that transcends this antinomy. Third, I look at the responses of Cupitt to the challenge of radical orthodoxy in order to show how he (mis)responds to it by treating the dispute as one within his own framework rather than between two different frameworks. We shall see that he refuses its alterity and interprets it in terms of the very framework it is concerned to reject. Finally, I suggest that we must take leave of the realist/anti-realist framework altogether, not only because this would allow for a more fruitful and less distorting "combat" with radical orthodoxy but also because such a framework is inextricably bound up with the very modernist paradigm that Cupitt professes to reject. So I argue that if nihilist textualism is to become properly postmodern, the realist/anti-realist framework must be left behind.

Wittgenstein on Disputes and Frameworks

I begin by considering the character of disputes within and between frameworks from a Wittgensteinian perspective. Wittgenstein said that to combat a point of view, one first has to establish whether that point of view is within or outside one's own framework. That is, one has to establish whether the combat is to be a dispute *within* a framework or *between* frameworks. For Wittgenstein, this was of the utmost importance if one was to avoid falling into confusion. This is because whereas disputes *within* a framework proceed by means of reasoned arguments that are held fast and validated by that common, surrounding framework, disputes *between* frameworks do not proceed within a common milieu, and so the common validity of reasoned arguments subsides. Thus, a dispute between frameworks has to proceed by means of quite different methods of persuasion and charm.

In *On Certainty*, Wittgenstein warns against using reasons from one framework to judge or combat another. He imagines that we meet a certain people: "Instead of the physicist, they consult an oracle. (And for that we consider them primitive.) Is it wrong for them to consult an oracle and be guided by it?—If we call this 'wrong' aren't we using our language game as a base from which to *combat* theirs?"[1] This would be an illegitimate move, primarily because our reasons will simply have no force. Reasons are held fast (are given force or validity) by all that surrounds them, that is, the framework. Thus, such reasons lose their status outside that framework. But we should not think this precludes us from saying that the practice is "wrong." To abdicate such judgment would be to attempt to speak from a neutral (nonexistent) metaframework. So we must continue to say that the practice is wrong while also recognizing that we do so only within our framework. The dispute then becomes a dispute between frameworks, which is the ultimate form of disagreement: "Where two principles really do meet which cannot be reconciled with one another, then each man declares the other a fool and heretic."[2]

So how do we move beyond this to a more fruitful combat, given that we have moved beyond the use of reasons? Wittgenstein continues, "I said I would 'combat' the other man,—but wouldn't I give him *reasons*? Certainly. But how far do they go? At the end of reasons comes *persuasion*. (Think what happens when missionaries convert natives.)"[3] And it is possible that such persuasion could succeed in inducing one to take leave of a framework or language game: "Certain events would put me in a position in which I could not go on with the old language-game any further. In which I was torn away from the *sureness* of the game."[4]

But how exactly is one torn away from the sureness of the game? How is one persuaded to take leave of a framework? Clearly, such a movement would not be governed by reasons, since we have left those behind. In his "Lectures on Aesthetics," Wittgenstein considers this question. He articulates the process of persuasion as follows: "If someone says: 'There is not a difference', and I say: 'There is a difference', I am persuading, I am saying 'I don't want you to look at it like that!'"[5] So the process of persuasion is simply a matter of rhetorically inducing individuals to change their point of view, their perspective, their style of thinking. As Wittgenstein goes on, "I am in a sense making propaganda for one style of thinking as opposed to another. I am honestly disgusted with the other."[6] Furthermore, he says that after he pulls an opponent's proof to bits, that opponent may well say that "the proof had a charm for him. Here I could only say: 'It has no charm for me. I loathe it.'"[7] So according to Wittgenstein, the success of the persuasion or otherwise is simply a matter of charm. A "propaganda for one style of thinking" will be effective only if the hearer deems the propaganda or the persuasion to have a certain charm. In disputes between frameworks, where there is an absence of common or foundational "reasons," it is ultimately only the presence or absence of charm that will determine whether or not there is to be a move from one framework to another.

From this analysis, it is clear that if one misinterprets a dispute between frameworks as being a dispute within a common framework, the result will be confusion and distortion. For one framework will combat the other by appealing to reasons and criteria of evaluation that the other will deny. This will result in combative deadlock. Furthermore, insofar as the "otherness" of each framework is denied, the distinctive essence and character of each framework is distorted. This is because each framework will be perceived through the interpretative grid of a fundamentally alien framework. It is my contention that such confusion and distortion occur when Cupitt attempts to address the challenge of radical orthodoxy. Before demonstrating that this is the case, however, it is first necessary to identify the particular philosophical framework within which Cupitt is located, in order to show that it is a fundamentally different framework from that occupied by radical orthodoxy.

Realism and Anti-Realism

It appears that Cupitt is located in a philosophical framework that allows only for a realist or anti-realist analysis of language. In this respect, Cupitt shares a common framework with modernist theological liberals such as John Hick. This is not to deny the fundamental disagreement between a realist like Hick and an anti-realist like Cupitt. The fundamental nature of this disagreement is emphasized by both of them. Hick insists that "my position is as different from Don's as religious realism is from religious anti-realism,"[8] while Cupitt says that "liberal theologies are always very realist, and . . . therefore represent the very antithesis of my own outlook."[9] I show, however, that this admittedly fundamental disagreement is nevertheless one that takes place *within* a common philosophical framework.

First, it is important to note that "anti-realism" is essentially a parasitical concept. As the term suggests, its meaning would be unintelligible without the "realism" against which it reacts and defines itself, in much the same way as we saw "postmodernism" to be unintelligible without "modernism." In an early and classic statement of the meaning of the term *realism* and of its antithesis, *anti-realism,* Michael Dummett characterized realism as "the belief that statements of the disputed class possess an objective truth value, independently of our means of knowing it: they are true or false in virtue of a reality existing independently of us. The anti-realist opposes to this the view that statements of the disputed class are to be understood only by reference to the sort of thing which we count as evidence for a statement of that class."[10] So the anti-realist concept of truth is less a theory of truth in its own right than a reaction against a specifically realist theory of truth. This is particularly evident when Cupitt defines anti-realism simply as "the contradictory of realism, its straight antithesis."[11] So the anti-realist concept of truth is simply a dialectical movement to the antithetical extreme of realism; it is what one is left with once realism has been subverted. It is therefore essentially parasitic, in the same way that Michael J. Buckley claims that atheism is parasitic on theism.[12] This does, therefore, at least suggest a common philosophical framework for the realism/anti-realism debate.

That realism and anti-realism are indeed two extremes of a common philosophical framework was repeatedly asserted by both Wittgenstein and Martin Heidegger, though they usually referred to anti-realism as "'idealism." Wittgenstein said, "From the very outset, 'Realism', 'Idealism', etc., are names which belong to metaphysics. That is they indicate that their adherents believe that they can say something specific about the essence of the world."[13] As Fergus Kerr points out, Wittgenstein suggests that where a dispute in philosophy seems so cut and dried, there must be some assumptions that are common to both sides—a common framework—the removal of which will lead to the end of the disagreement.[14] Kerr says that, for Wittgenstein, "the idealist's sceptical inclinations, but also the realists' bluff assurances, are equally dependent upon the myth that speaking, and *a fortiori* thinking and meaning, are, fundamentally, ostensive definition of physical objects."[15]

Heidegger independently made a similar point. His contention is that "from time immemorial truth has been a 'problem of logic' but not a basic question of philosophy."[16] The question of truth, he argues, is caught in the trammels of logic. He characterizes the traditional determination of truth as follows: "Truth is the correctness of the representation of a being. All representing of beings is a predicating about them, although this predication can be accomplished silently and does not need to be pronounced."[17] He says that truth is to be found in the most immediate way in the assertion, the "simple proposition," the λόγος: "Truth has its place and seat in λόγος. The more precise determination of truth then becomes the task of a meditation on λόγος, a task of 'logic'."[18] In the course of time, Heidegger says, objections were raised against this traditional or "realist" conception, leading to a view that he calls idealist but that may also be described as anti-realist. On the latter view, our representing gives us only something re-presented by us and so is itself a representation. All our knowledge therefore consists in the representation of representations and in a combination of representations.

Heidegger denies, however, that this "idealist" understanding of truth frees one from the philosophical framework of "logic" wherein the realist is located. He says that idealists "believe they have 'critically' purified and surpassed the usual determination of truth as correctness. But this 'belief' is mistaken. The doctrine that knowledge relates only to representations (the represented) merely restricts the reach of a representation; yet it still claims that this restricted representation conforms to the represented and *only* to the represented. Thus even here, a standard or measure is presupposed, to which the representing conforms. Even here truth is conceived as correctness."[19] Thus, Heidegger's point is that realism and idealism, in spite of all their hostility, share a common philosophical framework, and that the dispute between them is therefore a dispute *within* a framework. He says that "these hostile brothers, each of whom likes to think himself superior to the other, are unwittingly in complete accord with regard to the essence, i.e., with regard to what provides the presupposition and the very possibility of their controversy: that the relation to beings is a representing of them and that the truth of the representation consists in its correctness."[20] So Wittgenstein and Heidegger independently agree that realism and anti-realism are two halves of the same "metaphysical" or "logical" error; they stand at opposite ends of the same philosophical framework.[21]

Indeed, we have already intimated such a conclusion in chapter 2, where we saw that Cupitt's movement from realism to anti-realism was linear, progressive, and logical, suggesting an internal movement within a framework rather than a shift from one framework to another. All of this, then, suggests that Hick and

Cupitt, for all their disagreement, are located in the same philosophical framework within which their dispute is conducted. The dispute between Cupitt and Milbank, in contrast, is a dispute between two different frameworks, even though, as we shall see, Cupitt does not recognize it as such.

But I further want to suggest that one can trace a movement or *paradigm shift* between these two frameworks. For as we saw in chapter 2, and as I have been suggesting above, Cupitt's non-realism emerges out of and remains ultimately indebted to an essentially modern philosophical framework, whereas we saw that the project of radical orthodoxy was literally *post*-modern. The latter may be viewed as a particular (theological) manifestation of a wider cultural, social, and philosophical paradigm shift away from the framework of modernity (even though we have seen that Milbank himself views his project as a theological critique of such a culture, rather than as a manifestation of it).

The concept of a paradigm shift has been extensively analyzed by Thomas S. Kuhn. His work has been restricted to an analysis of scientific paradigm shifts, although it has important implications for how such shifts should be understood in extrascientific contexts. Kuhn makes the point that "when paradigms change, the world itself changes with them. . . . In so far as [scientists'] only recourse to that world is through what they see and do, we may want to say that after a revolution scientists are responding to a different world."[22] Kuhn's point is that in such a paradigm shift, there is not simply a shift in the interpretation of the world; rather, there is a shift or a change in the world itself, because there is no neutral "world" that stands over and above these interpretations. Kuhn recognizes that what we mean and understand by the world is itself created by interpretations or paradigms. Furthermore, he says that such shifts do not usually result from "more accurate and objective" observations, but for reasons that are not always apparent, the old paradigm becomes "somehow askew"; it "no longer functions effectively," and so a new paradigm takes its place.[23] (There are affinities here, of course, with Foucault's analysis of shifts in *episteme*, as mentioned in chapter 1.)[24]

It may be said that the largest and most comprehensive paradigm shift in recent years has been that from the modern to the postmodern, a shift that crosses boundaries, disciplines, and cultures. Cupitt has apparently embraced this shift, but as we see below, he remains inextricably caught up in a realist/anti-realist framework that is itself bound up with modernity. Radical orthodoxy, by contrast, claims to have taken this paradigm shift to its consummation, taking it considerably further than the cultural paradigm shift I analyzed in chapter 1, which, these theologians claim, is also too closely linked with the modernity out of which it emerged. So any consideration of the respective frameworks of Cupitt and Milbank must be undertaken in the context of this paradigm shift. Both frameworks claim to have taken account of this shift, but it may well be that the distance between them is, in fact, its manifestation.[25]

Don Cupitt's Response
to Radical Orthodoxy

I shall now examine how Cupitt responds to the challenge of radical orthodoxy. Although I am taking the work of John Milbank as the definitive paradigm of a radical orthodox theology, it has to be said that Milbank has not directly discussed the work of Don Cupitt in any of his published writings. It has therefore fallen to Rowan Williams and, later, Graham Ward to articulate objections to Cupitt's project from perspectives that may broadly be characterized as "radically orthodox."[26] Williams has resisted any overt identification with the project of radical orthodoxy, although on the basis of his writings it would seem possible to substantiate a radically orthodox position for him.[27] Cupitt has responded to both Williams and Ward in the form of two short articles, which together constitute Cupitt's response to the approach of radical orthodoxy.[28] It is my suggestion that these (albeit rather meager) responses are highly significant in that they reveal a fundamental misreading of the challenge of radical orthodoxy. That is, Cupitt reads the dispute as one within his own framework rather than as one between two different frameworks.

At the beginning of his article "Religious Realism," Rowan Williams states his primary aim. Discussing the theological project of Don Cupitt, as articulated in the books *Taking Leave of God* (1980) and *The World to Come* (1982), Williams says, "I suspect that we are being presented with a false dichotomy here, and my aim in these pages is to question some of what it takes for granted."[29] This false dichotomy is that between realism and anti-realism, and Williams's questioning of "what it takes for granted" is clearly a questioning of the very framework that gives rise to it. Thus, Williams recognizes that his dispute with Cupitt is a dispute *between* frameworks, and we have seen that disputes between frameworks proceed not by means of reasoned refutation but by means of persuasion. Thus, Williams continues, "I should say that I am not at all sure that Cupitt can be 'refuted', insofar as he offers less a sustained argument than a particular kind of vision of the moral and spiritual world."[30]

So Williams's task is to persuade us that Cupitt's framework is less attractive than the one Williams is commending.[31] It is designed to ask whether Cupitt's vision is quite as "consistent, attractive and liveable" as it is made out to be, and whether the choices with which we are confronted are as sharply defined and as distinct as Cupitt presents them.[32] In the process of this persuasion, Williams makes numerous criticisms of various aspects of Cupitt's moral and spiritual vision. It should be said that many of these criticisms have gradually become outdated as the years have passed and as Cupitt's position has gradually evolved.[33] In this context, however, I am not so much concerned with providing a detailed exposition of Williams's individual criticisms as with Cupitt's response to the general challenge to his framework. It is this generally embracing challenge that has remained valid and has not been vitiated by time or by Cupitt's fluctuating position.

Williams takes issue with what he considers to be the predominance in Cupitt's work of a rhetoric of power—that if we are not to be "puppets of the divine will," then God must become the "tool of the finite will."[34] This antinomy is derived from the framework within which Cupitt is situated, with its straightforward choice between realism and anti-realism. But why is this framework at fault, and how does Williams persuade us to take leave of it? His numerous criticisms may, I think, be reduced to two fundamental points. First, such a framework is profoundly un-Christian. Williams's primary objection here is that in Cupitt's scheme, the idea of God becomes almost exclusively *functional*, and in this sense, it is profoundly irreligious. This is because a religious discourse "which denied not the extra-religious, but the extra-subjective, reality of God would hardly be intelligible. The element of praise would vanish, and the dimension of gratuity—or even what we might call play."[35] In other words, a discourse in which God is conceived as a useful tool for mankind's spiritual development would simply be alien to the grammar of belief. Cupitt moves God to the periphery by making God functional—a spiritual tool that can be discarded when one has reached one's goal. For Williams, such a conception distorts the true nature and intelligibility of Christian language.

Second, however, Williams persuades us to take leave of Cupitt's framework by suggesting that it is philosophically inadequate. Is language, he asks—and not just religious language—best understood in terms of the realist/non-realist dichotomy? Williams thinks not and complains that Cupitt thinks we have a pellucid choice between simple descriptive reference and the most drastic constructivism. He says that this is "neither adequate nor illuminating."[36] Elsewhere, Williams says that language is something people do as a way of "negotiating" their environment; it is a means of finding their way around in which questions of *representation* are far from being the most central.[37] It is precisely because both realist and non-realist accounts of language assume that representational questions are central that Williams claims both are inadequate. Thus, it may be said that Rowan Williams presents two fundamental challenges to Cupitt's intellectual framework—one theological and one philosophical. I now consider how, and indeed whether, Cupitt responds to these challenges.

In his reply, Cupitt observes that Williams has little to say in favor of theological realism of the type that he criticizes and produces no metaphysical arguments to defend it: "Instead he speaks of *religious* realism. On the evidence of his published writings, all this means is that he is a religious symbolist who takes his symbols seriously."[38] It is clear that both Cupitt and Williams are opposed to what the latter describes as "the starker paradoxes of classical theism in much contemporary Anglo-Saxon philosophy of religion."[39] Cupitt acknowledges this common ground but does not seem to recognize that Williams is as much opposed to Cupitt's non-realism as he is to the "lucid dissolutions" of foundational realism. Cupitt says that "it is clear that I as well as Rowan Williams affirm the value of *religious* realism—within the sphere of play. And he as well as I acknowledges that such religious realism (linguistic, attitudinal and so forth) needs to be qualified by irony, and is subject to in-built checks and balances—that also operate within the sphere of play. So it appears that *there is no significant difference between us.*[40] This move is, in fact, characteristic of a modern liberal framework, which is concerned to be all-embracing and nonexclusive. For radical orthodox theologians, it is a framework that promotes a politics of pacifism, but without an ontology of peace.[41]

How is Cupitt able to say that "there is no significant difference between us" when we have seen that Williams mounts a very substantial attack on the very philosophical framework that Cupitt occupies? I suggest that the answer lies in the fact that Cupitt regards his philosophical framework not as a contingent one that can be identified and criticized but as the a priori basis on which all philosophical and theological discussion takes place. Thus, for Cupitt, it is not conceivable that Williams could be attacking his framework from outside, because there is no "outside." So Williams must somehow be located "within" a framework in which the only philosophical options are realism and anti-realism. So if, as Cupitt recognizes, Williams rejects the sort of metaphysical realism that he himself opposes, then Williams *must* be a sort of anti-realist—as far as Cupitt is concerned, there is nothing else for him to be. And if Williams's anti-realism is not explicitly evident, then he must be a crypto anti-realist, an anti-realist in disguise, a "symbolist who takes his symbols seriously."

Yet, in spite of insisting that Williams is a crypto-nonrealist and that there is consequently "no significant difference between us," Cupitt simultaneously says that Williams "clings to realism."[42] But Williams manifestly does not "cling to realism" in the empirical and foundational sense in which Cupitt understands the term *realism*. Williams would no doubt join Wittgenstein in his quest for "not empiricism and yet realism in philosophy."[43] We have seen that Williams's "religious realism" is something not empirical and yet realist, and it is something that is not allowed for within Cupitt's framework. For Cupitt, Williams's espousal of religious realism must mean either that he is clinging to realism or that he is a "religious symbolist" or "active non-realist." In the same article, Cupitt accuses Williams of being both—the only two options available in Cupitt's framework. He seems unclear about which option Williams has, in fact, taken.

But this brings us back to the crux of the issue, for the reason that Cupitt has difficulty philosophically locating Williams is that the latter has rejected both these options. Williams's whole article may be viewed as an attack not simply on one as opposed to the other of these categories but on the very framework in which these are the only two possible options. Williams repeatedly makes the point that Cupitt "tends to take for granted a simple dichotomy between descriptive-scientific-objective langauge and symbolic-noncognitive-arbitrary language," and that "we are being presented with a false dichotomy here." For Williams, like Wittgenstein and Heidegger, realism and non-realism are two sides of the same coin; they are the opposite ends of the same framework, and it is the framework as a whole that Williams is concerned to jettison. The challenge to Cupitt, therefore, is to defend this framework against Williams's attacks. We have seen that Cupitt manifestly fails to do so. The fundamental problem is that the framework in which he operates precludes him from *identifying* the challenge, and consequently, he is unable even to begin to address it.

Cupitt's reply to Rowan Williams was written in 1984, prior to his explicitly postmodern turn with the publication of *Life Lines* in 1986. It may perhaps be expected that, subsequent to this turn, Cupitt's appraisal of the radical orthodox agenda would have become less caught up in the modernist antinomy between realism and anti-realism. But this appears not to have been the case, for in his most recent discussion of radical orthodox theology, Cupitt continues to make the same claims. Discussing the recent work of John Milbank, Catherine Pickstock, Graham Ward, and Gerard Loughlin, Cupitt again says that the "strangest and most obviously contradictory" feature of their project is their commitment to theological realism, but without "any new arguments for metaphysical realism."[44] Again, Cupitt fails to identify the true essence of the radical orthodox challenge, namely, that theological realism "overcomes" metaphysics, which, as we saw in chapter 2, these theologians maintain is an invention of modernity. Cupitt is, of course, quite entitled to take issue with this claim, but this is precisely what he does not do, and he simply reiterates his claim that "realism is a doctrine in metaphysics." And as with Williams, he again suggests that these radical orthodox theologians are "with me after all." He says, "It may be that in claiming to be theological realists these writers are only making a small but politically-necessary gesture. . . . They are indeed a group of my own former pupils, and they are perhaps all of them teaching versions of 'active non-realism.'"[45] So not only Rowan Williams but all the radical orthodox theologians are, in fact, non-realists in disguise: true deceivers, crypto anti-realists, symbolists who take their symbols seriously.[46]

Thus, we begin to see why there has been so little engagement between our two versions of postmodern theology—radical orthodoxy and nihilist textualism. The main reason is that Cupitt has failed to perceive the true nature of the radical orthodox challenge, and consequently has failed to engage with it. We have seen that this failure arises from his mistreatment of the dispute as one within his own framework rather than as one between two different frameworks. The result is a disabling blockage, which arises because Cupitt regards his realist/anti-realist framework as the a priori basis on which all philosophical and theological discussion proceeds, rather than as a contingent one that can be distinguished from and criticized by other frameworks. In this respect, at least, it would appear that he has not taken account of the contemporary postmodern paradigm shift I referred to above; for as we saw in chapter 2, this framework emerged out of an empiricist and logical positivist paradigm that has now passed away.[47] The important task confronting us now, therefore, is to remove this disabling blockage and prepare the way for a genuine dispute *between* frameworks. If a nihilist and textualist postmodernism is to provide an effective critique of radical orthodoxy, this will have to be a critique that moves beyond the realist/anti-realist framework.

Beyond Realism and Anti-Realism

Thus far, we have seen that if there is to be an effective critique of radical ortho-doxy from a postmodern perspective, it must be one that recognizes and is respectful of alterity. In other words, such a critique must recognize radical ortho-doxy as an "other" framework. Only in its otherness can the distinctive voice of radical orthodoxy be respected, identified, and challenged. In this chapter, we have seen that the realist/anti-realist framework manifestly fails in this endeavor. In Hegelian fashion, it subsumes the alterity of difference and therefore precludes the possibility of effective confrontation.

In the following chapters, I provide a critique of radical orthodoxy from a postmodern perspective. Although this perspective shares something with the vision of Don Cupitt, especially in its more explicit postmodern aspects, my vision is ultimately distinguished from his by, among other things, my repudia-tion of the realist/anti-realist framework. There are several good "reasons" for such a repudiation, quite apart from the fact that it precludes the possibility of an effective critique of radical orthodoxy.

First, the realist/anti-realist framework is too discredited by now and too incorrigibly bound up with the modernist paradigm to remain credible. We have seen that thinkers from Martin Heidegger to Rowan Williams have emphasized that both *realism* and *anti-realism* are terms that get their sense within a frame-work that is preoccupied with *representation.* In spite of their antithetical atti-tudes to this representation, both realists and anti-realists define themselves in terms of the extent to which language may be said to *represent.* We saw in chap-ter 2 that an obsession with representation is characteristic of modernity and, indeed, that this obsession may be traced back to Duns Scotus. But in the wake of the shift from a modern to a postmodern paradigm, the question of represen-tation is no longer paramount. In the move toward the genres of fictionalism and narrative modes of knowledge, as intimated in chapter 1 and as developed in the following chapters, we see that talk of representation becomes less acute and, indeed, descends into irrelevancy. With the repudiation of the priority of repre-sentation comes also the repudiation of both realism and anti-realism. It is in this sense that non-realist accounts (to quote Kuhn again) become "somehow askew" and "no longer function effectively."

A second "reason" for repudiating the realist/anti-realist framework lies in its refusal of alterity or otherness. We have already seen how such a framework refuses the otherness of radical orthodoxy, but as I argue more fully in chapter 6, it also refuses alterity per se. Cupitt's non-realism proclaims the "end of the Other" and insists that everything is fully present and presenced, that nothing is hidden. Once again, such a disposition is highly redolent of the paradigm of modernity, with its emphasis on the priority of presence and the presentation of presence by means of re-presentation: what is present is real, and what is absent is nothing, or, alternatively, nothing is absent. But with the shift from a modern to a postmodern paradigm, that which is repressed returns, and in particular, the repressed "other" returns, although of course, the "other" can never be "present." So, whereas modernity repressed the "other," in postmodernism the "other" is lionized. Again, the realist/anti-realist framework fails to take account of this aspect of the paradigm shift, and so it again appears to be too bound up with the modernity that this shift has left behind.

Interlude

In this chapter, I have shown how Cupitt's philosophical framework is so bound up with the paradigm of modernity that it precludes an effective critique of Milbank's radical orthodoxy. In the following chapters, I attempt to rectify Cupitt's failure in this regard. But in doing so, one finds that Cupitt's framework must itself be left behind; it is a framework that one must "pass by," not only because, as I have been demonstrating in this chapter, it is unable to provide an effective critique of radical orthodoxy but also because it seems to have let the postmodern paradigm shift itself "pass by." (The significance of the theme of "passing by" becomes evident in chapter 6.) So Cupitt's modern postmodernism must be developed into an accomplished postmodernism. Only then will the postmodern paradigm shift be recognized for what it is, and only then can the challenge of radical orthodoxy be confronted effectively and without distortion. And so we move onward, away from realism and anti-realism, away from representation and presence, away from modernity and toward that which eludes us, the "other," the unknown; toward a deferred destiny that is (perhaps?) infinitely deferred.

Chapter 4

Narrative, Metanarrative, and Theology: On Out-Narrating John Milbank

If one of my principal aims in this book is to mount a critique of John Milbank's project of radical orthodoxy from a postmodern perspective, then the preceding chapters may be regarded as a lengthy, though necessary, prelude to the task now at hand. Furthermore, if the critique now to be undertaken is to be effective, it must also be informed as to why previous endeavors in this regard have ultimately failed. This question was considered in chapter 3, where it was shown that a modernist philosophical paradigm, framed by the antinomy between realism and anti-realism, must necessarily fail in such a task. Having identified this failing, the way is now prepared for an effective critique of the radical orthodox theology of John Milbank.

This is by no means an easy task. That Milbank's project is marked by an intellectual brilliance and an impressively dense scholarship has been remarked upon so many times that it can no longer be said to be in any sense an original observation. Indeed, it seems that any discussion of Milbank's work must be prefaced by these apparently obligatory remarks. But the frequency of their occurrence does not in any way detract from the truth of their import. In short, Milbank's challenge is formidable. This inevitably means that any light dismissal or trivial "refutation" of Milbank's project cannot but have failed to comprehend the true essence of his challenge. In other words, to comprehend the challenge is also to recognize its compelling force. But to recognize this force (without, however, being persuaded) is simultaneously to demand a response. As Aidan Nichols says, "The subtlety and sophistication of Milbank's criticisms of a range of secular constructs for both thought and social action so broad as to include virtually the entire contemporary intelligentsia of Western Europe and North America will require a response of equal incisiveness from the inhabitants of these systems."[1] In this book (and particularly in this chapter), my aim is to respond to the challenge succinctly articulated by Nichols.

I shall first make some preliminary remarks with regard to method. Indeed, this is an area in which I concur with Milbank, insofar as we can at least agree about the way in which we disagree; for as we saw in chapter 3, the end of modernity brings with it the end of a certain mode of disagreement, according to which points of view are "refuted" by means of reasoned argumentation. As systems give way to narratives, so reason gives way to persuasion and refutation gives way to "out-narration." As Lyotard says, narrative knowledge "certifies itself in the pragmatics of its own transmission without having recourse to argumentation and proof."[2] So Milbank's project is not offered as, nor should it be regarded as, a sustained theological argument to be refuted.

In his discussion of *Theology and Social Theory*, Graham Ward says that "if we accept the correlation between our knowledge and our stories and that this book is a story, an invention, then there is no position available from which to claim that this story is right or wrong. We can only tell the story differently. *Theology and Social Theory* does not offer itself as an argument for refutation, only as theology in performance, as a continuing tradition, a socio-linguistic practice."[3] So in what follows, I do not attempt—indeed, I do not think it is possible—to "refute" Milbank's vision. Visions cannot be refuted; they can only be countered by alternative visions. Having said this, however, it must also be admitted that Milbank does not *merely* present his vision. He also seeks rhetorically to subvert rival visions, showing their inadequacies, failings, and ultimate inferiority. An adequate response, therefore, must engage in a similar act of rhetorical persuasion or subversion. It will not be enough merely to present an alternative vision; one must also counterpersuade, countersubvert, and out-narrate.

So my concern in this chapter is to question the internal consistency, viability, and ultimately persuasiveness of Milbank's narrative. First, I claim that a totalizing, absolute metanarrative, such as that espoused by Milbank, must necessarily entail a certain violence and exclusion of difference in spite of his claims to the contrary. Another danger of such an absolute metanarrative is that it will forget its fictive status, and in so doing, its structure will become akin to that of a speculative metanarrative. Second, I show that such violence can be resisted only by a supplement that reminds the metanarrative of its fictional status. I argue that such a supplement must necessarily be "external" to or "other" than the metanarrative itself and, indeed, that within Milbank's project there is abundant evidence of such external supplementation. I claim that the existence of this external supplement deconstructs the metanarrative *as* a metanarrative, and therefore, the concept of an absolute metanarrative that is simultaneously fictional is actually an illusion; for every (meta)narrative is "supplemented" and "positioned" by yet another (meta)narrative, and so the attempt to single out any one (meta)narrative as the "beginning" or "foundation" of the rest is misguided. Indeed, I show how Milbank himself cannot avoid this infinity of supplements, and that part of his own supplement is inextricably bound up with the nihilism that he otherwise refuses. I raise these and other questions in what follows to suggest that in spite of the undoubted brilliance of Milbank's project, it is by no means unproblematic.

Milbank, Narrative, and Metanarrative

Milbank's early studies were in the areas of social and political thought, and in particular, he undertook an extensive analysis of the thought of the eighteenth-century thinker Giambattista Vico, initially in his doctoral dissertation and later in published form.[4] It was his work on Vico that gave rise to his development of a "poetical" or "narrative" theology, as expressed in *Theology and Social Theory* (1990). Between the publication of this book and *The Word Made Strange* (1997) we may detect a subtle shift of emphasis. Although Milbank continued to insist on the radical linguisticality of all reality, he nevertheless moved away from an explicitly narrativist mode toward a more substantive "ontological" one. (I consider what Milbank understands by the ontological in the next chapter.) In this chapter, however, I concentrate on the narrativist character of his project, without which the later, ontological stage would have been inconceivable.

In chapters 1 and 2, we saw that Milbank is both "for" and "against" postmodernism in that he embraces many postmodern insights only subsequently to turn them against postmodernism itself. Much of this ambivalence revolves around the peculiarly postmodern concerns with the concepts of "narrative" and "metanarrative." We saw that Milbank embraces the emphasis of Lyotard and others on the primacy of the narrative mode but that he rejects Lyotard's narration of the "end" of metanarratives and the subsequent free play of "little" narratives (*petit récits*). Indeed, it may be said that the crux of Milbank's argument lies in his assertion of the *necessity* of a metanarrative.

But for Milbank, the return of the metanarrative cannot be a simple return of what went before; it cannot, for instance, be a return of the speculative metanarratives of Hegel and Marx. Milbank says that the return of the metanarrative does not mean that we should follow Hegel in seeking "once again to establish an 'encyclopedia' of knowledge, in which all significant reality is included, and rationally demonstrated as necessary existence. If one takes this to be the centre of the Hegelian enterprise, then it is forever dead."⁵ Similarly, Marx mistakenly prioritized the necessary over the contingent. He failed to realize "the sheer contingency of the capitalist system as a whole, and to see that it can only be morally criticized and opposed in the name of another, equally contingent vision and practice."⁶ It would seem, then, that the essential difference between Milbank's conception of metanarrative and the metanarratives of Hegel and Marx would be that Milbank (like other postmodernists) knows his metanarrative to be a "fiction" whereas Hegel and Marx did not. This point has been made by Gerard Loughlin, who says that the difference between these two contrasting conceptions of metanarrative would seem to be that between "fiction" and "myth": "A myth is a fiction which forgets that it is only a story. A story based on faith knows itself to be only fictive (after Nietzsche): a story based on reason (dialectic) does not."⁷

Milbank proclaims the necessity and inescapability of the metanarrative on the basis of two main considerations, one philosophical and one theological. Philosophically, Milbank claims that the attempts of Lyotard and other postmodernists to write without a metanarrative are illusory. This is because in telling their story of the end of the metanarrative and the triumph of the little narrative, postmodernists are, in that very act, reinstating another metanarrative that tells (explains and interprets) how all the little narratives relate to one another, namely, arbitrarily and with infinite unsettlement. Actually, we have already observed that postmodernists are not completely unaware of this paradox. As Paul Julian Smith puts it, "We may doubt whether Lyotard's proposed 'war on totality' can take place without just a little help from those master discourses he is so anxious to displace. . . . Lyotard adopts the authoritative voice of the metadiscourse at the same time as he announces its death."⁸ And Lyotard himself recognizes this when he says that the "great narratives are now barely credible. And it is therefore tempting to lend credence to the great narrative of the decline of great narratives."⁹ This is, of course, an aspect of the postmodern predicament itself—that one deconstructs that which makes the deconstruction at all possible. Whereas Lyotard and other postmodern philosophers are happy to live with this paradox or even to embrace it as being of the essence of the postmodern condition itself, Milbank claims that the metanarrative is an inescapable fatality, and that the way must be prepared for the *return* of the metanarrative.

Theologically, however, Milbank proclaims the necessity of the (particular theological) metanarrative because he claims that unless theology, as the ultimate metanarrative, "positions" all other discourses, the inevitable result would be a critical "reserve" that is independent of God. And, as we saw in chapter 2, wherever a system of thought has such a "reserve," it will inevitably culminate in nihilism. If nihilism is to be avoided, therefore, theology must be accorded the status of a metanarrative. The crucial theological configuration here is that of "participation," as derived from Plato and developed by Christianity. Participation "refuses any reserve of created territory, while allowing finite things their own integrity."¹⁰ This means "every discipline must be framed by a theological perspective" to guard against it being "grounded literally in nothing."[11] It is said that the appearances of worldly phenomena are saved by being exceeded: "By appealing to an external source for bodies, their art, language, sexual and political union, one is not ethereally taking leave of their density. On the contrary, one is insisting that behind this density resides an even greater density—beyond all contrasts of density and lightness (as beyond all contrasts of definition and limitlessness). This is to say that all there is *only* is because it is more than it is."[12] So what there is may be said to *be* only because what there is participates in the Divine. This is, of course, to repudiate Duns Scotus and to embrace Thomas Aquinas, particularly his concept of analogy; for we saw in chapter 2 that genuine analogy is possible only through participation, which in turn is possible only if the ontological transcendence of God is preserved. Such preservation is possible only, it is maintained, for a theology conceived as metanarrative.

I want to claim, however, that both these philosophical and theological contentions may be called into question. First, I suggest that Milbank's philosophical point lacks a certain nuance. It is typical of Milbank's either/or approach that he claims that, because it is not possible to do without a metanarrative at all, then it must be necessary to embrace one in the most absolute and totalizing way possible. For although Milbank is right to point out, against Lyotard, that the specter of a metanarrative continually "returns" in spite, or perhaps because, of our attempts to repress it, this return is itself inherently unstable and tends toward a self-deconstruction. It seems that a metanarrative is both an unavoidable necessity and an unstable impossibility. I suggest that this is a typically postmodern paradox that should be embraced rather than "resolved." The problem is that Milbank wants to resolve this paradox in his assertion of the absolute "presence" of the metanarrative. But as we shall see, his "resolutions" are themselves inherently unstable. Milbank too often tends to ignore or elide the nuances of postmodern narrative complexity in favor of his pellucid either/or choice between the absence or presence of the metanarrative.

Second, with regard to his theological justification for the return of the metanarrative (namely, that any other configuration leads to nihilism), this point must, I think, be conceded to him. For we saw in chapter 2 that the metanarratives of modernity do indeed deconstruct themselves and logically culminate in nihilism, and that a premodern or postmodern theological metanarrative is the only effective way of guarding against a nihilistic outcome. Having said this, however, nihilism is only to be regarded as necessarily undesirable from within Milbank's metanarrative. If, as I intend to show in this chapter, there are good "reasons" (or persuasive considerations) for not adopting his metanarrative, then this a priori rejection of nihilism becomes groundless and subsides. In the light of this subsidence, I develop a more nuanced, positive, and less pejorative account of nihilism in chapters 5 and 6. Furthermore, at the end of this chapter, I argue that even Milbank cannot avoid elements of nihilism in his own metanarrative. It seems that a certain nihilism is intrinsic to any self-reflexively postmodern narrative.

If it is the case, therefore, that both the philosophical and theological justifications for Milbank's espousal of theology as metanarrative may be shown to be questionable, then the way is prepared for a refusal of Milbank's vision. Indeed, this encapsulates my aim in this chapter. I begin by demonstrating the instability of Milbank's metanarrative, showing the extent to which it appears to embody much of what it professes to repudiate.

Milbank and Dualism

Thus far, we have seen that the only possible relationship between Milbank's theological metanarrative and all other (meta)narratives is one wherein the former negates, subordinates, and positions the latter. As Milbank puts it, if "theology no longer seeks to position, qualify or criticize other discourses, then it is inevitable that these discourses will position theology."[13] What is characteristic about this formulation is that it is once again presented in terms of an either/or dichotomy. Milbank thereby confronts us with a straightforward antinomy: *either* theology will "position" other discourses *or else* other discourses will "position" theology. This blatant dichotomy is simply assumed and taken for granted, and at no point does Milbank give consideration to the possibility of a subtler account of narrative interaction.

One of the main difficulties with presenting the issue in the way Milbank does is that the presentation itself pertains to a dualism. This dualism is performatively installed, and because the metanarrative that positions is so totalizing and all-embracing, it gives rise to a whole series of other dualisms and oppositions that are all-pervading and ever present. These include dualities between peace and violence, sacred and secular, nihilism and Christianity, and, ultimately, theology and philosophy. These oppositions appear throughout Milbank's narrative, with priority being ascribed to the Christian side of the dualism in each case. The prominence of such dualisms, however, at the very least sits uncomfortably alongside Milbank's commitment to overcome dualism. As Steven Shakespeare has suggested, Milbank's overcoming of dualism "depends upon a more fundamental dualism."[14] In particular, Milbank is committed to overcoming the dualisms that are derived from the metanarratives of modern philosophy. Let us therefore pause for a moment to consider the way in which dualism is inextricably linked with the philosophical epoch of modernity.

Michel de Certeau locates the founding of the dualism of modernity in certain movements in the thirteenth century not unrelated to those I discussed in chapter 2. He identifies in particular the influence of Ockhamism, which gave rise to a "'realism' of linguistic 'representation'" which "postulated a divorce between words and things." Language now became "separate from that real that it intended, depicted, and was confronted with."[15] Inseparable from this dualistic science of representation was a prioritizing of the visible and the transparent over the invisible and the hidden. De Certeau points out that there was a new preoccupation with *seeing*: "Vision slowly invaded the previous domain of touch or of hearing. It transformed the very practice of knowledge and signs. Even the religious field was reorganized in function of the opposition between the visible and the invisible."[16] Thus, de Certeau demonstrates out that "the utopian impetus already behind the drive toward transparency is the same that assumes, in the seventeenth century, the (epistemological) guise of 'representation'."[17]

Stephen Toulmin has said that at the base of this (Cartesian) epistemology of "representation" lay a distinction between *rational freedom* in the human world of thought and action and the *causal necessity* of mechanical processes in the natural world. This distinction cut so deep that it gave rise to a whole host of associated dualisms that formed a prominent part in the "framework of modernity."[18] These dualisms, therefore, all derive from the fundamental modernist division between nature and humanity, a division that Toulmin traces back to Descartes. He says that "the Cartesian division of matter from mind, causes from reason, and nature from humanity, was endorsed and continued by Isaac Newton, and ceased to be of concern to natural philosophers alone. From then on, it played a major role in social and political thought as well."[19] And it is clear that in this division between humanity and nature, subject and object, it was humanity that was accorded the priority. The "framework of modernity" prioritized the subject. But this prioritizing of the subject also gave rise to countless other prioritized dualisms, for instance, the priority of experience over expression. The experience was the basic, pure, prelinguistic essence that was conveyed by a secondary, less-adequate approximation in language—the subsequent expression. Hence, the experience was primary and the expression secondary.[20] In a similar way, modernity was concerned to ascribe priority to truth over myth, to history over narrative, to the universal over the particular, to the text over the reader, to philosophy over theology. Most, if not all, of these priorities derived from the priority of the subject and its capacity to determine rationally the "way the world is."

Postmodernism, by contrast, seeks to overcome all these prioritizations. It is maintained that an experience without expression would be unintelligible as an experience. It is the expression that gives meaning and intelligibility to the experience and thereby brings it into being *as* an experience, just as the expression would be meaningless without the experience that gave rise to it. So neither experience nor expression is prior or more foundational, but both are simultaneous and mutually founding. Similarly, truth is not prior to myth but is conveyed through myth, just as history is conveyed through narrative. So, too, the text is not prior to the reader but is made a text through the reader's reading of it, just as the reader is made a reader through his or her reading of the text.

Milbank generally concurs with this postmodern overcoming of prioritized dualisms. He recognizes that the dualisms of modernity necessarily entail a privileging of one side of the dualism over the other, as, for instance, in modernity's privileging of the subject over the object. Interestingly, Milbank thinks that premodernity was conversely guilty of prioritizing the object over the subject. In contrast, he recognizes that objects and subjects both get their sense from within their narration in a story, and that without such a story, the concepts would become unintelligible. If this is the case, then it must mean that neither subject nor object can be privileged. He says, "If subjects and objects only are, through the complex relations of a narrative, then neither objects are privileged, as in pre-modernity, nor subjects, as in modernity. Instead, what matters are structural relations, which constantly shift; the word 'subject' now indicates a point of potent 'intensity' which can re-arrange given structural patterns."[21] Again, whereas modernity dictated that a dichotomy between "above" and "below" would privilege the "below," whence all sensible theology would begin, Milbank maintains that "postmodernity implies that conceptions of the 'below'—of human subjectivity and relationship are only constituted within the narrative that simultaneously postulates the 'above'."[22] Milbank's point is that these dualisms are overcome, not in the sense that we no longer speak of a "subject" and an "object," of "above" and "below," but in the sense that no side of the dichotomy is thought to be prior. Each side of the dualism mutually founds and mutually constitutes the other.

It is therefore initially surprising to find that Milbank's reinstatement of the Christian metanarrative gives rise to a whole series of privileged and prioritized dualisms. With regard to overcoming modernity's priority of philosophy over theology, he does not overcome it but reverses it. So modernity's priority of phi-losophy is not overcome but is reversed into the priority of theology. So, too, modernity's priority of the secular is not overcome but is reversed into the prior-ity of the sacred. Whereas Milbank wanted to overcome modernity's priority of the subject *and* premodernity's priority of the object, when it comes to the dual-ism between theology and philosophy, the sacred and the secular, he does not want to overcome *both* modernity *and* premodernity but explicitly wants to return to the premodern. This is because Milbank wants to return to the medieval position whereby philosophy is absorbed and made possible by theology. But the result is another prioritized dualism and a mirror image of modernity's reduc-tionism. As John D. Caputo has said of Milbank's project, "Simply to negate modernity is to oppose the reduction of the religious to the secular in modernity with the opposite reductionism, of the secular to the religious. The result is a war of competing reductionisms."[23]

This "war of reductionisms" is itself profoundly dualistic, and it gives rise to a series of derivative dualisms that replace the prioritized dualisms of modernity. It is not, of course, inconsistent for Milbank to replace the latter dualisms with the former ones; for whereas the modern notions of "subject" and "below" and so forth were thought to privileged *prior* to a narrative, theology and the sacred are prioritized *within* the particular Christian metanarrative. It is, however, slightly incongruous, and the dividing line between the two types of dualisms (namely, prior to a narrative and internal to a narrative) is a very thin one. This is because the modernity-privileged notions of "subject" and "below" were, in fact, privileged within a narrative, namely, the modern metanarrative of secular reason, even though this metanarrative was nonreflexive and therefore unaware of the fact. So what Milbank has done is replace one sovereign metanarrative with another, thereby replacing the dualisms of the rejected metanarrative with the dualisms of the accepted one. This is hardly an overcoming of dualism; rather, it is simply the replacement of one set of dualisms with another.

Furthermore, if Milbank wants to jettison both premodernity's prioritizing of the object and modernity's prioritizing of the subject, would it not be more consistent for him correspondingly to jettison both premodernity's prioritizing of theology and modernity's prioritising of philosophy? For as long as such priority is maintained, the sort of dualism that Milbank is so eager to overcome will inevitably result. He would no doubt want to claim that dualism in his project is mitigated by the doctrine of "participation," as discussed above.[24] For if the creature *participates* in the Divine, then the sense in which the creaturely and the Divine are set over and against each other (as in modernity) is overcome, and thus the consequent dualism of modernity is similarly overcome. But although the doctrine of participation may overcome (or at least minimize) the dualism *within* the Christian story as presented by Milbank, the dualism that results from Milbank's absolute conception of the theological metanarrative remains; for now theology and philosophy are set *over and against each other,* and this, we have seen, gives rise to yet another form of dualism. We are told that theology must "position" other discourses if other discourses are not to "position" theology. For Milbank, this antinomy cannot be escaped, and consequently, the resulting dualism cannot be escaped. It is an inevitable corollary of his conception of metanarrative. It seems as though Milbank minimized the dualism at the level of the Christian story only to reinstate it at the level of his own metastory. (I return to this point in more detail in due course.) Furthermore, it may be said that this dualism, which pervades Milbank's project, gives rise to an inevitable warfare, a violence, that again sits uncomfortably with his professed aims. It is to this question that I now turn.

Milbank and Violence

Having suggested that Milbank ultimately fails to overcome the dualism he claims to overcome, I now want to suggest that his metanarrative is also characterized by an inescapable violence. If I am at all justified in this suggestion, this would prove problematic for Milbank's project, for two reasons: first, because so much of Milbank's apologetic or rhetoric on behalf of Christianity revolves around the narrative's promotion of peace over violence. Indeed, this is ultimately Milbank's only defense against postmodern nihilism—that Christianity tells a "much better story" insofar as it is a story that promotes the ontological priority of peace rather than the ontological priority of violence. If Milbank's presentation of this story is marked by precisely such a violence, however, then this must considerably weaken its force. Second, it is claimed that the Christian story is one of peace insofar as it respects, by subsuming, difference. But if the violence of

Milbank's presentation is such that it obliterates difference, this again must weaken the force of his case. On both counts, therefore, the presence of violence in Milbank's project is particularly problematic.

So whence does this violence arise? We have just observed that Milbank's metanarrative gives rise to a dualism that pictures a warfare, a violence. Milbank seems to envisage a "battle" or "combat" between theology seeking to "position" other discourses and other discourses seeking to "position" theology. A meta-narrative, by definition, positions other narratives, other discourses, and not only is this act of positioning itself violent, but it also gives rise to distorted or violent readings of the very discourses that are positioned. To a certain extent, therefore, every metanarrative is necessarily violent. In positioning, explaining, and encompassing other narratives, particularly (but not exclusively) narratives that claim to be rival metanarratives, it inevitably and necessarily does violence to them; for in becoming subservient to the metanarrative, these narratives are intrinsically altered. This is particularly evident in Milbank's treatment of the so-called postmodern nihilists. As Graham Ward says, "Each analysis is sub-servient to [Milbank's] grand narrative. Because of this there emerges an element of distortion. The abstraction that homogenizes the postmodern projects of Derrida, Lyotard, Deleuze and Foucault, for example, inevitably borders on over-simplification. . . . There is, then, a necessary idealism, a necessary 'vio-lence' one might say, as Milbank retells the history of ideas within the Christian superstory."[25] If all narratives are indeed subservient to Milbank's metanarrative, this means that the narratives he adopts or utilizes are just as "positioned" by it as are those he rejects.

Milbank himself has never concealed the fact that his recovery of premodern modes of theological thought necessarily entails them being "changed." He con-cedes that there cannot be a "restoration of a pre-modern Christian position."[26] Indeed, even if such a restoration were possible, he insists that it would not in any case be desirable, because "patristic and mediaeval thought was unable to overcome entirely the ontology of substance in the direction of a view which sees reality as constituted by signs and their endless ramifications."[27] For Milbank, therefore, theology must consist of a *repetition* of patristic and medieval modes of thought, but this is a theology that must now be repeated *differently*. In this, Milbank appeals to Kierkegaard, saying, "For Kierkegaard and his successors, we never have access to a single, isolated, original instance, and it follows as a corol-lary of this that the irreducible reoccurrence is nonetheless not an identical rep-etition, for otherwise we would be able to regard the second instance as a mere echo of a first that is free-standing in its own right."[28] Milbank says that for Kierkegaard, "Christ is that universal identity which arises through its happen-ing again, differently."[29] So what Milbank recovers is not the tradition itself (whatever that may be) but, as Cupitt more pejoratively puts it, a "laundered fac-simile of tradition."[30] Thus, in adopting an Augustinian narrative, for instance, he simultaneously subordinates it to his own metanarrative and, consequently and inevitably, distorts it.

Now, it should be pointed out here that if all metanarratives necessarily do violence to the narratives they organize or explain, then Milbank's project cannot be deemed to be vulnerable on the grounds that it does likewise, particularly if he acknowledges that this must necessarily be the case. Having said that, however, it should also be pointed out that there are varying degrees of violence, more and less sensitive ways of respecting the integrity of the narratives that are being positioned. In the next chapter, I demonstrate the ways in which Milbank does undue violence to the thought of the father of postmodern nihilism, Friedrich Nietzsche. But here I want to look briefly at how he does violence to the thought of his own theological father, St. Augustine.

We saw in chapter 1 that Milbank's most significant extraction from Augustine's theology was the ontological priority of peace. For Augustine, this peace was to be secured not by a mere mitigation of the severity of conflict within and between differences but by means of a "musical" ontology wherein all differences are subsumed and gathered up into a *concentus musicus*. Augustine prays for this gathering up into one unity in which all is included, at the end of *De trinitate*: "So when we do attain to you, there will be an end to these many things which we say and do not attain, and you will remain one, yet all in all, and we shall say one thing praising you in unison, even ourselves also being made one in you."[31] Augustine's vision here is that of a peaceful, unified community, a vision that Milbank says was "at the centre of his theology. . . . The heavenly city meant for Augustine a substantial peace; but this peace could also be imperfectly present in the fallen world, in the sequences of time, and time redeemed through memory."[32] There are, however, different ways of securing this peace, and in declaring his preference, it may be said that Milbank makes a move away from Augustine. He says that one can attempt to secure peace by drawing boundaries and excluding the "other," and that most polities and religions do precisely this. But, he says, "the Church has misunderstood itself when it does likewise. For . . . nothing really positive is excluded—no difference, whatsoever—but only the negative . . . namely any stunting of [a] person's capacity to love and conceive of the divine beauty; this inhibition is seen as having its soul in arbitrariness. But there is no real exclusion here; Christianity should not draw boundaries, and the Church is that paradox: a nomad city."[33]

The difficulty here, however, is that, as Wayne Hankey points out, Augustine was the "Hammer of Heretics, who not only drew boundaries between orthodox Christianity and heresy, but even used Imperial coercion against Donatists and Pelagians."[34] To a certain extent, Milbank attempts to account for this in his discussion of Augustine's coercion of the Donatists. He says that in the latter's "overconcern for purity of attitude, and for association only with the pure, the Donatists are thought by Augustine not merely to underrate the objective validity of the sacraments, but also the importance of visible unity to which it is inseparably tied."[35] He says that the Donatists' "heresy" lies in their separating themselves from the shared beliefs and practices of the main Christian body: "They fail to see that the unity and inter-communion of Christians is not just a desirable appendage of Christian practice, but is itself at the heart of the actuality of redemption."[36]

Commenting on this, Robert Dodaro says that, "for Milbank, Augustine's cri de coeur for unity stands over against Donatist interiority, an interiority which is both heresy and privatization."[37] This is in contrast to Milbank's Augustine, who instead manifests a public, symbolic exteriority. As Milbank puts it, Augustine's "typological apologetic for accepting Donatist baptism—that some true children of Israel were born from the slave-wife Hagar, not the free wife, Sarah— shows also an insistence on the Church as a historical community bound together by a historical transmission of signs, whose dissemination will necessarily be muddled, imperfectly coordinated with 'true belief', and not fully subject to prediction or control."[38] Thus, according to Milbank, Augustine's actions against the Donatists were taken in the name of an open-ended exteriority, as opposed to the closed interiority of the Donatists.

Dodaro, however, has wondered whether Milbank's response is sufficient here. He says that one may doubt "whether Milbank pays sufficient attention to the violence at the heart of what he terms Augustine's quest for 'the unity and inter-communion of Christians'."[39] He points out that Milbank's account of Christian coercion is restricted to the coercion of the Donatists, and that Milbank does not discuss the Pelagians, who would have been more problematic. Furthermore, even his discussion of the Donatist coercion is limited to the areas of church-state relations and the ontology of punishment: "As a result, his discussion never arrives at the question of the legitimacy of pluralism for Augustine. Milbank's account of Donatist ecclesiology is largely dismissive and prejudicial; his account of the 'peace' at the center of Augustine's church is apologetic and optimistic."[40]

Dodaro says that there is a "tension" in Augustine's thought between his own understanding of self-knowledge and his treatment of others. Dodaro details numerous parallels between Augustine's self-criticism and the errors for which heretics and others are themselves condemned. Given such parallels, one might have expected less violent and uncompromising condemnations on the part of Augustine. Indeed, Augustine himself is, at times, acutely aware that judgment of others should be tempered by an awareness of one's own faults. Dodaro quotes Augustine exhorting magistrates and provincial administrators to judge the accused in accordance with the leniency with which their own consciences have judged themselves: "See how you interrogated yourself and listened to yourself and punished yourself, and yet you spared yourself. Listen to your neighbor in the same way."[41] According to Dodaro, this text "best expresses Augustine's understanding of the interplay between self and other in the determination of justice,"[42] and yet he notes that this understanding does not seem to have been applied to Augustine's treatment of the excluded others, the heretics. He therefore asks, "Does Augustine ever view the heretic or the theurgist *in interiore modo*, in a symmetry to himself, and therefore as an 'other' for whom his invitation to dialogue ever amounts to anything more than a rhetorical pose?"[43] There is thus a dialectic within Augustine's thought between inte-riority and exteriority, and as Dodaro and Hankey make clear, it is a dialectic that Milbank obscures. Hankey therefore says, "It is precisely the positive Mil-bankian transformation of the postmodern deconstructive *agon* which blinds him to a feature of Augustine's dialectic. Milbank's critics are correct; his peace-making narrative excludes."[44]

This is not the place for a full analysis and evaluation of Milbank's interpre-tation and appropriation of Augustine. But this brief discussion at least provides one example of how narratives are "creatively" or "violently" subsumed by Mil-bank into his own metanarrative. For Milbank, the great virtue of the Augustin-ian narrative is the way in which difference is subsumed within the Christian ontology without being obliterated. Difference is unified while still being respected as different. But the difficulty with Milbank's metanarrative is that it is precisely this difference that seems not to be respected. It cannot but do undue violence to the narratives that it positions. And the example of the Augustinian narrative is particularly instructive, because it shows how this necessary violence is inflicted on those narratives that Milbank positions affirmatively, as well as on those that he positions pejoratively. Indeed, we have seen that Milbank does vio-lence to Augustine's narrative in order to conceal a certain violence that lies at its heart.

As we shall see below in the section on "Milbank and Nihilism," however, this violence is perhaps most evident in Milbank's positioning of the narratives he wants to out-narrate, particularly those of "nihilism." The dualistic and con-frontational way in which, as we have seen, Milbank frames the debate between theology and nihilism does not help alleviate this violence. Indeed, it seems to *promote* an agonistic and violent strategy that eradicates a genuine commitment to difference.

Now, it may be admitted that this violent positioning of other narratives is demanded by Milbank's commitment to Christianity *as metanarrative*. If this is the case, however, then we are brought back to the question of the desirability of the singularity and exclusivity of Milbank's metanarrative. And it is not simply that the violence necessarily entailed by Milbank's metanarrative is undesirable in itself; it is also that there seems to be an inconsistency, or at least a tension, between espousing a narrative on the basis of its peaceful content, on the one hand, and expounding it in a way that seems at odds with its content, on the other. As with our consideration of dualism, we seem to find here that Milbank has eradicated violence within the Christian story itself, only to reinstate and "inflate it at the meta-narrative level."[45] Furthermore, once we recognize the degree of violence (albeit provisional) that Milbank's metanarrative necessarily entails, this must at least weaken the force of his attack on the "nihilistic" post-modernists for their own supposed ontology of violence. I consider this point in more detail in chapter 5. But I shall now consider another corollary of the char-acter of Milbank's absolute metanarrative, namely, its tendency to forget its own fictive status.

Milbank and Mastery

A metanarrative, precisely because it is a metanarrative, must seek to "explain" and "position" *everything*, that is, every other narrative and every other interpretation of the world. This is because, for a metanarrative, there can be no *remainder* or *reserve*. Such a conception of metanarrative may be said to have been most fully consummated in the thought of G. W. F. Hegel. For Hegel, all intellectual configurations are to be understood and "positioned" from the vantage point of Absolute Knowing or Spirit. He says that this goal "has for its path the recollection of the Spirits as they are in themselves and as they accomplish the organization of their realm. Their presentation, regarded from the side of their free existence appearing in the form of contingency, is History; but regarded from the side of their [philosophically] comprehended organization, it is the Science of Knowing in the spheres of appearance."[46]

For Hegel, therefore, all other forms of consciousness are manifestations of a journey toward something greater and constitute apparent knowledge, as opposed to Absolute Knowledge. The vantage point of Absolute Knowledge is the vantage point of the metanarrative, from which all other configurations are positioned and understood for what they really are. Hegel says that apparent knowledge is "the way of the Soul which journeys through the series of its own configurations as though they were the stations appointed for it by its own nature, so that it may purify itself for the life of the Spirit, and achieve, finally, through a completed experience of itself, the awareness of what it really is in itself."[47] When this awareness is finally accomplished, "when consciousness itself grasps this its own essence, it will signify the nature of absolute knowledge itself."[48] At this point, every other intellectual configuration gets its meaning and its legitimacy only from the place accorded to it within Hegel's metanarrative. From the vantage point of Absolute Knowledge, everything is "explained," everything is "positioned," everything is "mastered"; indeed, this vantage point constitutes the "mastery" of reality.[49]

This is the inevitable corollary and, indeed, the avowed aim of any speculative metanarrative, and it is a corollary that Milbank himself avoids only with difficulty. We may even go so far as to question the extent to which Milbank succeeds in avoiding it at all. For the *effect* of both the speculative metanarrative of Hegel and the fictive metanarrative of Milbank is that they both appear to "explain" and "master" reality. Indeed, their close proximity may help explain why Milbank is so eager to distance his own project from that of Hegel in this respect. We have already observed that Milbank proclaims Hegel's quest for an "encyclopedia" of knowledge to be "forever dead," and that he claims to espouse a theology "aware of itself as culturally constructed."[50] But to what extent does Milbank himself emerge with precisely this sort of "encyclopedia"? He comes perilously close to doing so, primarily as a result of his insistence on the theological necessity of an absolute and all-embracing metanarrative. Graham Ward states the difficulty here as follows: "All metadiscourses (including the Christian one) do set out to explain, and do so by forgetting they are narratives. And so, not surprisingly, there are moments when John Milbank appears to stumble into a positivism whose tenets he undermines."[51]

This tendency to stumble into the system of a speculative metanarrative is manifested in Milbank's work in several ways. It is evident, for instance, in the all-knowing, "omniscient" character of Milbank's narration; in the "rational," logical, and pedestrian style of his writing; and in his tendency to lapse into a form of apologetics. All these aspects of Milbank's narrative are characteristic of a mythical (nonfictive) speculative system and seem to suggest a tendency toward a "fictive forgetting." At times, it seems as though Milbank's metanarrative forgets that it is only a fiction. Let us consider each of these manifestations in turn.

To a certain extent, Milbank's "omniscience" is once again a necessary outcome of his commitment to theology as metanarrative. For Milbank, it seems that one must be all-knowing in order to know anything at all. As he says, "We *have* to say 'how things are in general' to be able to say anything at all."[52] Given that a metanarrative is necessary and inescapable, we have seen that Milbank espouses the *Christian* metanarrative, as opposed to any other, because it is the *only* metanarrative that can take account of difference in a peaceful way. For Milbank, it is this peacefulness that enables the Christian metanarrative (uniquely) to resist mastery: "This is why it is so important to reassert theology as a master discourse; theology, *alone*, remains the discourse of non-mastery."[53] The narrator speaks with a manifest omniscience here, for the obverse of the claim that theology *alone* is the discourse of nonmastery is the claim that *every other* discourse must be a discourse of mastery. Paradoxically, this very claim seems to subvert itself; for is not claiming to be the *only* metanarrative to avoid mastery an act of mastery par excellence? And on what basis can Milbank claim such an omniscience? Is he not adopting a "God's eye" view here, of the very kind to which he is so vehemently opposed?[54]

Correspondingly, Milbank also claims that *every other,* nontheological discourse must ultimately culminate in nihilism. Commenting on this, Gerard Loughlin has said that "it is clear that this claim goes beyond its warrants, since neither Milbank nor anyone else has carried out the comparison by which such a difference could be displayed. Milbank's own narration of the difference between Christianity and other cultures remains entirely occidental, and does not even begin the linkages required for the rigorous espousal of his claim."[55] It seems that Milbank's omniscience as a metanarrator stands in need of deconstruction. His authoritative self-assertion may be viewed as either a divine or a human omniscience—either a "God's eye" view or a Cartesian or Hegelian "mastery." Without such a deconstruction, there is the danger of a "fictive forgetting" or a relapse into positivism.

It is inevitable, however, that such an assumption of divine omniscience will bring in its wake a corresponding claim to authority. In the particular guise of John Milbank, the theologian speaks with an authority that is almost divine. This is a point that has been made (from their quite different perspectives) by Graham

Ward, Oliver Davies, Steven Shakespeare, and Gareth Jones. For both Shakespeare and Jones, the most revealing of Milbank's passages in this respect is to be found in the opening of *The Word Made Strange*. Here, Milbank writes of theology as a reflection on Christian practice. And yet, with such practice in disarray and with the theologian unsure as to where to find it, he "feels almost that the entire ecclesial task falls on his own head: in the meagre mode of reflective words he must seek to imagine what a true practical repetition would be like. Or at least he must hope that his merely theoretical continuation of the tradition will open up a space for wider transformation."[56] Commenting on this, Shakespeare says that the "humble tone masks an unprecedented self-importance," with its portrayal of the theologian as the true continuation of the church and therefore of Christ's incarnation. "A happy coincidence between human narrative and divine self-disclosure is assumed. . . . However, to preserve this assumption, it becomes necessary to divinize the narrator—the Church—and when the unreality of the ideal church becomes apparent, to divinize the intuitions of the individual theologian."[57]

It would appear, therefore, that the status of the individual theologian has become unduly inflated. But how does this sort of "divinized" inflation come about? Oliver Davies suggests that it derives from the emphasis that Milbank places on the role of language and culture in human life. Although such an emphasis is, in many ways, a welcome one, Davies says that it nevertheless has an unfortunate corollary for theology in that it unduly emphasizes the role of the solitary individual. This is because it "understands culture to be a task to which the exceptionally 'poetical' or gifted Christian individual is summoned in the interests of creating Christianity anew as transfiguration and theophany. Deconstructed language, no longer tied to reality or to other speakers, becomes the vehicle for a heroic re-sacralisation of the world carried out on behalf of the community by a solitary individual who possesses exceptional powers of divine poeticity."[58] Davies says that this emphasis on the solitary individual, arising from the concepts of "radical incommensurability" and "writing," gives rise to "monological readings of history" in which dialogue is downgraded. Furthermore, he says that this tendency is most clearly manifested in Milbank's attenuated understanding of the term *narrative* and, in particular, in the apparent assumption that there is only one Christian narrative: "The *de facto* assumption that there is a single Christian narrative again bypasses areas of difficulty, and supports the single voice as solitary herald of unified Christian tradition."[59] I return to Milbank's insensitivity to the multiplicity of Christian narratives below, in the section on "Milbank and Christianity." At this point, however, it is clear that Milbank's "omniscience" as theologian gives rise to a "mastery" that his metanarrative is (uniquely) thought to avoid.

Furthermore, these tendencies toward mastery are not alleviated by Milbank's style of writing. For although he extols the literary genres of narrative, rhetoric, story, and persuasion, as opposed to those of system, rationality, argument, refutation, and so forth, his writing style curiously seems not to embody these preferences. It is a directly pedestrian, dry, and logical style, which makes its points with such beguilingly reasonable logic and with such a cumulative effect that its conclusions seem almost rationally irresistible.[60] Whereas other postmodern writers play with writing, employ word games, and create linguistic tricks, Milbank's style can appear tame and rather heavy in comparison. This would not be all that remarkable were it not for the fact that it seems incongruously at odds with Milbank's actual message. The content of what he says is one thing; the form in which he says it seems to be quite another.

This observation has been made by Gillian Rose, who says that the incongruity of Milbank's writing style is even more marked when compared with the writings of Mark C. Taylor: "Taylor offers a montage of text and illustration, accruing grammatical, phonetic and graphological juxtapositions and complications, learnt, it would seem, from *Finnegans Wake*; Milbank offers a treatise . . . with sober, sustained argumentation, paced temporally and spatially from beginning to end. In tone, Taylor is masked, ironic, transgressive and extravagant; Milbank is straight, logical—in spite of his ontology of narration—severe, authoritative and original."[61] At this point, one begins to wonder at the extent to which Milbank really does persuade rather than argue; for at times, he does appear to slip into a mode of argumentation. For all his repudiation of refutation, it sometimes appears as though all other (nontheological) modes of thought are being "refuted"; it seems as though we are being compelled or coerced rather than persuaded. For all his espousal of rhetoric, narrative, persuasion, the reality of his writing style seems rather to embody argument, reasons, and coercion (and this, of course, is not unrelated to our discussion of Milbank's violence). Consequently, it can also appear as though Milbank engages in apologetics in spite of his resolute refusal of such apologetics. Let us now consider this suspicion.

Traditionally, theological apologetic consists of attempts to argue for a theological perspective, as opposed to alternative perspectives, on the basis of common criteria that are independent of the perspective being defended. Such criteria are usually derived from a modernist canon of rationality. Thus, although apologetics is an ancient discipline, Stephen Sykes says that it is now usually associated with "the common eighteenth-century topics of God, freedom, and immortality, including such subjects as miracle, prayer and providence, but generally abstracted from any consideration of the doctrines of creation, election, redemption, or the last things."[62] It is precisely such an understanding of apologetics that Milbank rejects. He insists that if his Christian perspective is persuasive, then this persuasion should be intrinsic to the Christian *logos* itself, and "not the apologetic of a universal human reason."[63] He says that the only argument for a tradition is the story of the development of that tradition—in the case of Christianity, a story of "preachings, journeyings, miracles, martyrdoms, icons painted and liturgies sung, as well as of intrigues, sins and warfare . . . and not just the story of arguments concerning a certain X (for example the nature of human virtue) lying outside the story."[64]

And yet, one is left wondering whether Milbank has really escaped from the clutches of apologetics. For in spite of his insistence that the only argument for

Christianity can be the telling and performance of the Christian story, it is quite clear that Milbank does not simply "tell and perform." He also argues, deconstructs rival viewpoints, and attempts to demonstrate that the Christian narrative is the only one that can construe difference in a peaceful way. But here, in a typically apologetic style, Milbank seems to appeal to a common ground that he shares with his rivals, namely, the desirability of peace, and the desirability of an ontology that embodies this peace. It is the assumption that his rivals share this sense of the desirability of peace that gives his argument its force, that gives strength to his case.[65]

A distinction should be made here between, on the one hand, speaking from within the Christian narrative, so that one claims that "peace is our eschatological goal, and consequently is ontologically prior" and, on the other hand, speaking in a manner that is at least semidetached from the Christian narrative, so that one asserts the desirability of conceiving of difference in a peaceful manner and *on that basis*, asserts the priority of the Christian narrative. In the former instance, the priority of the Christian narrative is *assumed*, whereas in the latter, the priority of the Christian narrative is *argued for* in an apologetic manner. In his theory, Milbank affirms the former approach, but in his "practice," we may say that he actually performs the latter. This is not to say, of course, that Milbank is here resorting to a "universal human reason," and if one takes this as the essence of apologetics, then he is clearly not providing an *apologia* for Christianity. But if the essence of apologetics is thought to lie in the assertion of the priority of a point of view on the basis of some sort of common ground that is external (as well as internal) to that point of view, then Milbank's actual "practice" or "performance" is much more susceptible to the charge of apologetics than he would have us believe.

Milbank himself has recently acknowledged that this is the case, saying that the quest for "an absolutely internal Christian discourse" is actually a misplaced one. He says that just as there are no uncontaminated, neutral "abstract" starting points, so, too, there cannot be particular narrative traditions uncontaminated by "abstract" notions. Indeed, he says that the notion of a completely internal Christian narrative is simply the result of an extreme reaction against apologetics based on a neutral starting point. Consequently, he says that "the concreteness of the gospels is also a mosaic of inherited general and vague notions and images, and there is no sheerly Christian language which will not be somewhat understood by non-Christians. . . . Thus I, at least, do not apologise for residual apologetics, as it is the questionable duality of internal discourse versus *apologia* which I seek to surpass."[66]

But this raises the further question of the status of the "peace," for example, on which Milbank's apologetic rests. Is it a uniquely Christian category, or is it one of the "general and vague notions" that Christianity has inherited? The fact that the notion of peace plays such an indispensable role in Milbank's "discursive developments of [Christian] faith that are to a degree convincing even to those outside faith's circle"[67] suggests that it must be one of the latter. But if this is the case—if peace is one of the "inherited general and vague notions"—this must further call into question Milbank's claim that Christianity is "uniquely" able to secure this peace. For if the notion of peace is an inherited rather than a uniquely Christian category, this at least raises the question of the extent to which such peace may be secured by alternative intellectual configurations. That Milbank assumes it cannot again seems to constitute an unwarranted omniscience. In any case, what also emerges from this is that if Milbank does not simply "tell the Christian story" but also provides an apologetic supplement to that story, then there are clearly two stories here. This, in turn, raises the question of which story is actually being prioritized by Milbank—the Christian story (which Christian story, in any case?) or Milbank's story. Which narrative is actually the *meta-narrative*? This question is of crucial importance, and I return to it in more detail below.

Thus far, we have observed in Milbank's metanarrative an apparent omniscience and authoritative self-assertion, a logical and coercive style of writing, and an apparent resort to apologetics, all of which suggest a forgetting of the fictive status of his own narrative and a dissolution of the boundary between a "speculative" and a "fictional" metanarrative. How is this danger of slipping into an incipient positivism to be avoided? According to Loughlin, it can be avoided only if, after Nietzsche, theology "acknowledges its own fictivity, and, in performance, attains to a certain playfulness and to a lightness of touch."[68] But this answer in turn gives rise to the question of where this acknowledgment of fictivity comes from. Loughlin again answers this question by claiming that it must come from *within* the Christian metanarrative itself. He says that "it will have to be at the level of the *content* that the story resists mastery, since the *effect* of any master-narrative as such will be the same, to position not simply the story in which it is implicated and from which it is unfolded, but all other stories as well."[69] In this, Loughlin concurs with Milbank, for whom the fictive awareness must also come from *within* the Christian metanarrative. It cannot come from outside that meta-narrative simply because there is no "outside." More particularly, this fictive awareness derives from and is ontologically grounded in the doctrine of the Trinity.

Milbank says that the "harmony" of the Trinity is "not the harmony of a finished totality but a 'musical' harmony of infinity. Just as an infinite God must be power-act, so the doctrine of the Trinity discovers the infinite God to include a radically 'external' relationality. Thus God can only speak to us simultaneously as the Word incarnate, and as the indefinite spiritual response, in time, which is the Church."[70] The effect of this understanding of the Trinity as a "musical harmony of infinity" is that knowledge of God ceases to have anything to do with "truth," correspondence, or positivism and instead pertains to the character of rhetoric, narrative, and fiction. Milbank says that in contrast to Aristotle and the neo-Platonists, Augustine and Dionysius redefined Being as that which is itself different. The consequence of this was that "God, or the first principle, can no longer be arrived at by dialectics, by the discipline of 'truth', or by the careful distinguishing of that which remains self-identical. A knowledge that is rather the infinite maximal tensional harmony of difference has to be something persuasively communicated. . . . Hence the relationship of God to the world becomes, after Christianity, a rhetorical one, and *ceases to be anything to do with 'truth'*, or, in other words with the relation of reality to appearance."[71] Milbank's point here is that the fictive status of his metanarrative—the reminder that his metanarrative is to be fictively distinguished from the speculative and positivist metanarratives—derives from the content of that metanarrative itself, in this case, the particular content of the doctrine of the Trinity.

But to what extent does the doctrine of the Trinity necessarily give itself to be read in this way? Although it may be legitimate for Milbank to read the doctrine in terms of persuasion, rhetoric, and narrative, it cannot be said that the doctrine necessarily *demands* to be read in this way; for the fact is that the doctrine of the Trinity has been subject to a bewildering variety of interpretations, many of which are antithetical to Milbank's own, yet all of which claim to derive from the doctrine itself.[72] And although Milbank adopts a specifically Augustinian reading, we have already seen that this is a *different* repetition of Augustine's thought. To what extent, therefore, can Milbank's reading of the doctrine be said to be derived *solely* from within the doctrine itself? If we are to avoid essentialism, we must recognize that the doctrine does not necessarily demand to be read in *any* way. On the contrary, the doctrine becomes meaningful and intelligible through the acts of reading and interpretation. Milbank's thinking necessarily lapses into circularity here. This is because his recognition of the fictional character of his metanarrative may be derived from the doctrine of the Trinity, but it can be so derived only if the doctrine is first read and interpreted in that particular "narrativist" and "fictionalist" way. After essentialism and foundationalism, such circularity is unavoidable, and its effect is a deconstruction of the idea of an absolute metanarrative, which is itself unfounded but which is the foundation of everything else.

Indeed, this point may be addressed to Milbank's reading of the Christian narrative more generally. We have seen that Milbank wants to interpret Christianity as being *internally* postmodern. But the difficulty with this is that Christianity is clearly not *intrinsically* postmodern. Milbank acknowledges this when he says that Christianity "can *become* 'internally' postmodern in a way that may not be possible for every religion or ideology. I mean by this that it is *possible* to *construe* Christianity as suspicious of notions of fixed 'essences' in its approach to human beings, to nature, to community and to God, even if it has never fully escaped the grasp of a 'totalising' metaphysics."[73] So Christianity can *become* postmodern; it is *possible* to *construe* Christianity in a postmodern way; but it is not necessarily and intrinsically postmodern. There is, of course, no such thing as an unmediated, contextless Christianity to restore. So Milbank's "restoration" of the Christian metanarrative must, at the same time, be something new, something different.

If, therefore, Christianity is being transposed and construed in a new postmodern way that is not intrinsic to the Christian narrative itself, this transposition and this construal must come from somewhere "other" than that narrative. It must come from a "supplement" that will be inextricably linked with the context, the setting, within which the narrative is proclaimed. This has to be the case because the narrative has to be mediated. As Graham Ward says, theology "gives expression to an ongoing conversation between past texts and present contexts. It is a self-conscious form of what has come to be called 'intertextuality', in which one or more discourses are transposed by being re-articulated within another. Because the conversation is ongoing, because contexts are always contingent, so theological expression will constantly change."[74] This suggests that the process of positioning between theology and other discourses is not quite as unidirectional as Milbank likes to suggest. Not only does theology position other discourses, but other discourses also position theology—by these other discourses, theology is rendered in a particular way. Once again, there is a necessary circularity here. It seems this cannot be avoided; theology (and indeed, every other discourse) must always be supplemented by other discourses. If this is the case, however, it calls Milbank's conception of an absolute, all-embracing metanarrative into question, for if a metanarrative is "positioned" by something external to it, by a supplement, then by definition it ceases to serve as a *meta*-narrative. And, against Milbank, I suggest that such a situation is inescapable. We are always already in the middle. It is not possible to go back to an absolute beginning; we cannot posit an absolute metanarrative that is itself unfounded and that is the "beginning" and foundation of everything else. All metanarratives that claim to position other narratives are also themselves positioned by these other narratives.

Indeed, I am not only claiming that this mutual positioning and mutual founding is inescapable, but I am also suggesting that it is *required* by Milbank's narrative if it is to remain fictive and resist mastery. And I am further suggesting that not only is such a supplement required by Milbank's project but, indeed, that it is also *already present* within it. In other words, I am suggesting that Milbank's own metanarrative is *itself* a supplement to the Christian narrative, in spite of his tendency to obscure the distinction between the two. To some extent, I have already intimated such a conclusion, for I have argued that Milbank minimizes the dualism and violence within the Christian story, only to magnify them both at the level of the metastory. And the apparent apologetic element in Milbank's project further suggests that there is a distinction to be made between the Christian story on the one hand and his own metanarrative supplement on the other. It is now time to explicate this distinction more fully.

Milbank and Christianity:
A False Equation?

In this section, I suggest that within Milbank's project, the Christian narrative is itself "positioned" by Milbank's metanarrative, which, although derived from, is essentially "other" than the Christian narrative. It is thus Milbank's narrative, rather than the Christian narrative, that is promoted to the status of metnarra-tive in Milbank's vision, and therefore Christianity is once again positioned by another narrative, in spite of Milbank's protestations to the contrary.

I begin by looking at Milbank's articulation of the relationship between Chris-tian doctrine and the Christian narrative. Here, he offers an example of a rejec-tion of priority in favor of mutual constitution. He says that doctrine is "invented" in order to deal with interpretative undecidability with regard to the narrative. The doctrine therefore stabilizes this undecidability by setting bounds of legitimation—by distinguishing what is an illegitimate interpretation from what is a legitimate one. As such, doctrine is "excessive" in that it goes beyond what the narrative warrants. It is this excess that distinguishes doctrine from nar-rative; without such an excess, doctrine would be indistinguishable from narra-tive. The important point here, however, is that this doctrinal excess then has an impact on the narrative itself, in a mutually founding pattern.[75] Milbank says that this "second-order," "regulative," "excessive" discourse "makes its own peculiar contribution to the content of Christianity, thereby insinuating itself back into the first-order discourse from which it is only relatively distinguished."[76] So doc-trine goes speculatively beyond the narrative, and "nothing justifies this specula-tion except itself, and the way it then enriches the stories told, and re-doubles the perceived significance of Christian practices."[77] But, of course, this is itself a nar-rative. It is a narrative—Milbank's narrative—that makes a distinction between narrative and doctrine, and that tells a story about how each relates to the other.[78] This raises the question of the status of Milbank's narrative. It is not the Chris-tian narrative, nor is it a part of Christian doctrine (though it is clearly bound up with both), and yet it "positions" them. It tells how each relates to the other; it acts as a setting, a background against which both are understood. It serves as an "organizing logic," a metanarrative.

So, on the one hand, Milbank claims that he is simply "telling the Christian story," while on the other hand, he is providing a supplement, a prologue to that story, the status of which remains unclear. He claims that the task of the theolo-gian is "to tell the again the Christian *mythos*, pronounce again the Christian *logos*, and call again for Christian *praxis* in a manner that restores their freshness and originality."[79] And yet, at the same time, he acknowledges that his project seeks to articulate "an original, necessary and ongoing *supplementation* which is yet not violent and subversive in relation to the original."[80] So there are at least two stories; the Christian narrative and Milbank's supplement, and the contents of the two stories are quite distinct. We have seen that, for Milbank, the Chris-tian narrative is "a story of preachings, journeyings, miracles, martyrdoms, voca-tions, marriages, icons painted and liturgies sung, as well as intrigues, sins and warfare."[81] Milbank's narrative, by contrast, is a story of the end of modernity and secular reason; of the return and necessity of the metanarrative; of stories, rhetoric, and persuasion; of the futility of liberalism and nihilism. The supple-mentary story can be construed out of the Christian story, and it can also be used to construe the Christian story in a particular way, but it cannot be *conflated* with the Christian story, as Milbank sometimes seems to do; for the *contents* of the two narratives are quite distinct.

Indeed, not only does Milbank provide a supplementary story explaining how Christian doctrine is related to the Christian narrative, but he also provides a supplementary interpretation or even "translation" of Christian doctrine. Of course, to read something, whether doctrine or anything else, is simultaneously to interpret it; there is no reading without interpretation. We may well ask, however, whether Milbank's interpretation sometimes slips into "translation," that is, a process whereby the surface or manifest meaning of a doctrine is translated so as to reveal a hidden, latent, underlying meaning. Such a strategy is typically employed by modern liberal theologians (inherited from Kant and Hegel in particular), and it is one that radical orthodoxy has been concerned to resist.[82]

R. R. Reno, however, has argued that Milbank engages in the very strategy for which the liberals have been condemned. He says that when Milbank "engages the biblical text, [he] consistently *translates* the particular sense into a conceptual or speculative process. The Gospel stories are, for him, allegories of a participatory metaphysics."[83] Indeed, Reno argues that this is the case not only with Milbank's reading of scripture but also with his reading of creeds and the ecclesiastical tradition. In each of these areas, Milbank appears to translate particularities into "higher, purified and untainted forms."[84] To illustrate this, Reno turns to the example of Milbank's interpretation of the doctrine of the atonement, in which he says that Milbank provides "a determinedly conceptual reading of the redemptive significance of Jesus."[85] Here, Milbank gives two reasons to explain how our redemption becomes possible after the death of Jesus: "First, we speculatively grasp that sin is negation, arbitrary violence, the refusal of pure love itself, and this speculation is an *indispensable* and yet independent moment of faith. But secondly, the speculation is only occasioned by the horrifying and sublime compulsion of Jesus' death, whose concrete circumstance makes us feel that here we really 'see' sin, and at the same time the essence of human goodness."[86] Reno says that, in this account, Milbank accords the activity of "interpretive creativity" an indispensable role in the act of atonement itself, which thereby gives rise to the idea of "participatory atonement." Reno dismisses this interpretation as a "postmodern combination of theory and rhetoric" and says, "The 'speculative grasp' suggests a general tendency, in Radical Orthodoxy, to substitute the creative production of theological theory for the creative power of Christ."[87] But the important point here for our purposes is that Milbank provides a distinctive supplement that "interprets," "positions," and "translates" the theological narrative from which it is clearly distinguishable.

More specifically, Reno says that Milbank's explanation of the doctrine of the atonement is redolent of the explanations of modern theology, particularly as epitomized by Kant. He says that this is particularly evident in Milbank's account of a "poetic atonement" brought about "by the horrifying and sublime compulsion of Jesus' death." "Milbank's 'speculative grasp' may spin with a theoretical rotation, but the relation of Christ to believer differs hardly at all from Kant's account of the eternal will, aroused by Jesus, who is the sensuous manifestation of the archetype of moral rectitude."[88] To add insult to injury, Reno further suggests that Milbank's account of atonement mirrors Hegel's dialectic in that the lost identity of Christ is recovered only in the "ongoing career of Spirit." In light of this, Reno says that Milbank demonstrates "an overall ambivalence about the role of Scripture, creed and inherited ecclesial practice that moves in a modernist direction. Authority shifts out of the particularity of word and sacrament into a supervening theory or concept."[89] Again, the important point here is that authority is being relocated, away from the Christian narrative itself into Milbank's own metanarrative. And Reno's argument adds the further point that the content of Milbank's metanarrative, which interprets, positions, and translates the Christian narrative, is rather more "modern" than Milbank would have us believe. This argument is all the more striking given Milbank's trenchant opposition to modernity in general and to Kant in particular, as was detailed in chapter 2.

In attempting to account for this strategy on the part of Milbank and other radical orthodox theologians, Reno says that they "seek to render Christian truth so perspicuous, so clear and evident at the level of theory, that the nihilistic temptation of secularity will be impossible, and Radical Orthodoxy's peaceful consequences will be made plain."[90] If this is the case, then it must also call into question Milbank's rhetorical claim that the persuasiveness of his case is nothing other than the persuasiveness of the Christian *logos* itself, because it appears that, to be adequately "persuasive," the Christian *logos* stands in need of the "help" and "assistance" provided by Milbank's "theory." Thus, although Milbank's claim—that his own persuasiveness is nothing other than the persuasiveness of the Christian *logos*—appears as a commendable modesty, it turns out to be quite the opposite. This is because Milbank's claim here renders invisible, or at least obscures, the presence of his own metanarrative supplement. The result is that the supplement is collapsed into the Christian narrative itself, thereby investing the supplement with an authority deriving from theological endorsement. By the obscuring of the distinction between the Christian narrative and Milbank's supplement, the latter gains a theological authority. It seems that Milbank's narrative is being privileged by the Christian narrative, rather than vice versa.

To resist this strategy, it is important to remember that Milbank's supplement is precisely that. Furthermore, it is a supplement that, in relation to the Christian narrative, is contingent and provisional. As we saw in our discussion of the doctrine of the Trinity, the Christian narrative may allow itself to be construed in the way that Milbank wants to construe it, but it does not necessarily demand that it be construed in that way. Lyotard has noted that those who interpret postmodernism as an opportunity for the return of religious metanarratives have a tendency to make precisely this sort of move. He says that "the answer to the question 'Can we perpetuate the great narratives?' has become 'We *must* do this or that'."[91] Indeed, there does seem to be a slippage in Milbank's writings from saying that "this is one possible way of interpreting the Christian narrative, and I think it is the best way" toward saying that "this is the only theological way of understanding the Christian narrative, and it is demanded by that narrative itself." The former *may* be defended; the latter cannot be.

So Milbank's rhetorical claim to the Christian high ground is here unmasked. He may claim that his metanarrative is the best setting, the best context within which to tell the Christian story and explicate Christian doctrine, but he cannot claim that his metanarrative *is itself* the Christian narrative or that it is the *only* context for the Christian narrative. It is just one of any number of contingent metanarratives that may position the Christian narrative. And any one of these contingent metanarratives may be privileged by the narrator, but they cannot be privileged by the Christian narrative itself. Of course, one may claim that a metanarrative is more consistent with and does less violence to the Christian narrative than another metanarrative, but even then it is the narrator himself, rather than the narrative, who makes this judgment.

That Christianity must itself be positioned by yet another metanarrative cannot be escaped, just as Milbank insisted that the metanarrative itself cannot be escaped. But we should remember that whichever metanarrative positions Christianity, it is itself positioned by Christianity, in a mutually founding relationship. It is not possible to go back to a primary metanarrative, which is itself unfounded but which founds everything else, for we are always already situated in a mesh of mutually implicated narratives. Every metanarrative is already implicated in others that position it, just as it seeks to position them. As Lyotard says, "No phrase is the first. This does not only mean that others precede it, but also that the modes of linking, implied in the preceding phrases—possible modes of linking therefore—are ready to take the phrase into account and inscribe it into the pursuit of certain stakes, to actualize themselves by means of it."[92]

We have seen that, within Milbank's project, the Christian narrative is itself positioned by Milbank's metanarrative. But Milbank's metanarrative is also itself positioned, not only by the Christian narrative but also by all sorts of other historical, social, and cultural narratives; for, theology aside, he claims that there has been a fundamental paradigm shift that may be described as "the end of modernity, which is not accomplished, yet continues to arrive." This cultural or philosophical narrative is not derived solely from the Christian narrative, for it also opens the way for the return of the Christian narrative. Hankey recognizes this when he says that Milbank's theology "is specifically determined in its antiphilosophical stance by its specific location relative to the given philosophy of our time."[93] In other words, Milbank's assertion of the priority of theology over philosophy is itself philosophically situated and determined. His antiphilosophical theology is itself positioned by a particular philosophy, which Hankey identifies as a Heideggerian-Derridian-Wittgensteinian space.[94] So there is a multiplicity of narratives and metanarratives, all mutually implicated and enfolded, and the attempt to single out one of these as being prior, unfounded and yet founding, is, I suggest, misguided. It is an attempt to go "too far back."

When we recognize, however, that Milbank's narrative is not to be equated with the Christian narrative; that the Christian narrative is, to some extent, positioned by Milbank's metanarrative; that this metanarrative is one of any number of possible and contingent metanarratives; and that it is privileged by the narrator himself, then the compatibility of Milbank's narrative with the Christian narrative can no longer be assumed. Frederick Bauerschmidt has made precisely this point, suggesting that Milbank's narrative is not as compatible with Christianity as he assumes. Recognizing the philosophical dependence of Milbank's theology, Bauerschmidt says that "at times Milbank's commitments to certain philosophical positions regarding language push him in directions which seem to run counter to the stories and practices of the church, which movement is then subjected to a lesser 'containment' that often seems arbitrary."[95] More specifically, Bauerschmidt is concerned that Milbank's "desire to make the 'speculative excess' of Trinitarian and Christological doctrine integral to discourse about Jesus seems to run the risk of losing its grounding in the stories of the man Jesus."[96] The latter point connects to Reno's argument that Milbank prioritizes speculative theory over the concrete Christian narrative. This prioritizing gives rise to what Bauerschmidt perceives to be a "thinness" in Milbank's account of Jesus, Christian morality, and the sacramental and institutional life of the church. This thinness is such that it calls into question the compatibility of Milbank's metanarrative with the Christian narrative.[97]

Romand Coles has also suggested that Milbank's metanarrative sits uneasily with the Christian narrative it positions. She says that Milbank's metanarrative partly undermines Christianity "insofar as it conceives of generosity as sufficiently engendered and containable within a single—albeit infinitely elaborating—hegemonic meta-narrative. Such a conception deconstructs conceit at the level of individual selves only to inflate it at the meta-narrative level."[98] Also, we have already considered the possibility that Milbank's single, hegemonic metanarrative promotes an incongruously violent means toward the church's peaceful end. Thus, Milbank cannot simply take for granted that all other attempts to "position" the Christian narrative are incompatible with Christianity, while his own is uniquely privileged by the Christian narrative itself.

If I am correct in my suggestion that an absolute metanarrative is inherently unstable, and that it must ultimately deconstruct and dissolve itself in its necessary dependence on supplementation by other metanarratives, and if Milbank is simultaneously correct in his suggestion that without an absolute metanarrative, nihilism will be the inexorable result, then we may legitimately expect to uncover a certain implicit nihilism within Milbank's own project. In the next section, I show that this is indeed the case. Having distinguished between Milbank's own narrative and the Christian narrative, and having identified Milbank's narrative as a supplement that is apart from (though bound up with) the Christian narrative, I now want to suggest that Milbank invokes yet another supplement—a "meta-metanarrative"—that tells a story of how his metanarrative "combats" other metanarratives. I argue that the content of this "meta-metanarrative" converges remarkably with the nihilism that Milbank wishes to "out-narrate." Having suggested that Milbank's narrative is more apart from the Christian narrative than he would have us believe, I now want to suggest that it is also more bound up with the nihilist narrative than he is willing to admit.

Milbank and Nihilism:
A False Dichotomy?

In a world in which there is not only a plurality of narratives but a plurality of competing, incommensurate narratives, a metanarrative has to be invoked in order to understand how these various narratives relate to one another and interact. Each metanarrative positions within it all competing narratives. Rival metanarratives are subsumed into the privileged metanarrative(s) and are thereby reduced to being mere narratives within the metanarrative in question. So Milbank's radical orthodoxy and Lyotard's postmodernism, for instance, are rival metanarratives, but within Milbank's metanarrative, Lyotard's is reduced to being a mere narrative that is positioned by and within, and indeed is negated by, Milbank's metanarrative.

The question then arises of how we are to understand and articulate what happens when these two metanarratives "combat" or "out-narrate" each other. Now, we have seen that when one analyzes and logically organizes "combats" between narratives, one emerges with a metanarrative. Correspondingly, when one analyzes and logically organizes combats between metanarratives, one emerges with what I shall rather inelegantly call a "meta-metanarrative" (and one could keep going back ad infinitum, which is why the concept of a final, absolute metanarrative is so inherently unstable). But for Milbank, there is nothing "beyond" the Christian metanarrative, nothing that positions it. It is, on the contrary, ultimate and final. I have already argued that, in Milbank's project, it is his own metanarrative that is ultimate and final, rather than the Christian narrative, as he claims. I now want to suggest that Milbank further invokes a "supplement to his supplement" or a meta-metanarrative, without explicit acknowledgment. I also want to suggest that at the meta-metanarrative level, there is a curious convergence with nihilist postmodernism.

So how is one to understand and articulate the confrontation of metanarratives? For the nihilist postmodernists, the answer is simply a reiteration of their metanarrative. Their metanarrative may be reinvoked at the meta-metanarrative level, for their story of a multitude of narratives conflicting, competing, and out-narrating one another can serve a dual purpose. It serves not only as an analysis of disputes between narratives but equally well as an analysis of disputes between *meta*-narratives. For Milbank, by contrast, the question is more difficult, and there does seem to be an ambiguity in his thought with regard to how this question should be answered. On the one hand, he refuses the question. The Christian metanarrative is ultimate and final, and there can be no question of moving "beyond" it to a meta-metanarrative by which it is itself positioned. We have seen that the nihilist metanarrative must be downgraded to being a narrative within the Christian metanarrative.

This evasive strategy is problematic, however, for it envisages a series of metanarratives that do not combat, conflict, or interact with one another at all. Rather, each metanarrative exists in isolation from all the rest, each rehearsing its own internal rationale. The difficulty with this is that metanarratives do, in fact, confront each other and they do so not merely by reducing each other to being mere narratives within their own respective metanarratives. On the contrary, they confront each other as *rival* metanarratives that are to be combated and out-narrated *as* metanarratives. Indeed, Milbank's project appears both to assume and to be an instance of this, for it recognizes that nihilism is a rival metanarrative, one that must be countered by putting forward an alternative metanarrative that does not differ in form (it, too, is unfounded *mythos*), only in content (primarily, its "ontology of peace"). It would appear, then, that there are three levels here. In the above section, I distinguished between the Christian narrative and Milbank's metanarrative that interprets and positions it; these are the first two levels. But when Milbank writes of how his metanarrative counters others by out-narrating it, telling a better story, and so forth, he has, as it were, taken another step back. He is telling a story of how his metanarrative combats rival metanarratives, and in doing so, he invokes a third level, the level of the meta-metanarrative. Now, this meta-metanarrative is not some neutral vantage point. It is just as much a *mythos*, a "fiction," and just as unfounded as the metanarratives about which it speaks. Nevertheless, it is clear that we are at a different "level" here; a self-reflexive move has been made.

The questions that inevitably arise from this are that of the *content* of the meta-metanarrative and that of whence this perspective is gained. We have seen that what characterizes the content of Milbank's construal of the Christian narrative is that it embodies an ontology of peace—a *polis* that is a "musical, worshipping realm, when it is in the hands of those acquainted with the true 'art of government', which means those who understand how what is different can be combined, because they have a vision of their common superordinate origin."[99] But this is the content of Milbank's metanarrative, on which his meta-metanarrative comments. What of the content of his *meta*-metanarrative? What does it embody? What "setting" does it envisage for the telling of the metanarrative? According to Milbank, there are "infinitely many possible versions of truth, inseparable from particular narratives."[100] Each such version of truth is a *mythos*, a "fiction,"[101] and there is no possible way of deciding between them that is independent of these "fictions." The only resolution comes when there is a "rhetorical victory,"[102] when one "persuades"[103] from within one of these fictions that it is a "better" one[104]—when one narrative "out-narrates" another.[105] I have extensively annotated the sources of these words and phrases in order to emphasize that this is *Milbank's* meta-metanarrative, his own understanding of how his metanarrative "combats" the nihilist metanarrative and, by implication, all other metanarratives. This point needs to be emphasized because one finds a remarkable convergence here with the nihilist metanarrative. When Milbank talks of victory, of a better story out-narrating others, he seems to be invoking a rhetoric of power. This is a power that Milbank does not account for; his own rhetoric accepts and, indeed, is made possible by it.

This is recognized by Oliver Davies when he says of Milbank's project that "it disconcertingly serves . . . to align Christianity as an exercise in 'persuasiveness' with other rhetorics, which can equally point to their power to persuade which, in Milbank's terms, must be taken as evidence of their 'truth'. . . . Further, rhetoric and persuasion are themselves consummately manifestations of privilege and power."[106] However peacefully Milbank may construe the content of the Christian narrative, it attains its preeminence by asserting its power over other narratives—by combating them, out-narrating them, and achieving victory over them. But this is precisely the way in which nihilist postmodernists claim that a narrative achieves victory over others. We find, therefore, a curious convergence between Milbank and nihilism. Milbank negates the nihilist ontology of power, conflict, and violence in his metanarrative, only to reinstate it at the meta-metanarrative level. As Shakespeare says of Milbank's project, it "rejects secular nihilism only through the assertion of its own ungrounded rhetoric. The resulting vision of the world is of endless conflict between mutually exclusive discourses all seeking to occupy the hermeneutical high ground. It remains complicit with the nihilism it seeks to overcome."[107] It appears that Milbank ultimately remains captive to the nihilist metanarrative and an ontology of violence. Indeed, we were already suspecting this was the case in the earlier parts of this chapter, for we saw that Milbank minimized violence, dualism, and mastery at the level of the Christian narrative, only to reinstate them at the level of his (meta-)metanarrative. These suspicions are now confirmed as this process is made explicit.

If even Milbank's own project is unable to avoid a certain nihilism, it would seem that his dualistic and bipolar opposition between theology and nihilism is oversimplistic and insufficiently nuanced. Perhaps it is the case that neither theology nor nihilism can be completely repressed. If, as I have been suggesting, a metanarrative is simultaneously both a necessity and an impossibility, then the reality of this paradox would seem to preclude the ascription of any final or absolute priority to either theology or nihilism. If theology is always haunted by a certain nihilism, so, too, we shall see, is nihilism always haunted by a certain theology—in which case we would do well to move away from a discussion dominated by the dualistic opposition between theology and nihilism. Milbank's either/or must be left behind in favor of something else, something "other."

Interlude

In this chapter, all my criticisms of Milbank's project may be regarded as variations on a single, fundamental objection, namely, a protest against his absolute and ultimate conception of theology as metanarrative. This single objection is comprised of two constituent parts. First, I argued that such a conception of metanarrative is undesirable in its necessary effects—its dualism, violence, and mastery. Second, I argued that a metanarrative is, in any case, an inherently unstable concept that must ultimately deconstruct and dissolve itself. We have seen that these two aspects of my critique are intimately linked, for we saw that the undesirable effects of Milbank's metanarrative are installed at a "higher" level. They are minimized in Milbank's reading of the Christian narrative, only to be reinstated at the level of Milbank's theoretical positioning of the Christian narrative, a positioning that we have seen to be remarkably complicit with modernity in its form and with nihilism in its content. If Christian theology is being rendered and positioned in a particular way by Milbank's theoretical meta-metanarrative, and if the latter is itself philosophically and culturally situated and determined, then we begin to see how the very idea of an "absolute Christian metanarrative" itself begins to dissolve. It seems impossible to contain this process of positioning, and therefore impossible to identify an absolute beginning. This is why the possibility of an unfounded metanarrative that is the foundation of everything else will always elude us. Indeed, this impossibility is manifested in Milbank's own metanarrative.

Although I identified three "levels" of metanarrative positioning within Milbank's project, it would be possible to identify more such narrative linkages, indefinitely and in all directions. This gives rise to an infinite process of movement in which it is impossible to identify a beginning or an end. This is why, I suggest, the concept of an ultimate and final metanarrative must ultimately deconstruct itself; it is an attempt to go back to an impossible beginning, an attempt to go "too far back." And yet, we have also seen that we can never entirely overcome the metanarrative. As Milbank made clear in his critique of Lyotard, a metanarrative, an "organizing logic," will always unwittingly reinstate itself. Some form of ultimate linguistic ordering is always unavoidable. And so, it seems, a metanarrative is as necessary as it is impossible. In the following chapters, I develop an account of how we may negotiate this paradox. But in the wake of this paradox, in the absence of an unproblematically absolute metanarrative, Milbank is right to point out that some form of nihilism is inevitable. Thus, when the metanarrative of Milbank's project has been deconstructed, one should not be surprised to find a latent nihilism in that project itself. When the absolute metanarrative has dissolved, a certain nihilism must result. But must this nihilism necessarily promote an ontology of violence, as Milbank claims? And to what extent does this nihilism remain vulnerable to Milbank's virulent attacks? It is to these questions that I turn in the next chapter.

Chapter 5
(A/)Theology and Nihilism

We have seen that much of Milbank's theological rhetoric is directed against nihilism. Indeed, he concurs with Nietzsche to the extent that he regards nihilism as the inversion of Christianity, its straight antithesis. As such, it is secular, heretical, the apotheosis of modernity. Clearly, nihilism plays an indispensable role in Milbank's narrative drama. If Christianity (or rather, Milbank's Christianity) is the hero of this story, then nihilism is the hero's adversary. And the weapon with which Milbank slays his opponent is none other than that of out-narration.[1] But Milbank never quite locates his opponent, for he uses the term *nihilism* in a rather vague and undefined way. This is problematic, because there is not one nihilism in our present epoch; there are many.

In this chapter, therefore, I consider what exactly is meant and has been meant by the term *nihilism*. In particular, I distinguish between a metaphysical account of nihilism and a narrativist account. To return to the terminology I invoked in the previous chapter, this is to distinguish between nihilism as myth and nihilism as fiction. I argue that although Milbank presents nihilism as a fiction in order to open the way to an effective out-narration of it, in the actual process of this out-narration, he nevertheless reverts to an account of nihilism as metaphysics, a positivist deviant. For rhetorical purposes, he thus out-narrates a nihilism repudiated by most nihilists, and I suggest that this makes his task of out-narration too easy. I argue that only a narrativist or "fictional" nihilism can be an accomplished nihilism, for a "metaphysical" nihilism, as Gianni Vattimo points out, ultimately refuses all nihilistic implications. It is precisely such a fictional nihilism that Milbank does not confront and that thus remains untouched by many of his criticisms. When metaphysical nihilism is overcome, the violent dualistic dichotomy between "positivist" nihilism and "narrativist" theology (which is, perhaps, another incarnation of the realist/anti-realist debate) begins to subside. The way is then opened for both a fictional nihilism and a fictional theology, where any final priority is infinitely deferred.

The Advent of Nihilism

When did the nihilistic journey or movement of departure "begin"? The question of the beginning being as problematic as ever, I shall here identify a number of "defining moments" in the emergence of nihilism. Nietzsche is clear that nihilism "begins" with the death of God and is accomplished only when the shadows of the dead God have been finally and completely eradicated. With the eradication of these shadows comes the dazzling whiteness of nihilism. But when did God begin to die? Michael Gillespie has argued that the birth of nihilism may be traced back to Descartes's construction of a "bastion of reason" to shield man from the terrifying, transrational, transnatural God of nominalism. This was a God whose absolute will and power threatened to reduce nature to chaos, because everything owed its existence to the fiat of an omnipotent inscrutable will. As such, creation appeared unintelligible to finite human beings, without order, intelligibility, or connections. Nature was thus reduced to a "chaos of radically individual and unconnected beings."[2] Descartes's response was to transfer this problematic concept of will from God to man. Gillespie says that the Cartesian notion of will became increasingly explicit in continental thought from Fichte to Nietzsche: "It was this idea of an absolute will that gave birth to the idea of nihilism, for if the I is everything, then, as Jacobi pointed out, God is nothing."[3] For Gillespie, therefore, the birth of nihilism may be traced back to Descartes.

We saw in chapter 2, however, that Hans Urs von Balthasar traces it back a stage further, to Averroes and his followers of the thirteenth century. For Balthasar, and subsequently for John Milbank and Catherine Pickstock, the long journey toward nihilism was embarked upon with the turn to modernity. In particular, we saw that they maintain that it was Duns Scotus's turn to univocity that laid the foundations for the philosophical project of modernity, a project that masks a nihilist metaphysics. For Milbank, this nihilist metaphysics was first unmasked by the eighteenth-century "radical pietists" Johann Georg Hamann and Franz Heinrich Jacobi. Indeed, he suggests that it was Jacobi who first "thematized" the notion of nihilism.[4] It is important to note, therefore, that in both Gillespie's philosophical genealogy and in Balthasar's theological genealogy, the birth of nihilism is located several hundred years before Nietzsche.

If Jacobi first thematized the notion of nihilism, however, he did so in a pejorative way. For him, nihilism was something to be "left behind" in favor of theology. In less than a hundred years, however, this leave-taking was reversed in that theology was being left behind in favor of nihilism, which was coming to be established as a new creed, particularly among intellectuals in the towns and cities of Russia. This new phenomenon was first reflected in published form in Ivan Turgenev's novel *Fathers and Sons*, which was published in 1862, some ten years before the publication of Nietzsche's first book, *The Birth of Tragedy*. The nihilist of the story is Evgeny Bazarov, whose character is based on at least three individuals whom Turgenev knew.[5] The first was N. A. Dobrolyubov (1836–1861), who was a follower of and collaborator with N. G. Chernyshevsky (1828–1889), an intellectual involved with the publication of the radical journal *The Contemporary*. Another contributor to *The Contemporary* on whom the character of Bazarov was based was a certain Preobrazhensky (Nikolai Sergeevich), a friend of Dobrolyubov. Of Chernyshevsky, Richard Freeborn says, "His advocacy of scientific materialism, utilitarian aesthetics, rational egoism and a variety of other ideas (mostly drawn from the left-wing Hegelian Feuerbach) educated a whole generation of intelligent young Russians in the need to criticize and reject everything—social institutions, the church, the political status quo and so on—which did not conform to the laws of the natural sciences."[6]

But perhaps more important than either of these was a Dr. Pavlov (1823–1904), a young provincial doctor whom Turgenev knew at his hometown, Orël. Turgenev himself wrote of him: "In this remarkable man were embodied—in my eyes—that scarcely conceived, still fermenting principle which later received the name of nihilism. . . . I was upset by the following fact: not in a single work of our literature did I come across so much of a hint of what I sensed everywhere."[7] But what exactly was this nihilism that Turgenev "sensed everywhere" and that seemed to have been embodied in a young provincial doctor? Freeborn says that what Turgenev sensed about this man was, above all, "his commitment to science and materialism, his negative cast of mind, his self-assurance, cynicism, energy, repudiation of aesthetic feeling and everything 'romantic'. He sensed, in fact, the reality of the 'new man' whom Chernyshevsky and Dobrolyubov had been so keen to foster through their radical journalism."[8]

What is characteristic of this nihilism, then, is its positivism, empiricism, utilitarianism, and scientific materialism. In all this, it was quite clearly the latest manifestation of the metaphysics of modernity. When Bazarov's disciple Arkady Petrovich is asked by his father and uncle to clarify what exactly is meant by the term *nihilism*, he replies, "A nihilist is a man who doesn't acknowledge any authorities, who doesn't accept a single principle on faith, no matter how much that principle may be surrounded by respect."[9] But such critical demolition was not particularly revolutionary, for it was, after all, just another incarnation of Descartes's realization that it was necessary "to demolish everything completely and start again right from the foundations if I wanted to establish anything at all in the sciences that was stable and likely to last."[10]

What distinguished Russian nihilism of the late nineteenth century from the modernist metaphysics that preceded it was its rejection of God, and consequently its rejection of the notion of progress and of any action beyond the purely utilitarian. Whereas, for Descartes, God was the only guarantee of the existence of the external world, the nihilists' rejection of God meant there could be no such guarantee—in which case, however, the logical outcome of this rejection ought to have been more radical than it was. One might have expected them to come to a realization of their own nothingness and the nothingness of their own thinking, as well as of the external world.[11]

But this did not quite happen. Pavel Petrovich may have challenged Bazarov and Arkady to "see how you get on in a vacuum, in airless space,"[12] but a vacuum was precisely what they did not occupy; for they retained their confidence in science, in materialism, in rationality, and in utilitarianism. As Arthur C. Danto says, they believed "in a crudely materialistic interpretation of science. It was basically in the name of science that they proclaimed, as invalid, the principles they inveighed against. But inasmuch as their understanding of science was filtered through a version of materialism which they mistook for science itself, or which, if more sophisticated, they took to be the only attitude compatible with and justified by science, there was an undeniable component of belief, indeed of faith, which interpreted their nihilism and rendered it halfhearted."[13] Their nihilism was half-hearted because it was too metaphysical. That Nietzsche was dissatisfied with this form of thinking is evident in his remark, "Nihilism in the St Petersburg style—i.e., belief in unbelief to the point of martyrdom for it, shows always, and above all, the *need* for belief."[14] Thus, the Russian nihilists continued to think under what Nietzsche would call "the shadows of the dead God."

Metaphysical Nihilism:
Heidegger's Nietzsche

Friedrich Nietzsche's revolutionary contribution to the development of nihilism lay in his relentless efforts to eradicate these shadows. For instance, the significance of the famous declaration of the madman was not so much to announce the death of God—the spectators were aware of that happening, indeed, had committed the act themselves. Rather, the madman's concern was to announce the *implications* of this death. He cries, "But how have we done this? How were we able to drink up the sea? Who gave us the sponge to wipe away the entire horizon? What did we do when we unchained this earth from its sun? Whither is it moving now? Away from all suns? Are we not plunging continually? Backward, sideward, forward, in all directions? Is there any up or down left?"[15]

Nietzsche's realization was of the absolute nothingness that must inevitably follow the death of God; that nothingness which the Russian nihilism of Bazarov had failed to realize. Bazarov's confidence in reason, materialism, and science is destroyed by Nietzsche. It is at this point that the nihilistic metaphysics of modernity is unmasked. In contrast to Bazarov's confidence in rationality, Nietzsche says that "the irrationality of a thing is no argument against its existence, rather a condition of it."[16] So, for Nietzsche, the death of God brings with it a picture of the world as irrational nothingness. The total nature of the world is "to all eternity chaos, not in the sense that necessity is lacking but in that order, structure, form, beauty, wisdom and whatever other aesthetic notions we have are lacking."[17] And this chaotic world is a theater of conflict, a stage upon which the governing principle of the will-to-power plays itself out.

It is at this point that we come up against a paradox, indeed, perhaps *the* paradox, in Nietzsche's thought. For we are led to question the status of Nietzsche's nihilistic world of chaos and the extent to which it may be regarded as "reality." Is this not a metaphysics of the nothing, the nothing that "is"? And is the will-to-power not a metaphysical principle that represents the "truth" of the human condition? In other words, does Nietzsche really overcome the metaphysics of modernity, or is he merely bringing it to its culmination and therefore still caught in its web? Indeed, this is the paradox that has consistently bedeviled Nietzschean scholarship. Alexander Nehemas presents the dilemma as follows: "Does he or does he not, then, think that his views of the self, of morality, of history, many of which are themselves apparently paradoxical, are true? If he does, how can this possibly be consistent with his view that all views are only interpretations? If he does not—that is, if he does not think that his views are true—why does he make the effort to present them in the first place?"[18] Nehemas says that, faced with this dilemma, some scholars have emphasized the "positive" or "substantive" elements in his thought, while others have emphasized his "perspectivism." In other words, some scholars have wished to read Nietzsche as a metaphysical nihilist (where nihilism is the "truth" of the human condition), whereas others have wished to read him as a fictional nihilist (where nihilism is just one interpretation among others).

The ambivalent style of Nietzsche's writings, however, precludes any final decidability, and it is this that gives rise to the disputes and complexity in Nietzschean interpretation. This ambivalence may be regarded as an inevitable consequence of the fact that Nietzsche was writing from within the language of the metaphysics of modernity while simultaneously writing to overcome it. This may, perhaps, be regarded as an early manifestation of the postmodern strategy referred to above, namely, that one must deconstruct that which makes the deconstruction at all possible. As Michel Haar says of Nietzsche, "When making use of current metaphysical oppositions (which, for him, all come down to the Platonic opposition between the 'true world' and the 'apparent world'), he does so with a view to eradicating and abolishing these very distinctions; there is thus inevitably an ambiguity weighing upon his use of terms having a precise meaning within the tradition, terms such as 'true' and 'false', 'good' and 'evil'."[19] The crucial question is thus whether Nietzsche is so tied into the old language of metaphysics that his work can be regarded as no more than its culmination.

Martin Heidegger was convinced that Nietzsche was the last metaphysician, although Heidegger shared Nietzsche's preoccupation with the questions of the meaning of the death of God and of nihilism. For Heidegger, however, Nietzsche's articulation of nihilism and his attempt to overcome it remained trapped within the logic of metaphysics. He argued that Nietzsche was as one with Descartes, Kant, and Hegel in that "they all leave untouched the essence of truth itself. No matter how far removed Nietzsche is from Descartes and no matter how much he emphasizes the distance between them, in what is essential, he still stands close to Descartes."[20] He says that, for Nietzsche, "truth" means "as much as the true, and the true what is known in truth. Knowing is a theoretical-scientific grasp of the actual in the broadest sense. That suggests in a general way that Nietzsche's conception of the essence of truth keeps to the realm of the long tradition of Western thought, no matter how much Nietzsche's particular interpretations of that conception deviate from earlier ones."[21]

As we saw in chapter 3, Heidegger's concern was to rescue the notion of "truth" from the clutches of "logic," whereby truth is conceived as "correctness," as "representation." For Heidegger, the crucial difference between his thought and Nietzsche's was that whereas he wanted to call this definition of truth into question, Nietzsche overturned this conception of truth without calling it into question. Thus, Heidegger says, "Every philosophy is theology in the original and essential sense that the conceiving λόγος of beings as a whole asks about the ground of Being, and this ground becomes named as θεός, God. Indeed, Nietzsche's philosophy, for instance, in which an essential saying states 'God is dead' is in accord with this saying 'Theology'."[22]

For Heidegger, therefore, Nietzsche's attempt to overcome nihilism also remains within the boundaries of the metaphysical and thus ultimately fails to overcome nihilism. This overcoming is constituted by the crucial and central notion of the eternal recurrence. Heidegger interprets its meaning as that of the creative life, especially art: "Art and truth, creating and knowing, meet one another in the single guiding perspective of the rescue and configuration of the sensuous. With a view to the conquest of nihilism, that is, to the foundation of the new valuation, art and truth, along with meditation on the essence of both, attain equal importance."[23] But just as Nietzsche's notion of truth remains unquestioned, so, too, does his notion of art, according to Heidegger. In particular, his inversion of Plato, with regard to the hierarchy of sensuous and nonsensuous, is insufficiently radical. Heidegger says, "A path must be cleared for a new interpretation of the sensuous on the basis of a new hierarchy of the sensuous and nonsensuous. It does not wish to put what was at the very bottom on the very top. A new hierarchy and new evaluation mean that the ordering *structure* must be changed. To that extent, overturning Platonism must be a twisting free of it."[24] It is just such a "twisting free" that Heidegger claims Nietzsche cannot attain, for his thought is merely an "inverted Platonism." As Gillespie says, "Heidegger thus can argue that the doctrine of the eternal recurrence, which Nietzsche regarded as his great victory, is his most telling defeat because it represents his inability to dwell in the vicinity of the great *question* that nihilism opens up and his turn back to a metaphysical *answer* to the question."[25]

Fictional Nihilism:
Postmodern Nietzsche

Heidegger's reading of Nietzsche, however, was subsequently subjected to severe questioning. Inadequacies in Heidegger's interpretation were first identified by Walter Kaufmann, although, as Gillespie points out, his break with the Heideggerian reading was tentative. He continued to maintain that Nietzsche was an integral part of the inherited philosophical tradition and, unlike later commentators, that Nietzsche's conception of the Dionysian was also compatible with previous philosophy.[26] He was determined to show that there is an underlying unity beneath Nietzsche's aphorisms, and that behind them "there is a whole philosophy."[27] Similarly, Arthur C. Danto was concerned to emphasize the "systematic" character of Nietzsche's philosophy and endeavored to domesticate it in order to render it less offensive to the analytical philosophical tradition. He insisted that Nietzsche's nihilism is "a positive and, after all, a respectable philosophical teaching."[28]

A more revolutionary overturning of Heidegger's interpretation, however, has been brought about by a number of postmodern philosophers, such as Gilles Deleuze, Jacques Derrida, Sarah Kofman, and Gianni Vattimo. These postmoderns have also disagreed among themselves, however, with regard to what should replace the old Heideggerian reading. Vattimo, for instance, thinks that Deleuze places Nietzsche within the framework of an "energetic" or "vitalistic" ontology—a framework also endorsed by Michel Foucault and Pierre Klossowski and influenced by Henri Bergson and Georges Bataille. Vattimo, by contrast, prefers a hermeneutic interpretation that "comprehends (includes and understands) more aspects of Nietzsche's philosophy than any other, and avoids contradictions and ambiguities which inhere in the others."[29]

Although Gillespie ultimately disagrees with the postmodern readings, he nonetheless concedes that they have much to commend them, particularly in their insistence that Heidegger "did not confront the most profoundly antimetaphysical moment in Nietzsche's thought."[30] Gillespie says that, to a great extent, this was because of Heidegger's conception of "Nietzsche" (Heidegger said that the *name* of the thinker stands as the title for the *matter* of his thinking). Heidegger argues that all of Nietzsche's writings were preparatory to his true "systematic" work that was never completed, *The Will to Power*. So Heidegger tries to reconstruct this work, to think Nietzsche's thought that was unthought owing to insanity or an inability to think it through.[31] Thus, Jacques Derrida says that Heidegger's reading is directed at "gathering together the unity and the uniqueness of Nietzsche's thinking," at positively claiming that his thinking is one, that he has only one name, that he names himself only once. But, Derrida asks, "who ever has said that a person bears a single name? Certainly not Nietzsche."[32]

So Heidegger attempts to gather Nietzsche's thought into a unity and a totality, when unity and totality were precisely what Nietzsche jettisoned. And with regard to the unfinished *Will to Power*, Gillespie says that Nietzsche may simply have recognized that this work "would have taken him back to metaphysics and thus decided not to take it. This interpretation is supported by the fact that Nietzsche had actually discarded most of the material included in *The Will to Power*."[33] Furthermore, Gillespie says that Heidegger's understanding of the eternal recurrence as an incorrigibly metaphysical concept is based on his repression of the role of Dionysus, which, he says, is clearly the most antimetaphysical moment in Nietzsche's thought. It is Heidegger's neglect of this that gives rise to his metaphysical misreading: "Heidegger does not lay great weight upon Dionysus, emphasizing instead the pantheistic and metaphysical side of Nietzsche's notion of the eternal recurrence. This . . . is a serious lacuna in his interpretation of Nietzsche. Indeed, one might well argue that it is only by deemphasizing this ecstatic element that Heidegger is able to characterize Nietzsche as a metaphysical thinker at all."[34] Gillespie goes on to suggest that a deeper investigation of this Dionysian element might have led to an ecstatic openness to the mystery of existence similar to that sought by Heidegger himself.[35]

If Gillespie thinks that Heidegger has neglected the Dionysian element in Nietzsche's thought, Derrida maintains that it is Heidegger's repression of the "idea becoming female" theme that is most crucial. Nietzsche maintains that truth is like a woman, as may be seen in *Beyond Good and Evil*, for instance, which opens with precisely this supposition. If woman is truth, she at least knows that there is no truth. Nietzsche says, "She does not *want* truth—what does woman care for truth! From the very first nothing is more foreign, more repugnant, or more hostile to woman than truth—her great art is falsehood, her chief concern is appearance and beauty."[36] Derrida says that, previously, the idea was Platonic and the philosopher was equated with truth, but in the second age, the idea is "becoming female." He says this notion is crucial to Nietzsche's thought, and it is a notion that Heidegger represses: "Much as one might skip over a sensible image in a philosophy book or tear out an illustrated leaf or allegorical representation in a more serious volume, Heidegger analyzes all the elements of Nietzsche's text with the sole exception of the idea's becoming-female (*sie Wird Weib*). In such a way does one permit oneself to see without reading, to read without seeing."[37]

Thus, Heidegger's Nietzsche became increasingly discredited, particularly by postmodern philosophers, and a postmetaphysical, hermeneutic Nietzsche took its place. One of the leading interpreters of Nietzsche in this direction has been Gianni Vattimo. For Vattimo, Nietzsche's doctrine of eternal recurrence was not intended as a "description" of the true reality of being. He says, "The thesis that there are no facts, only interpretations, is probably only an interpretation itself, 'and so much the better'. Can we really think that Nietzsche's polemic against all kinds of metaphysics (all kinds of 'true' essences of reality) resolves itself into a theory stating that the true reality of all being is *fluxus* and will to power?"[38] Vattimo, however, acknowledges that Nietzsche's writings are ambivalent, with the result that they can have multiple "uses" and can be utilized in support of and against almost every philosophical thesis. In particular, he identifies a number of "contradictions" or "polar tensions" in Nietzsche's thought, the most important of which is the opposition "between the thesis that there are no facts, only interpretations, and the metaphysics of the will to power and the eternal recurrence."[39] There is thus a tendency to conceive the interpretative character of all reality in a metaphysical sense. The result of this tendency is that "will to power and eternal recurrence appear as a *metaphysical* description of the *true reality* in a world in which there are no facts, only interpretations; but, taken in a metaphysical sense, they are *not* only interpretations."[40] For Vattimo, however, if this tension is to be resolved, it must be in the direction of an hermeneutic ontology, rather than a metaphysical one, because the latter ultimately refuses all nihilistic implications.[41] In contrast, "an accomplished nihilism, like the Heideggerian *Abgrund*, calls us to a fictionalized experience of reality which is also our only possibility for freedom."[42] So Vattimo's nihilism is a fictionalized nihilism. Nihilism is thus no more than a story.

Derrida agrees with Vattimo that Nietzsche did not intend his own interpretations of reality to be accorded the status of "truth." He says that there is no such thing as "the truth of Nietzsche or of Nietzsche's text. In fact, in *Jenseits*, it is in a paragraph on women that one reads 'these are only—*my* truths' (*meine Wahrheiten sind*). The very fact that '*meine Wahrheiten*' is so underlined, that they are multiple, variegated, contradictory even, can only imply that these are not *truths*. Indeed there is no such thing as a truth in itself. But only a surfeit of it. Even if it should be for me, about me, truth is plural."[43] For Derrida, Nietzsche's multiple styles, the heterogeneity of his text, are crucial in that they are deliberately intended to preclude a metaphysical reading. Indeed, Derrida claims that it is the style(s) rather than the content of Nietzsche's texts that is of primary importance. He says, "The question posed by the spurring-operation (*opération-éperonnante*) is more powerful than any content, thesis or meaning. The stylate spur (*éperon stylé*) rips through the veil."[44] Derrida says that this "stylate spur" ruptures any reading of totality into Nietzsche's texts, "even a fragmentary or aphoristic one," and thus it also precludes any reading of Nietzsche's nihilism as metaphysical.[45]

It would appear, then, that although interpretations of Nietzsche have been diverse and complex, it is nonetheless possible to identify two dominant readings: one that interprets Nietzsche as the last metaphysician, expounding a nihilistic metaphysical doctrine of "the way the world is," and another that interprets Nietzsche as the first philosopher to overcome metaphysics, clearing the way for a hermeneutic understanding of philosophy, where nihilism is just one story among others.

The Nihilistic "Movement of Departure"

I now want to suggest that these two Nietzschean interpretations correspond to two dominant readings of nihilism itself: a substantive nihilism and nihilism as a story; metaphysical nihilism and fictional nihilism. The former may be viewed as a culmination of metaphysics, while the latter may be viewed as a "twisting free" from it. But I shall further suggest that these two forms of nihilism are not detached and alternative interpretations that are free-standing and independent of each other. On the contrary, the distinction between them arises only as a result of a "movement of departure" from one form to the other, from metaphysics to fiction. I shall suggest that metaphysical nihilism itself induces this movement of departure and therefore itself gives rise to a fictional nihilism. It may even be said that nihilism *is* this very movement, for an accomplished nihilism is not a position or a system (which is why a solely metaphysical nihilism can never be an accomplished nihilism) but is rather a dis-position, a process, a movement. As Vattimo says, it is "an indefinite process of reduction, diminution, weakening."[46] Let us now consider this movement of departure.

Metaphysical nihilism speaks of the void, of emptiness and arbitrariness, of the world as a stage on which indifferent forces violently compete with each other. This is a representation, a philosophical realism—an attempt to articulate the "truth" of the world. As such, it is the culmination of modernity. Metaphysical nihilism is unaware of itself as such, however, because, as Vattimo observes, the essence of modernity becomes visible to us only as we distance ourselves from it.[47] Similarly, Catherine Pickstock says that "the power of modernity is the power to *disguise* itself."[48] Thus, metaphysical nihilism is not aware that it is representing or that it is philosophically realist. (Metaphysical nihilism is frequently accompanied by a denial of "objective truth.") Rather, it believes itself to be an accomplished nihilism at the end of metaphysics and of modernity.

But if metaphysical nihilism is indeed engaged in the act of representation, what exactly does it seek to represent? It is at this point and in answer to this question that I invoke a third form of nihilism, what I shall call a "pure" nihilism. It is, however, distinct from the other two forms of nihilism in that it cannot be expressed. Indeed, the more one speaks about it, the more one distances oneself from it. It is that which metaphysical nihilism yearns to represent, and in its attempt to do so, it ceaselessly moves further on. But this movement never reaches its goal; its journey never comes to an end. Metaphysical nihilism never reaches its goal of "pure" nihilism because the latter *cannot be represented*. Metaphysical nihilism thus has an impossible object, and as such, it is destined to die of its own impossible goal. Thus, in its (impossible) quest to achieve this pure nihilism, metaphysical nihilism undergoes a process of purification in which it purges itself of its metaphysical baggage.

This process of purification has a number of stages. The first stage begins with a self-conscious and self-reflexive movement on the part of metaphysical nihilism. At this stage, there is a realization that in speaking of the nihilistic void, one has not grasped the *nihil* in itself; one has merely produced another linguistic representation, another fiction. There is a recognition here that in order to grasp the *nihil* and overcome metaphysics, one must repudiate representation. So, in answer to the question of the "way the world is," one no longer speaks of a nihilistic void, because this is now unmasked as another metaphysical representation. Thus, one can now answer only with "silence." But at a stage further, one realizes that one cannot even answer with the word *silence*, because as Mark C. Taylor has said, "to say 'silence' is to break silence. Silence inevitably withdraws in and through its articulation."⁴⁹ So to say "silence" is again to represent the world as "silence." It is equally futile, however, to answer the question with a wordless silence, because as Jean-François Lyotard has said, silence is itself a "phrase," an effect of language, just as language is an effect of silence.⁵⁰

So the metaphysical quest for a pure nihilism collapses in recognition that, ultimately, it must be deprived of its goal. It is attempting to represent something that can be attained only with a renunciation of representation. Yet, if representation is renounced, how can it ever be attained? It is with the realization of this dilemma that metaphysical nihilism dies, in that it comes to perceive that its object, that which it is trying to represent, is unrepresentable. So it is here that one twists free of metaphysics and of the quest for the pure nihilism that was never attained and emerges on its far side—into fictionalism. One takes leave of the unattainable antinarrative of pure nihilism and moves on to embrace the narrative of fictionalism. This is both the accomplishment and the overcoming of nihilism. It is the accomplishment of nihilism because metaphysics is now overcome. Metaphysical nihilism was not an accomplished nihilism precisely because it was a *metaphysical* nihilism, that is, a representation, a philosophical realism. In taking leave of this metaphysics, of this frustrated attempt at representation, nihilism is accomplished. It is also an overcoming of nihilism, however, because nihilism is now fictionalized along with everything else. Here, insofar as the nihilist story is still told, it is told precisely *as* a story. The absoluteness of nihilism is thus overcome, its privilege dissolved; for now nihilism is a story just like any other. Thus, the nihilism that once relativized everything else has now relativized itself.

So "pure" nihilism is a conceptual chimera, an endless deferral, something sought but never attained. It is not a conceptual space within which we may dwell, because it is a self-negating concept. It is something that always eludes us. Clearly, as something unattainable, it is also something inexpressible, and as such, it is antinarrative. It can be alluded to only by means of our two main concepts of nihilism—as representation and as fiction. We have seen that it induces the nihilistic movement of departure from metaphysics to fiction. Metaphysical nihilism journeys away from itself in order to reach its impossible goal of pure nihilism. Having thus departed, it finds that its object has slipped away and that it has instead journeyed into the terrain of fictionalism.

But "pure" nihilism never slips away entirely, even after the nihilistic movement of departure has been accomplished. Rather, it stands on the margins of the fictional text, as an "other" that cannot be expressed, which forever haunts it and induces new departures. The antinarrative of pure nihilism always induces one to take leave of the narrative(s) of fictional nihilism, for fictional nihilism can never come to rest in a single narrative but keeps moving from one narrative to another, prompted to do so by the pure nihilism that transcends them all. There are deliberate echoes here of the "movement of departure" and the "heterology" narrated by Michel de Certeau. I return to explore these echoes in the next chapter. At this point, however, I turn to John Milbank's interpretation, analysis, and "out-narration" of nihilism.

Milbank's Nihilism

As we observed at the outset of this chapter, Milbank concurs with Nietzsche to the extent that he believes nihilism to stand as the antithesis of Christianity. Indeed, nihilism is not something that stands alone in its own right; rather, it is merely the negation of Christianity. As such, it is profoundly secular and heretical, and the only appropriate Christian reponse to nihilism must be that of "out-narration." It is time now, however, to consider exactly what Milbank understands by *nihilism* and to examine where his understanding is located in relation to the various accounts of nihilism we have been considering in this chapter.[51]

For Milbank, nihilism is inextricably linked with postmodernism precisely because postmodernism *is* nihilistic. Furthermore, both concepts are also inextricably bound up with modernity, for nihilism is a more virulent form of modern secular reason—its final postmodern incarnation[52]—while postmodernism itself is, in many ways, an "exacerbation" of modernity.[53] Postmodernism constitutes the new challenge to theology in the wake of the death of modern social science, and it does so by relativizing and questioning claims to universality: "Its more insidious method reveals no secret behind the *mythos*, but merely points to other 'truths', and shows how these are suppressed or denied by a totalizing perspective. Yet the obvious implication of 'many truths', or rather 'many incommensurable truths', is that every truth is arbitrary, every truth is the will-to-power."[54] Thus, for Milbank, nihilists are secular postmodernists, and they include Nietzsche, Heidegger, Deleuze, Lyotard, Foucault, and Derrida.

In Milbank's narratives, however, the two main forms of nihilism I have identified appear to coexist; for at the same time that Milbank insists that nihilism is metaphysical, a representation, with a positivist genealogy of history and an ontology of difference, he also appears to recognize that nihilism is nothing more than an unfounded *mythos*, a fiction, a story. He says that nihilism "is also no more than a *mythos*. To counter it, one cannot resuscitate liberal humanism, but one can try to put forward an alternative *mythos*, equally unfounded, but nonetheless embodying an 'ontology of peace', which conceives differences as analogically related, rather than equivocally at variance."[55] So nihilism as metaphysics and nihilism as fiction both appear within Milbank's texts.

But how are these two nihilisms reconciled within Milbank's narrative? The answer is not always clear, but there appear to be three levels of interpretation here. On the first level, nihilism claims to be merely a narration of differences, a story told to unsettle the reader.[56] Yet, for Milbank, this narration actually entails a "joyfully" nihilistic positivism, and this positivism is most apparent in Nietzsche's *Genealogy of Morals*. So, on the second level, nihilism always ends up by telling a positivist story about the evolution of power and knowledge.[57] Milbank maintains, however, that such a positivism is unsustainable, and he thus "unmasks" nihilism as being nothing more than a mythology. Milbank's revealing of nihilism as mythology is therefore the third level. He thereby opens the way for the out-narration of one unfounded *mythos* by another.[58]

But what is the purpose of this triple interpretation of nihilism, whereby Milbank rejects nihilism as a fiction only subsequently to reinstate it? It would appear that in order to clear the ground for Milbank's out-narration of nihilism, he must first insist that it is an unfounded *mythos* in the same manner as the Christian *mythos* with which he wishes to replace it. But to facilitate the actual process of out-narration, he must also insist that nihilism contains within it a necessary and disguised positivism. But to what extent can such a reading be justified? I suggest that this interpretation makes Milbank's task of out-narration too easy, and that the nuances of Nietzsche's nihilism are rather more complex and subtler than Milbank would have us believe.

A Historicist Genealogy?

Milbank claims that nihilism has two necessary aspects: first, a historicist "genealogy" and, second, an "ontology of difference." I shall consider each of these in turn. First, on the historicist genealogy, Milbank refers to Nietzsche's *Genealogy of Morals* and asks whether the narrated genealogy is just one possible interpretation, a story told with a bias to induce unsettlement. He replies that for Nietzsche and Foucault, it is not. Rather, "genealogy is not an interpretation, but a new 'joyfully' nihilistic form of positivism which explains every cultural meaning-complex as a particular strategy or ruse of power. No universals are ascribed to human society save one: that it is always a field of warfare. And yet this universal history of military maneuvers is also to be regarded as in some sense liberating, as assisting the emergence of an *übermensch*, or a post-humanist human creature."[59] Thus, Milbank says that Nietzsche espouses a positivist nihilism, and he thereby aligns himself with a Heideggerian interpretation of Nietzsche as the last modernist metaphysician. According to Milbank, Nietzsche's claim is that an "economic" mode of behavior has been the secret truth of every society, which has now been unmasked. So, although genealogy claims to be merely a narration of differences, Milbank says that "because nihilism proclaims an ahistorical and transcendental identity of reason with power, it always finishes up by telling, after all, a positivist story about the evolution of power/knowledge."[60]

But let us pause to examine Milbank's understanding of the nihilistic geneal-ogy here. What is immediately evident in Milbank's account as I have just pre-sented it is, once again, his penchant for hyperbole, his tendency to make the sweeping statement, the gigantic claim, the totalizing and thus obliterating obser-vation. With regard to his interpretation of Nietzsche, Milbank does exactly what Derrida accused Heidegger of doing—he gathers Nietzsche's thought into one single unity and totality. He "names" him once. And yet this is precisely what Nietzsche resists. As Derrida asks of Heidegger's unifying gesture, "Is it anything more or less than the desire (a word effaced in Heidegger's Nietzsche citation) for a proper name, for a single, unique name and a thinkable genealogy? Next to Kierkegaard, was not Nietzsche one of the few great thinkers who multiplied his names and played with signatures, identities and masks? Who named himself more than once, with several names? And what if that would be the heart of the matter, the *causa*, the *Streitfall* ('point of dispute') of his thinking?"[61]

We may indeed suspect Milbank of the desire for "a single unique name and a thinkable genealogy." Why? Because a single name and a thinkable genealogy are that much easier to out-narrate. In other words, Milbank's unifying of Niet-zsche's thought is perfectly understandable from the standpoint of pejorative rhetoric. My survey of the complexities of Nietzschean interpretation in this chapter was conducted precisely to highlight Nietzsche's resistance to any unify-ing and totalizing gesture. One gets no sense of such ambivalence in Milbank's treatment of Nietzsche. Furthermore, it is not just Nietzsche who is "named once" in Milbank's texts but also Heidegger, Deleuze, Lyotard, Foucault and Der-rida. Indeed, not only is each of these thinkers "named once" individually, but their unique and diverse thoughts are treated collectively as "one." They are all named by the same name: *nihilist*. And on Milbank's account, they are therefore all "positivists" as well. In a particularly violent act, therefore, Milbank obliter-ates all differences both within as well as among these thinkers. This must surely weaken the force of his case, for the "nihilism" that appears in Milbank's texts would surely be jettisoned by these writers themselves. And so the suspicion inevitably presents itself to us: is the "nihilism" that appears in Milbank's texts merely a straw man?

To answer this question, let us first of all return to the nihilist "genealogy of history." How are we to understand Nietzsche's conception of genealogy in par-ticular? Can it really be as "positivist" as Milbank claims? Thus far, we have seen that Nietzsche's philosophy is, above all, ambivalent. As Eric Blondel says, any attempt to systematize Nietzsche "leads to leaving out a huge quantity of non-logical, non-'philosophical', 'artistic' material, that one tends in a *dualistic* approach, to discard eventually as irrelevant, purely aesthetic, sensible or, to put it mildly, as rhetorical residue (not to say: waste!). This common attitude among philosophical students of Nietzsche is in fact typically inconsistent with Niet-zsche's conception of style and with his antidualistic idea of philosophy."[62] There are certainly aspects of Nietzsche's genealogy that suggest a metaphysical or pos-itivist self-understanding, and it is possible to highlight them in order to construe

Nietzsche's genealogy in a metaphysical way. Such highlighting, however, as Blondel suggests, must inevitably entail a corresponding concealment of those antimetaphysical moments that continually return to call such accounts into question.

One such moment is Nietzsche's insistence on the close connection between genealogy on the one hand and interpretation on the other. In the preface to *On the Genealogy of Morality*, he says that an aphorism "has not been 'deciphered' just because it has been read out; on the contrary, this is just the beginning of its proper *interpretation*, and for this, an art of interpretation is needed. In the third essay of this book I have given an example of what I mean by 'interpretation' in such a case:—this treatise is a commentary on the aphorism that precedes it."[63] So the third essay is the one that most exemplifies Nietzsche's understanding of genealogy as interpretation, and as David C. Hoy points out, it is anticipated in sections 373 and 374 of *The Gay Science*.[64] Hoy says that in this passage Nietzsche asks what grounds he can have for preferring his own interpretation above those of others. He asks whether there can be any "ground floor" for our interpretations and says that because we cannot ask what reality is like outside our conceptual framework, it "cannot be decided" whether reality exists independent of our interpretations or, indeed, whether the idea of uninterpretable reality makes sense. For Hoy, this "undecidability" is significant because it suggests that Nietzsche knows "that to claim the essence of existence is such that there are only interpretations would be tantamount to saying paradoxically that the essence of things is not to have an essence."[65] The important point about this "undecidability," therefore, is that it seems to suggest that Nietzsche is concerned to avoid any relapse into metaphysics or positivism in his genealogical accounts.

Nietzsche says that the color that is most important to the genealogist is *gray*, which is to say, "that which can be documented, which can actually be confirmed and which has actually existed, in short, the whole, long, hard-to-decipher hieroglyphic script of man's moral past."[66] So reality is a "hieroglyphic script" that is to be read and deciphered. As Blondel puts it, "Nietzsche's philosophy is that of a *philologist*, i.e. of someone who tends to consider reality as a text (that is to say *not* as a thing which can be intuitively or conceptually seen as it is, but as a set of rich, ambiguous and even mysterious signs which can only be interpreted, deciphered and construed, almost as an enigma), and who therefore never ceases to read more and more in texts."[67] Thus, Nietzsche's genealogy is a reading of a text of ambiguous signs and, like all readings, is an interpretation and a construal and not an a/historical positivism.

So why does Milbank insist on reading Nietzsche as a positivist? Part of the answer is to be found, I believe, in the fact that Milbank tends to conflate the genealogy itself with Nietzsche's own interpretation and understanding of it. This is suggested by the fact that Milbank's account of Nietzsche's *Genealogy* is founded almost entirely on essays one and two, at the almost total expense of the preface and essay three.[68] This is significant because whereas essays one and two present an alternative genealogy to call into question more traditional accounts of morality, the preface and essay three are concerned more with the concept of genealogy itself and what Nietzsche understands by "interpretation." The importance of the preface, of any preface, should not be underestimated, for in the preface, we find a reinscription, a rereading, and a rewriting of the text that is to come. In effect, the preface turns the text into a new text, a new reading. If the preface is repressed, therefore, the text itself is turned into a different text and is thereby read differently.[69] Thus it is that Milbank's repression of the preface turns Nietzsche's *Genealogy* into a different text, and he thereby reads it differently. Furthermore, we have already seen that in Nietzsche's own preface, he points forward to essay three as an example of what he means by "interpretation." In a sense, therefore, the third essay is an extension of the preface, and together they provide a rereading of essays one and two and thereby turn them into a new text.

If we recuperate Nietzsche's rereading of his own text, we find that a positivist reading is continually unsettled. Nietzsche repudiates refutation and says that he is concerned only to replace the improbable with the more probable and, sometimes, to replace one error with another.[70] He says that we must journey through the land of morality with new questions and, as it were, with new eyes, so that we virtually discover this land for the first time. This discovery is not the discovery of something that was always there but the discovery of a new meaning through a reading of the hard-to-decipher hieroglyphic script.[71] But for this new meaning, this text, to be "readable," one must first be able to practice the requisite *art* of reading.[72] The great triumph is to renounce faith in one's own ego and to deny one's own reality. This is a triumph not only over the senses but also over appearance, "an act of violation and cruelty inflicted on *reason*: a voluptuousness which reaches its peak when the ascetic self-contempt and self-ridicule of reason decrees: '*there is* a realm of truth and being, but reason is firmly *excluded* from it!'"[73]

We are warned against a "pure, will-less, painless, timeless, subject of knowledge" and against such contradictory concepts as "pure reason," "absolute spirituality," "knowledge as such." To think such concepts is to "think an eye which cannot be thought at all, an eye turned in no direction at all, an eye where the active and interpretative powers are to be suppressed, absent, but through which seeing still becomes a seeing-something, so it is an absurdity and non-concept of an eye that is demanded." We are reminded that there is *only* a perspective seeing, *only* a perspective "knowing."[74] The thought of a "presuppositionless" knowledge is unthinkable; "a 'faith' always has to be there first, for knowledge to win from it a direction, a meaning, a limit, a method, a *right* to exist. (Whoever understands it the other way round and, for example, tries to place philosophy 'on a strictly scientific foundation', first needs to *stand not only philosophy on its head* but truth itself as well: the worst offence against decency which can occur in relation to two such respectable ladies!)."[75] Science and asceticism are on the same foundation in that they both overestimate truth, that is, they share the same faith that truth cannot be assessed or criticized.[76]

To draw attention to these aspects of Nietzsche's reading of Nietzsche is merely to draw attention to that which has been repressed in Milbank's reading of Nietzsche. It is not to conclude decisively that Nietzsche was a "fictionalist," for any such attempt to conclude anything decisively about Nietzsche is a conclusion too far. It does, however, seriously unsettle Milbank's reading of Nietzsche's genealogy of history as a positivist account of nihilism. It renders much more plausible an understanding of Nietzsche's genealogy as "a story told with a bias to induce unsettlement." So Milbank commits the double error of, first, gathering up Nietzsche's thought into a unified totality and, second, presenting this unity as a positivism. While resisting any unity or decisive conclusions, I should prefer to "read" and "interpret" Nietzsche's genealogy, with Hoy, as "an interpretation, not an explanation of the sort that would deduce a single necessary conclusion from universal principles and observable facts."[77]

An Ontology of Difference?

Let us now turn to the other "necessary aspect" of nihilism as Milbank understands it, namely, its "ontology of difference." For Milbank, every narrative assumes an ontology. That is, every narrative assumes a "setting" against which the narrative is told and within which it gets its sense. The nihilist narrative (understood in a positivist sense) assumes a "setting" or ontology of difference or violence. Thus, Milbank says that "an *a priori*, transcendental discourse which secures ontological violence, is a necessary supplement for every nihilist genealogy."[78] This supplement is one where violence and conflict are ontologically prior, necessary, and "natural." He says that "to understand one's own proffered words or actions as just arbitrary, itself implies a speculation on the arbitrariness of the process in general."[79]

But why does Milbank assume that there is a "speculation" on the part of the nihilists? It should be said that in moving from narrative to ontology, Milbank is doing no more than moving from one story to another; for what distinguishes ontology from narrative is not the form of the stories (i.e., they are both *stories*) but their contents.[80] This is as true of Milbank's ontology as it is of the so-called ontology of the nihilist postmodernists. Milbank, however, seems to suggest otherwise, namely, that in moving to ontology, we are moving to a discourse regarding the "way things are"—a speculation. It would seem, however, that such an assertion is sustainable only if, like Milbank, one holds to a "positivist" or "metaphysical" account of nihilism. Clearly, if we understand nihilism as metaphysics, if it is "true" that the processes of the world are abitrary, constituted by contingent differences that compete and conflict with one another in a violent and warlike manner, with victory being won by the most powerful, then such a metaphysics must posit a (nonfictional) ontology. Nihilism must then be a description of "the way things are," and an ontology of violence must be the inevitable corollary. To that extent, Milbank is right. It has to be said, however, that such a conception of nihilism seems to be held more by those who are concerned to out-narrate nihilism than by those who actually espouse it.[81]

If nihilism is understood as a "fiction," as just another story, then it becomes difficult to justify any sort of ontology at all. Insofar as there is an ontology, it, too, will be just another story. Furthermore, this point can equally be made against Milbank's own ontology. He clearly regards his theological ontology as more than "just another story." We have seen that, for Milbank, "a 'metacritical' perspective, as Hamann and Herder realized, makes a constitutive and not merely regulative metaphysics an inescapable aspect of our historical destiny."[82] This assertion is, however, a very weak one because, as Phillip Blond points out, Milbank does not give this ontology any phenomenology, and without phenomenology, it remains "hopelessly noumenal." Blond says that "a pragmatic account that wishes to be theologically realist requires some sort of theological account of the real. Otherwise it is difficult to see how a theological realism could differ, or escape from, a pragmatic and possibly voluntaristic account of what is realisable for human experience."[83] Blond blames Milbank for this lack, whereas I applaud him for it. But the point is that without such an account, the move to ontology is not a "speculation" about "how things are"; rather, it is a move to yet another story. As Loughlin says of such a move, "We have not moved from a story to a discourse—from a narrative to an 'idea'—but from a story to another story."[84]

If this is the case, however, then we are led to ask what exactly it is that distinguishes the nihilists' metanarrative from their ontology, for the contents of both stories are exactly the same. As we saw in chapter 4, the metanarrative is replicated exactly at the level of ontology (or the level of the "meta-metanarrative"), and if the form of both stories is also exactly the same—that is, they are both *stories*—then it may well be said that the distinction between the postmodernists' metanarrative and ontology becomes superfluous. May we not do better to say that they *refuse* ontology? This would indeed be more consistent with what the nihilists themselves want to say. They would refuse any suggestion that they are "speculating" about the "way things are" and, as we have seen, would say that nihilism is itself merely (?) a *mythos*. As Vattimo says, "The world in which the truth has become a fable is in fact that place of an experience that is no 'more authentic' than that offered by metaphysics. This experience is no *more* authentic because authenticity—understood as what is 'proper' or as reappropriation—has itself vanished with the death of God."[85]

So the postmodern nihilist (meta)narrative is itself a fable, a story, a *mythos*. It refuses ontology and speculation about the "way things are," and the "setting" of the metanarrative *is* the metanarrative itself. There *cannot* be a distinction between the two in form, and there *is* no distinction in content. In this case, it may be said that Milbank has misconstrued his "combat" with nihilism as being a dialectical battle between ontologies—an ontology of peace over against an ontology of violence. This is a misconstrual for two reasons: first, because we have seen that the dispute is rather one between a metanarrative that assumes an ontology and a metanarrative that does not—it is the dispute between the *contents* of two metanarratives—and, second, because Milbank's rhetoric against the violence of the postmodernist ontology (or rather, metanarrative) loses much of its force when we realize that Milbank negates violence at the metanarrative level, only to reinstate it at a "higher" level—the level at which he narrates a story of how his metanarrative "combats" the nihilist metanarrative.

Milbank's metaphysical reading of nihilism with its "ontology of violence" also gives rise to his insistence that nihilism is already an ethics, and more specifically, a malign ethics of fascism. He says that although nihilism "does not prescribe particular evaluations, it also teaches the needlessness of regret, and the necessity for resignation to the whole process, where all is equally necessary and equally arbitrary; where everything depends on everything else, and dependence is enacted through constant struggle and counter-resistance."[86] Milbank asks what it means to enact such an ontology and answers that the implication of posthumanism is that "freedom is only a reality as power," and this gives rise to "the promotion of the strongest, the most enduring, the most all-pervasive."[87] Milbank claims that postmodernists such as Foucault, Deleuze, and Lyotard reapply the Nietzschean reduction of liberty to power: "The neo-Nietzscheans cannot, in consequence, wriggle out of the implication that, while nihilism may be 'the Truth', it is at the same time the truth whose practical expression must be fascism."[88]

But to what extent does nihilism necessarily commit one to an ethics whose practical expression must be fascism? It is my contention that this is necessarily the case only if one holds to a metaphysical conception of nihilism. For if nihilism is more than just a story, more than just an interpretation, and is instead conceived to be a description of an ontological structure, then Milbank is absolutely right to point out that this makes societies that promote conflict and warfare and the tyranny of the strongest more "spontaneous" and more "natural." They would be more spontaneous and natural in that they correspond to "the way the world is." As Vattimo has pointed out, Nietzsche's concepts of the will-to-power and eternal recurrence are not facts but interpretations. He says, however, that "taken in a metaphysical sense, they are *not* only interpretations. This is probably one of the reasons that Heidegger considered Nietzsche as a thinker still belonging to the history of metaphysics. Even the 'nazi' mis-interpretation of Nietzsche's philosophy could be brought back to this contradiction: if one assumes the universality of interpretation as a metaphysical description of an ontological structure, the result cannot be but a view of reality as a permanent conflict of forces, in which only the strongest is right."[89] But if we move beyond such a metaphysical nihilism (which is not thoroughly nihilistic at all) into a fictional nihilism, then such tyranny is overcome.

This happens because, as we have seen, when nihilism becomes fictional— that is, when nihilism is both accomplished and overcome—it thereby loses its privileged status. The nihilism that relativized everything else is now itself relativized and becomes a story just like any other. The nihilistic story now promotes fictionalism and narrativity. Ethics are now grounded not in a nihilistic conception of the "way the world is" but in particular fictions and narratives. The nihilist narrative is still told, however, in order to remind us that these fictions and narratives (including itself) are indeed fictions and narratives and nothing more.

Thus, for a fictional nihilism, it is simply not true that nihilism "refuses adherence to a particular tradition," as Milbank claims.[90] This may well be true of metaphysical nihilism, but for fictional nihilism, it is quite the contrary. Fictional nihilism precisely *opens the way* for a commitment to particular traditions by a reduction and weakening of its own ontological status. To quote Vattimo again, "The meaning of nihilism, . . . if it is not in its turn to take the form of a metaphysics of the nothing—as it would if one imagined a process at the end of which Being is not and nothing is—can only think of itself as an indefinite process of reduction, diminution, weakening."[91]

As such, nihilism induces a fictional disposition, but this in no way precludes a commitment to tradition. As nihilism empties itself ontologically, one is invited—indeed, compelled—to commit oneself to particular narrative traditions, even if this commitment is informed and marked by a fictional disposition. Indeed, it is fictional nihilism that prevents our commitment to narrative traditions from becoming absolute and totalizing. But if nihilism thinks of itself in this way, as an indefinite process of reduction, diminution, and weakening, it is precisely such a nihilism that Milbank does not confront. It is significant that although Milbank "names" Nietzsche, Heidegger, Deleuze, Lyotard, Foucault, and Derrida, he does not consider Vattimo. It is significant because we have seen that it is in Milbank's rhetorical interests to confront a *metaphysical* nihilism. If Milbank were to discuss Vattimo, he would have to discuss an accomplished, fictional nihilism, which would complicate his process of out-narration. Indeed, it would make all of his antinihilistic polemic superfluous, because confronted with a truly fictional nihilism, there would be nothing for him to do but "tell the Christian story."

Theology and Nihilism

If it is the case, as I have suggested, that fictional nihilism opens the way for a commitment to particular narrative traditions, then the nihilistic prohibition of theology is overcome with the result that the antithetical opposition between theology and nihilism is deconstructed. Indeed, of all narrative traditions, it may be theology, more than any other, that calls us most strongly, because (for reasons that become clear in the next chapter) the disposition of fictional nihilism inevitably confronts us with heterological questions of "otherness" that theology is uniquely placed to address. In this case, it may be that fictional nihilism stands in need of a theological supplement just as theology stands in need of a fictive and nihilistic supplement. Perhaps theology returns to haunt and deconstruct nihilism just as nihilism returns to haunt and deconstruct theology. Perhaps each is impossible without the/its other. Perhaps we are destined to dwell in the space between theology and nihilism, a space in which ultimate priority is infinitely deferred. Indeed, even Milbank recognizes that theological truth "may indeed hover close to nihilism, since it, also, refuses a reduction of the indeterminate,"[92] even though this proximity is often masked by the virulence of his antinihilist rhetoric. And we have further seen that, although Milbank mounts a theological critique of nihilism, it is precisely this nihilism that opens the way for such a critique and makes it possible. It is precisely this ambivalence, unsettlement, and mutual "positioning" that Milbank obscures. Others, however, have provided a more nuanced account of the relationship between theology and nihilism.

Jean-Luc Marion has argued that Nietzsche's declaration of the "death of God" does not mark the end of theology but rather opens the way for the recovery of an authentic theology. He says, "The 'death of God', as death of the 'moral god', confirms the twilight of an idol; but, just because it has to do with an idol, the collapse entails, even more essentially than a ruin, the clearing of a new space, free for an eventual apprehension, other than idolatrous, of God."[93] Laurence Hemming develops this insight from a Heideggerian perspective, arguing that, for Heidegger, it is nihilism, most particularly in the declaration "God is dead," that makes it possible to think about the essence of God at all. The God that is declared dead by nihilism is only the God of metaphysics and not the God of faith. Thus Hemming says, "In the light of Heidegger's work, in the proclamation 'God is dead' or 'God does not exist', might the contested meaning be not the word 'God' but the word 'exist', so that what 'God' names is able to be secured in itself apart from existence and only contestable when *brought into* the realm of existence (being)? Might it not just be that Nietzsche's proclamation of the death of God leaves open the question of God's essence?"[94] For Hemming, the metaphysical God is the trace of my "I," its universalization. It is nothing but myself, projected and made transcendent.

If nihilism overcomes metaphysics, it is also nihilism that overcomes this metaphysical God. Hemming says, "Nihilism proclaims this 'I' dead, and so open to question. The 'I' that is this reflection becomes questionable in and *as* nihilism. As 'I' become questionable in nihilism, which means as 'I' enter the question, God, as the universal 'I', is no longer transcendent being but 'dead' in favour of something else transcending."[95] Thus, nihilism is that situation which opens up the possibility of the "death" of the God of metaphysics in favor of the "return" of the God of faith. Hemming concludes that theology "is not in the least bit ruled out by taking seriously nihilism's claims about God, faith and theology. On the contrary, taking nihilism seriously means being able to turn into the modern situation of nihilism and proclaim there that redemption in Christ which is to be proclaimed and faithfully kept."[96] Thus, Hemming explicitly says what Milbank only implies, that a postmetaphysical theology is, at least to some extent, made possible by nihilism.[97]

If it is indeed the case that a postmetaphysical theology is made possible by nihilism, and if Milbank is right in his contention that a postmetaphysical theology is, in many ways, a return to premodern theology, then one may expect to find a similar indebtedness to nihilism in the thought of premodern theologians. Indeed, Nick Land has suggested that such an indebtedness may be found in the thought of Aquinas, although he neglects to add that Aquinas's thoughts on creation and the *nihil* were derived from the prior writings of Augustine.[98] The crucial question here is: what is creation if not the negation of the *nihil,* and to what extent is creation *conceivable* without the *nihil?* Augustine says that "we correctly believe that God made all things from nothing" (*de nihilo*).[99] But creation is not a single act whereby the *nihil* is finally overcome. Rather, it is a continuous act of preservation or conservation, because, as Augustine puts it, all created, and therefore mutable, beings "tend to nothingness" and are held out of nothingness only because God "preserves them by his supreme loving-kindness."[100] Thus, as Joseph Torchia says, "In the absence of God's gratuitous generation of being, we would not now exist; in the absence of his ongoing conservation of being, we would cease to exist altogether."[101]

So nihilism is never finally destroyed. It is always there, but repressed and negated, and if God were to cease God's "conservative" activity (as, according to Augustine, God can but will not), nihilism would spontaneously reassert itself. It would appear, then, that there is an ambiguity in ontological priority here, for God did not create the *nihil;* God created out of it. And although the creature is created by God, the creature is nevertheless created out of the *nihil.* And if God's conservation were to cease, the repressed *nihil* would immediately return.

To invoke here an *improper* theological reading of Augustine, one could say that the *nihil* is the "other" that theology represses in order to establish its own priority—in which case, one may also say that the advent of nihilism in our contemporary condition marks the "return" of that which theology "repressed." Just as postmodernism "returns" to interrogate the stabilizing and totalizing pretensions of modernity, so nihilism "returns" to disrupt the absolute priority of theology. Continuing the analogy, however, we saw that postmodernism is also parasitically dependent on the modernity that it interrogates, and thus we are never completely finished with the modern; modernity never finally "ends." So, too, nihilism's interrogation of theology is simultaneously dependent on that theology. Thus it is that theology is never completely overcome; theology never finally "ends." Thus, we find ourselves in a condition of suspension, in which any final priority between theology and nihilism, God and the *nihil,* is deferred. As Nick Land puts it, "God and the *nihil* squabble over creation as jealous rivals fight over a shared lover, except that the creature—however much it might respect God—is torn by its desire in quite the other direction, whilst the *nihil* has all the tantalizing indifference that naturally flows from incomparable powers of seduction."[102] In light of this improper theological reading, we may ask: is God conceivable without nihilism, and indeed, is nihilism conceivable without God? To what extent is it possible to posit an absolute priority or "beginning" at all? Does not even Augustine's theological metanarrative deconstruct itself?

Interlude

It seems that any attempt to ascribe a final priority to either theology or nihilism must ultimately collapse. As Mark C. Taylor says, "If structuralism and post-structuralism have taught us anything, it is that identity is inescapably differential; there can be no religion apart from its opposite."[103] Whereas Milbank is quick to point out that nihilism is inconceivable apart from theology, he obscures the extent to which theology is inconceivable apart from nihilism. To this extent, he is complicit with the metaphysical nihilism he seeks to out-narrate, for both present us with an unambiguous either/or. Whereas Milbank ascribes an ultimate priority to theology, a metaphysical nihilism ascribes an ultimate priority to (ontological) nihilism. In Milbank's out-narration of the latter, however, what drops out of vision is the fictional nihilism I have been defending in this chapter. Refusing both Milbank's prioritizing of theology and metaphysical nihilism's prioritizing of (ontological) nihilism, fictional nihilism recognizes that the question of priority can never be settled. Without a settled priority, without a "beginning" (or a "foundation"), without a final metanarrative, one can never come to rest. As it becomes evident that every so-called metanarrative is "positioned" by countless others, which are themselves similarly positioned, every metanarrative must ultimately deconstruct itself. This infinite process of positioning that never begins or ends is precisely that: a process, a movement. This movement is the movement of fictional nihilism, and it is a movement that is made possible by the weakening of the ontological status of nihilism itself. We have seen that Vattimo refers to this movement as a process of reduction, diminution, weakening. In the next chapter, we shall see that Michel de Certeau refers to it as a movement of perpetual departure, a process that must keep moving in the name of the "other."

All of this, of course, raises the question of the extent to which fictional nihilism itself becomes yet another prioritized metanarrative. Insofar as this is the case, to what extent does it avoid the difficulties inherent within Milbank's metanarrative? In the previous chapter, I registered my objection to any pellucid dichotomy between the presence and absence of a metanarrative, for both are equally problematic. We saw that Milbank was right to point out that there can never be a complete absence of metanarrative. But in rejecting the possibility of a complete *absence* of metanarrative, Milbank moved in dialectical fashion to the opposite extreme, in asserting the absolute and ultimate *presence* of metanarrative. But in this and the previous chapter, I have attempted to show that the presence of metanarrative is just as problematic as the absence of metanarrative. It seems that a metanarrative is as impossible as it is unavoidable. Fictional nihilism attempts to articulate and to dwell within this infinitely unsettled paradox.

In this and the previous chapter, we have seen that Milbank wants to remove himself from this paradox by "resolving" that which resists resolution. He wants to overcome the very nihilism that makes his theology possible. Yet I have argued that the fact that nihilism has made Milbank's theology possible means that he can never finally overcome that nihilism. We have seen that his Christian metanarrative is itself supplemented by a nihilistic "meta-metanarrative." As such, it is more indebted to and more mutually implicated with nihilism than he would have us believe. Furthermore, his ostensive refusal of nihilism is what gives rise to the totalizing, absolute theological metanarrative that "positions" all other narratives, and which yet refuses to recognize the extent to which it is itself positioned by these other narratives.

In chapter 4, we observed (with Loughlin) that theology can resist mastery only if it acknowledges its own fictivity and attains a performative "playfulness and lightness of touch." But is it not the case that the best way to maintain this fictivity, playfulness, and lightness of touch is to tell the story of nihilism, which fictionalizes everything, including itself, and which itself opened the way for the return of theology? Milbank rightly points out that the danger of a totalizing, metaphysical nihilism is fascism, but there is also an obverse side to this. For the danger of a totalizing Christianity (the potential for which is opened up precisely by the end of modernity and the overcoming of nihilism) is the proliferation of various fundamentalisms, sects, and Christian fascisms that threaten to engulf us at the end of modernity. But is it not the case that these phenomena proliferate precisely because they have forgotten the very nihilism that made them possible? And, I would suggest, what guards Milbank against this fate (although he is loath to recognize it) is a certain nihilistic supplement in his own texts that appears as the repressed other that is never finally overcome. Indeed, the question of the "repressed other" is crucial here, and it is to this that I turn in the next chapter.

Chapter 6
(A/)Theology and the "Other"

What would a writing of fictional nihilism look like? It would certainly not be a "system," for, as we have seen, fictional nihilism is more of a disposition (dis/position) than a position. It would, however, maintain a sense of fictivity and lightness of touch. It would entail playing with writing in a manner that is never fixed but always in process, constantly moving, negating, shifting. It would never come to rest in a single metanarrative but would reply to each contender for metanarrative status, "not that . . . not that . . . not that" or, alternatively, "*nada, nada, nada, nada, nada*," "until the end of one's strength."[1] We have seen that this movement is induced by an unnameable, unpresentable, and unre-presentable "other." This "other" is, in effect, a condition for the possibility of a fictional nihilism. I have improperly "named" this "other" as a "pure nihilism," that which induces one to take leave of a metaphysical nihilism and that which continues to haunt a fictional nihilism, always inducing new departures.

The logic here, then, is a "neither/nor," a logic that replaces both the "either/or" of modernity and the "both/and" of modern postmodernism. More particularly, in this context, it is *neither* the radical orthodoxy of John Milbank *nor* the nihilist textualism of Don Cupitt. In this chapter, I look at three instances of fictional nihilism, as manifested in the writings of Don Cupitt, Mark C. Taylor, and Michel de Certeau. In the first part of this chapter, I suggest that the chief difficulty with Cupitt's presentation of nihilist textualism lies in its eradication of the "other." Without this "other," without a "principle of travel," without a "movement of departure," Cupitt's fiction is always in danger of becoming nonfictional. It appears to be insufficiently narrativist, insufficiently reflexive, and insufficiently *post*-modern. Indeed, it is Cupitt's eradication of the "other" that distinguishes him most sharply from his fellow textualist Mark C. Taylor, for whom the "other" is lionized. But, although Taylor's concern for the "other" sends him on a journey of perpetual departure, it is a journey that is insufficiently "embodied." Refusing every location and habitation, Taylor is exiled to the nonplace of nowhere: the desert. In effect, he refuses the movement from antinarrative to narrative that is characteristic of fictional nihilism.

In light of this, I suggest that the movement of fictional nihilism is best exemplified in the work of the French Jesuit Michel de Certeau. Although he is also sent on a journey of perpetual departure motivated by the return of the "other," this movement is one that does not merely *pass over* locations, narratives, and traditions but actually *moves through* them. De Certeau is therefore more able than Taylor to respect difference, embodiment, and community. Finally, I argue that although there is a sense in which theology "returns" for de Certeau, theology itself must nevertheless also be left behind on the journey of perpetual departure; for although theology, as a heterological narrative, is one that de Certeau wants to "move through," it must also be exceeded and moved beyond. Against Graham Ward, therefore, I argue that without such a movement *beyond*, de Certeau's profound concern for heterology would be betrayed. His "endless exodus of discourse" must continue. I conclude that, like the mystic discourses to which he devotes so much attention, de Certeau's wanderings show us not so much the way forward as the way to get lost. Losing oneself, one moves beyond the either/or of both Milbank's radical orthodoxy and Cupitt's nihilist textualism.

Don Cupitt and the Eradication of the "Other"

We have already observed some of the ways in which Don Cupitt's nihilist textualism is inadequate as a postmodern alternative to John Milbank's radical orthodoxy. We have considered the inadequacy of the realist/anti-realist dilemma by which Cupitt's project is framed. We saw that this framework was yet another manifestation of the dualism of modernity, and we saw that it failed to comprehend, let alone confront, alternative viewpoints (such as radical orthodoxy) that repudiate this framework. I shall now consider how Cupitt's project eradicates any conception of an "other," a concept that is unavoidable for any postmodern project that wants to take seriously questions of alterity and difference.

It may be said that Cupitt's eradication of otherness is a direct resu
philosophical commitment to monism and naturalism. He says that he p.~p----
"an interpretation, from a one-world or naturalistic point of view, both of what
religion has been in the past and of what it may become in the future."[2] Cupitt
describes his philosophical outlook as a *Lebensphilosophie* and portrays the flux of
life in a way that is both biological and sociocultural. Such a portrayal appears
much more indebted to modernity than to postmodernism, an indebtedness
Cupitt himself acknowledges when he says that "as an outlook, religious naturalism goes back at any rate to Spinoza."[3] He says that after Spinoza, this naturalistic
outlook was developed by Ludwig Feuerbach, Karl Marx, and Charles Darwin,
a deeply "modernist" canon if ever there was one. Graham Ward has drawn out
the implications of this monistic and naturalistic outlook, saying that it is tied to
the metaphysical notion of correlation; as such, it is perceived as a "truer" outlook
insofar as it corresponds to "the way the world is." He says that Cupitt "is continuing to write theological apologetics based upon the liberal notions of correlation, a primary monism, and the exponential pursuit of human emancipation."[4]

What is this primary monism? Cupitt says that his outlook "is monistic in the
sense that everything, including the objective world, language and the world of
subjectivity is made of only one sort of stuff; and it is naturalistic in the sense that
everything is contingent."[5] In this monistic and naturalistic vision, any intima-
tion of transcendence or otherness is precluded. Everything is visible and nothing is hidden. Thus, Ward says that the iconoclasm of Cupitt and his fellow
nihilists "is only in the name of a more foundational monism. . . . They are indis-
solubly linked, therefore, to a certain conception of history (a profoundly
unpostmodern part-and-whole metanarrative). And this is the direct legacy of the
historicism, romantic idealism, and neo-empiricism of the nineteenth century."[6]
For Ward, this foundational monism is not only metaphysical; it also eradicates
and excludes that profoundly postmodern concern with otherness—that which
escapes mastery. Of Cupitt and his fellow nihilists Ward says, "Each theology
aims to eradicate difference or otherness because of the philosophical monism of
their commitment to a general 'life-force.' They each interpret Nietzsche's Eternal Recurrence as the dissolution of identity and difference and this flies in the
face of postmodernism where difference is lionized."[7] It would appear, then, that
Cupitt's nihilism is a version of the metaphysical nihilism that I considered in
chapter 5. His religious naturalism and foundationalism appear more metaphysical than fictionalist, in spite of his protestations to the contrary.

This is a point that has been made by Gerard Loughlin, when he says that "the
chief problem with textualist theology is that it is not textualist enough. It tells
us that there are only stories, but it tends to obscure the fact that in that case, textualism also is only a story."[8] He quotes Cupitt saying, "The world remains fictional as it must. . . . Outside our stories there is still nothing but formlessness."[9]
Commenting on this, Loughlin says, "For textualist theology we tell stories
against the Void. There is nothing beyond our stories except white noise. This is
the master narrative: that there is, finally, only nothing."[10] Thus, Loughlin

suspects that Cupitt tells a story of the way the world is *beyond* stories. Beyond stories, there is formlessness, the Void, white noise. But what is the status of these characterizations? Are they created by stories, or do they somehow lie behind the stories? Loughlin thinks Cupitt is engaging in the modernist philosophical activity of "speculation," that is, he is attempting to provide an account of "the way the world is"—in this case, a formless void. If this is so, then Cupitt has not escaped the grasp of the "system."

Drawing on the work of Roland Barthes, Loughlin distinguishes between the "system" and "systematics." Barthes asks, "Is not the characteristic of reality to be *unmasterable?* And is it not the characteristic of any system to *master* it? What then, confronting reality, can one do who rejects mastery? Get rid of the system as apparatus, accept *systematics* as writing."[11] But what is meant by *systematics* here? Barthes says that systematics "is the play of the system."[12] Loughlin takes this to mean that "'reality'—text and world—is unmasterable; that we cannot hope to master it within writing but must accept the play of writing which is the movement of forces across the differential (system) of language. We must play with writing and in writing play."[13] Thus, it may be said that whereas the system is metaphysical, systematics are fictional; the former masters reality, whereas the latter plays with writing. For Loughlin, Cupitt's nihilist textualism still seeks to master reality and, as such, has not escaped the tyranny of the system.

It may be said that Loughlin's and Ward's most basic criticism is that Cupitt does not sufficiently incorporate the distinctively postmodern notion of *reflexivity* into his writing.[14] Their point is that Cupitt's statements about the narrative and fictional character of all reality seem to claim *for themselves* some exemption from the narrativity and fictionalism that they attribute to everything else; hence Loughlin's point that Cupitt tends to obscure the fact that his own system is also only a story. Similarly, Ward's claim is that Cupitt "deconstructs" in the name of a foundational monism, which is itself exempt from such deconstruction. Hence the reduction of all to the monistic "one" and the eradication of the "other."

Cupitt himself is certainly not unaware of the ever-present predicament of reflexivity. Indeed, he explicitly states the dilemma as follows: "Almost every large philosophical statement we may currently want to make seems to produce an effect of absurdity when applied to itself. Statements about universal transience, relativity, secondariness and so forth seem to be trying to claim *for themselves* some exemption from the general weakness that they attribute to everything else."[15] In addition, he says that one always wants to ask of any system whether it demonstrates internally the fulfillment of the conditions that make possible its own statement of itself. In other words, does the system contain itself within itself? "The fear is that we have all become so self-conscious about this question [i.e., reflexivity] that systematic completeness and 'closure' are now unreachable."[16] So, if Cupitt does indeed have the full measure of the problem of reflexivity, to what extent does he incorporate it into his own system?

Perhaps the most systematic presentation of Cupitt's "system" is to be found in *The Last Philosophy*. In this book, Cupitt expansively sets out his philosophical system and concludes with a twenty-four-point formal summary statement. He himself refers to this project as a "system," and it appears to embody many of the characteristics of a system, as Loughlin understands the term—a totalizing project that seeks to master reality. Thus, as we saw in chapter 1, it goes back to the *beginning* and builds on *foundations*—in this case, language, because this is our most solid foundation. But what is of particular significance here is that the predicament of reflexivity is conspicuous by its absence. If, for instance, we examine Cupitt's twenty-four-point summary statement, it is not until we have read and moved out of the "system" and into the subsequent footnote that we are cautioned that "having stated my system, I ought to cross it out, lest I be thought to have relapsed into an obsolete kind of metaphysics."[17] This footnote or appendix is, in fact, of crucial importance, for it serves as a *negation* or a *fictionalization* of all that has gone before. It is a retort to the system that has just preceded it—"no . . . not that." Cupitt concludes that "although my small summary is quite intricately composed it needs to be crossed out or put in scare quotes, lest I give the impression that I am claiming more than anyone can or should claim."[18] But the difficulty here is that it does often appear as though Cupitt is claiming more than he can or should claim, precisely because these negations or fictionalizations appear as mere appendixes or footnotes or subsequent comments that are external to the system itself. The system is thus negated from outside rather than from within. The result is that the system in itself can appear metaphysical, foundational, and nonreflexive. We may thus question whether Cupitt's system fulfills his own criterion that any genuinely postmodern system should contain within itself the conditions for its own possibility. If the negations and fictionalizations are so crucial here, they ought surely to be incorporated into the system itself and thus internally negate it *as* a system, rather than being relegated to a footnote or an external qualification.

Cupitt, however, evidently does think that his system is self-reflexive in that if it is "read aloud," it enacts that which it states. He says that "no secure starting-point or foundation for metaphysics can be found which does not generate paradoxes. . . . My opening paragraphs, if read aloud, *sidestep* the difficulty by simultaneously saying and showing and being an example of what there is, and indeed of *all* that there is. There is *this*—a language-formed discharge of energies, pouring forth and passing away."[19] The important point here is that Cupitt thinks that the difficulty of reflexivity can be "side-stepped"; it is something that can and should be overcome. Thus, Cupitt "incorporates" reflexivity into his system to overcome it, rather than to embrace it. This is again evident in the following discussion of reflexivity: "To *solve* this sort of difficulty and get going, I have elsewhere suggested that we should copy the old judo trick of turning the opponent's own strength against him. We should use reflexivity to *conquer* reflexivity, making the very utterance aloud of our doctrine reflexively self-confirming."[20] Again, therefore, reflexivity is a difficulty to be "solved" or "conquered." But in that case, to what extent is reflexivity genuinely *incorporated*? Far from being incorporated, it is something Cupitt appears to want to overcome.

Reflexivity, however, is not something that can be overcome; rather, it is an inescapable dimension of the postmodern condition itself. Thus, to overcome reflexivity, which is the same thing as to eradicate it, is to eradicate an essential aspect of postmodernism itself, namely, its concern with "otherness," aporias, that which escapes mastery. As we saw in the previous chapter, it is what makes Nietzsche's writings so ambiguous. It is also what hindered Heidegger's completion of *Being and Time*, and it is evident when Derrida deconstructs that which makes deconstruction possible. For instance, Derrida says that "I have had to . . . put aside all the traditional philosophical concepts, while affirming the necessity of returning to them, at least under erasure."[21] Further, it means that although a phrase presents, it cannot present that it presents. As Lyotard says, "The presentation entailed by a phrase is forgotten by it, plunged into the river Lethe. Another phrase pulls it back out and presents it, oblivious to the presentation that it itself entails."[22] What these thinkers have in common is that they are all committed to the inescapability of reflexivity and therefore embrace it internally, within their own writings. In contrast, we have seen that Cupitt seeks to "sidestep," "solve," and "conquer" reflexivity in his writings. The result is that the postmodern aporia is thereby closed, radical openness disappears, and the many become one.

Indeed, this closure is one that Cupitt himself explicitly wants to embrace, at least insofar as he wants to eradicate the "other." He argues that there is nothing hidden or mysterious and that everything is present: "Otherness disappears in the infinite free-associating hospitality of mediaspace. . . . The new globalized culture breaks down the barriers of space and time, Otherness and Difference, and returns everything into the superabundant virtual present."[23] In this "superabundant virtual present," which gives priority to presence and what is present, otherness disappears. What Cupitt thus does here is mend that which should remain broken. This means we are already in danger of turning back to unity and closure: to *modernity*. Indeed, Graham Ward has suggested that this prioritizing of the "present" and repression of the "other" is coterminous with modernity itself. He says that the space of modernity presupposes that "all that is is visible; there is nothing hidden, occult or mysterious. All things exist insofar as their properties are perceptible and an account can be made of them; as such, all things are inert. This is a non-mythical form of realized eschatology: the truth of what is fully present and presenced."[24]

Thus, it would appear that the content as well as the form of Cupitt's "system" retains all the characteristics of a modernist, foundational, metaphysical description of the world, even though that system has been externally emptied of its foundationalism and metaphysics. But in this case, would we not do better to get rid of both the form and content of the system as well? This would mean embracing fictionalism and reflexivity into the writing itself, rather than relegating them to a footnote. The fictional negation (the endless "not that . . . not that . . . not that . . .") would thus become constitutive of the fictional nihilist disposition itself, rather than an external appendix to a neofoundational system. The system would thereby subvert itself in its becoming a self-consuming artifact. We are thus moving toward a fable that resists the system, a constant movement of destabilization that never comes to rest, a movement that constantly "takes leave" and moves "away from here" in the name of the "other"—that which always exceeds, escapes, and eludes us.

Mark C. Taylor:
Nomad for the "Other"

Thus far, I have repressed the work of Mark C. Taylor in favor of that of Don Cupitt as a paradigm of nihilist textualism. At this point, however, it is important to bring Taylor into the discussion in order to highlight certain nuances in the work of Cupitt, Taylor himself and, later, Michel de Certeau. For if Cupitt seeks to eradicate the "other," then it may well be said that the "other" is lionized by Taylor. In this sense at least, it may be said that Cupitt and Taylor stand at opposite ends of the postmodern spectrum.[25] Although Taylor does not explicitly discuss Cupitt's work, it is clear that he would regard it as insufficiently *post*-modern. Taylor says that modernity is, among other things, the embodiment of a desire: "Modern culture expresses a deep and abiding longing for the presence of the present and the present of the presence."[26] We have seen that it is this desire that marks Cupitt's project, as he eradicates or represses the "other" in favor of a realized eschatology that embodies the "presence of the present and the present of the presence."

But for Taylor, as for other postmodern writers, postmodernism marks a return of the "other" that modernity repressed: "The other that 'inspires' and 'haunts' the same cannot be interiorized or assimilated. Alterity is inside as an outside—interior as an exterior—that 'obsesses' subjectivity. Neither present nor absent, the other is 'proximate'. The proximity of the other is, paradoxically, closer than every present yet more remote than every absence."[27] So, for Taylor, the same and the present is always disrupted and ruptured by the other and the absent. Reality can never be mastered because there is always an excess, a remainder, an other that calls such mastery into question: "While this exterior is never present (though it is not absent), it returns repeatedly to disrupt every present and all presence."[28]

It seems that Taylor would regard Cupitt's postmodernism as a form of the "logo centrism" of "modern postmodernism" (as opposed to the logocentrism of modernity and the "denegation" of postmodernism). The logo centrism of modern postmodernism revels in signs, images, representations, and figures that do not point beyond themselves but stage an endless play. Reality is logo centric because there is nothing beyond the image.[29] Taylor says that although logo centrism appears to reject or negate the logocentrism of modernity, any simple opposition between them is misleading. This is because "they are really contrasting expressions of a single impulse. Both logo centrism and logocentrism seek immediate union with the real. Within this similarity, an important difference emerges: contrasting interpretations of reality lead to alternative aesthetic strategies. While logocentrism struggles to erase signifiers in order to arrive at the pure transcendental signified, logo centrism appears to extend the sign to infinity by collapsing the signified into the signifier. Union with the real—regardless of how the real is understood—holds out the promise of overcoming alienation and achieving reconciliation."[30]

From our discussion of Cupitt's project, we have seen that it may be regarded as an embodied incarnation of Taylor's logo centric modern postmodernism, for Cupitt does indeed collapse the signified into the signifier, giving rise to a reality in which it is claimed that alienation is overcome and liberation is achieved. Furthermore, insofar as Taylor asserts that the logocentrism of modernity and the logo centrism of modern postmodernism are "contrasting expressions of a single impulse," he is as one with Wittgenstein and Heidegger. For we saw in chapter 3 that both Wittgenstein and Heidegger regarded "realism" and "anti-realism" or "idealism" as opposite sides of the same coin—two manifestations of the same metaphysical error. In the same way that Wittgenstein and Heidegger wanted to move beyond the either/or antinomy between realism and idealism, so Taylor wants to move toward a third "moment" that moves beyond both the logocentrism of modernity and the logo centrism of modern postmodernism.

This third reading of "disfiguring," which is a different version of postmodernism, "enacts what Freud describes as the process of 'denegation', through which the repressed or refused returns. Neither simply an affirmation nor a negation, de-negation is an un-negation that affirms rather than negates negation. The affirmation of negation by way of un-negation subverts every effort to negate negation."[31] Taylor says that in this third "moment" of disfiguring, the unfigurable "appears" by disappearing in and through the "faults, fissures, cracks and tears of figures." If it comes, in a certain sense, "after" modernism and postmodernism, then in another sense it also comes "before" them, in that it "always already haunts their presence and disrupts their present." He says that "such a nondialectical third entails the strange alogic of the neither/nor, which can be figured by *neither* modernism's either/or *nor* modernist postmodernism's both/and."[32] This neither/nor opens up a space in which otherness and difference are irreducible to identity and sameness. In this space, every habitation is uninhabitable, and every "location" is displaced or dislocated. This process of displacement or dislocation gives rise to a constant movement, a movement of exile, a movement of perpetual departure.

It may be said, then, that Taylor's moment of postmodern denegation is in close proximity to the movement of fictional nihilism to which I have alluded in my previous chapters. I have suggested that fictional nihilism is itself a movement, a process, a displacement or a dislocation that is induced by an "other" that I have improperly named a pure nihilism. This pure nihilism is neither inside nor outside the text but always haunts it, resisting settlement and stability and always provoking new departures. We saw that the "otherness" of pure nihilism cannot be domesticated and certainly cannot be represented. It can be "named" only improperly and can be alluded to only by distancing oneself from it. The more one tries to draw near to it, the more it eludes one and slips away. I suggested, therefore, that pure nihilism is a conceptual chimera, something sought but never attained, and certainly not a space in which we may dwell. But this raises the question of where we *are* then able to dwell. If every (meta)narrative and every location is to be refused or left behind in the name of the "other," and if the "other" itself can never be attained, does one not then become exiled to the non-place of nowhere?

For Taylor, this would appear to be the case. He says, "The nonplace of exile is the desert—the desert where a certain disaster lurks."[33] So, for Taylor, the refusal of every location and the departure from every habitation means that one can live and move only in exile, in the nonplace of nowhere—in the desert: "All re-fusals—be they archaeological or teleological, gardens or kingdoms—must be refused. Every habitation is uninhabitable, every *Heim, unheimlich.*"[34] But is this not also a refusal of the descent from the infinite to the finite, from the absolute to the particular, from the spirit to the body, from unity to difference, from anti-narrative to narrative? In the last chapter, we saw that in its quest for pure nihilism, metaphysical nihilism took leave of the finite, the particular, the embodied, and the different in order to attain the white light of pure nihilism. In the wake of the inevitable failure of this quest, we saw that there was a corresponding descent from antinarrative into narrative and a return to the finite, the particular, the embodied, and the different, even though one returned to them only in order to leave them behind. This simultaneous *return* and *departure* was seen to be the characteristic movement of fictional nihilism. Both are necessary because it is only when one has *returned to* and *moved through* particularities that one can *depart* and *leave them behind*. In other words, there is both affirmation and negation.

It is my suggestion, however, that Taylor's only affirmation is an affirmation of negation; for although he is undoubtedly committed to refusal and departure, there is a conspicuous absence of return and affirmation. We may distinguish here between two movements of perpetual departure; one movement *passes over* particular locations, narratives, habitations, and traditions, while the other movement *moves through* them. So, although both are movements of perpetual departure, the former moves through the nonplace of nowhere, erring in exile through a nomadic desert, while the latter moves through particular locations, habitations, and narratives, returning to them only in order to move through and beyond them. It is my suggestion that the perpetual departure of Mark C. Taylor is of the former type. Refusing all locations and habitations, Taylor passes over all particularities, moving and erring only through the nonplace of nowhere. But does this not leave Taylor open to Milbank's charge (as observed in chapter 5) that the postmodern refuses commitment to particular traditions and is therefore ethically impotent?[35] We saw that a fictional nihilism precisely *opens the way* to such commitments as a result of the weakening of its own ontological status.

Taylor's refusal of all habitations and traditions seems to preclude such commitments. Furthermore, to what extent does such a movement really respect *difference*? For Taylor's "nonplace of exile" seems to be the impossible nonplace of pure nihilism, an unattainable and unrepresentable unity and sameness where difference disappears. To move from the dazzling whiteness of pure nihilism to the particularities and distinctions of fictional nihilism is to move away from white ecstasy and toward the "land of shadows."[36]

Taylor himself is aware of the danger as well as the impossibility of this white light. This may be seen in his discussion of Arnold Schoenberg's music, which Taylor says attempted to strip away the uncanny veil behind which "altarity" withdraws. He says that Daniel Libeskind, who studied music in Israel and turned away from a career as a concert pianist to pursue architecture, was wary of Schoenberg's attempts in this respect: "Having lived through the pain of the Holocaust, Libeskind realizes that the white light of pure sound can also carry the shadow of a fire that is less than divine."[37] This is because the white light of pure sound or pure nihilism is the consummation of identity. Taylor says that "as identity approaches, difference withdraws. When identity becomes absolute, difference is consumed, leaving only the trace of ash and, perhaps, a cinder. The fullness that attracts also repels."[38] This state of pure nihilism, where identity becomes absolute and difference is consumed, is referred to by Michel de Certeau as a "white ecstasy," a participation in "a universal visibility that no longer is comprised of the cutting out of the individual, multiple, fragmentary, and mobile scenes which make up our perceptions . . . the whiteness that is beyond all division, the ecstasy that kills consciousness and extinguishes all spectacles."[39]

Taylor's attitude to this white light of "altarity" is ambivalent; it attracts as well as repels. Tellingly, he says that "Schönberg's X is duplicitous; it both implies the white light of the ovens and points toward the guiding light of the desert."[40] This duplicity brings out the proximity of Taylor's desert to the "white light of the ovens." In this vein, Graham Ward has suggested that the desire for "white ecstasy" is the desire for death,[41] in which case the desire for life is manifested in the throwing down of shadows, the affirmation of difference and distinctions, the return to locations, narratives, habitations, and traditions, even though these will be moved through and left behind in the name of an "other" that cannot be domesticated. This is the return to fictional nihilism, the descent from the antinarrative of pure nihilism to the narrative of fictional nihilism.

Thus, I suggest that we should return to the "land of shadows." We should leave behind the movement of perpetual departure that *passes over* particularities and return to a movement of perpetual departure that *moves through* them. If Mark C. Taylor provides an instance of the former movement, I now want to suggest that Michel de Certeau provides an instance of the latter. For de Certeau urges us to return to the "finite" place, the body, and to finitize what the mystics infinitize. He says that "we must leave the non-place"[42] and that we must "move through" mystics and explore the "body" that speaks therein, narratives of the body, bodies invented for the Other.[43] It is my suggestion that this return to the finite is a consummation of the movement from the antinarrative of pure nihilism to the narrative of fictional nihilism. This is not to suggest that the alterity of pure nihilism is overcome. On the contrary, it continues to haunt and disrupt every location and every settlement, thereby inducing new departures. But these departures take place through and within locations, rather than by passing over them. In this sense, I suggest that the work of Michel de Certeau opens up a postmodern space that is *neither* the radical orthodoxy of John Milbank *nor* the nihilist textualism of Don Cupitt. De Certeau shows us an embodied way to get lost: "It goes on walking, then, tracing itself out in silence, in writing."[44]

Michel de Certeau:
Writer of the "Other"

As with Mark C. Taylor, the alogic of Michel de Certeau's heterological wanderings is that of the neither/nor. Indeed, it may well be said that de Certeau's own life was a performative illustration of the heterological wandering he sought, in so many different ways, to narrate. He entered the Society of Jesus in 1950 and was ordained to the Roman Catholic priesthood in 1956. As a graduate student, he undertook a close study of Hegel, which made a lasting impression on him; it made him "definitely skeptical about 'absolute knowledge'."[45] He was initially commissioned to conduct research into the history and origins of the Jesuit order, but in the late 1960s and early 1970s, his theological interests broadened out from his earlier classically historical work. Frederick Bauerschmidt says that during this period, de Certeau attempted "to grasp the situation of Christianity in modernity and to rethink Christian theology in the light of that situation."[46]

But by 1974, this attempt to rearticulate Christian faith and theology had been abandoned. Bauerschmidt identifies this shift as follows: "In 1971 he had written that 'Jesus is the Other. He is the vanished one [*le disparu*] living ("verified") in his Church.' However, two years later he wrote that while a relation to the other remained as essential constituent of the modern self and modern society, 'this other is no longer God.' . . . He increasingly saw the formality of faith breaking free from its content; practices of departure are no longer tied to a determinable vocabulary of faith, nor to an institutional Christian place."[47] Thus, in the ensuing years, de Certeau's work ceased to be explicitly theological, as he began to publish books that were to become landmarks in the fields of social theory and historiography, such as *The Practice of Everyday Life* (1974) and *The Writing of History* (1975), in addition to countless articles and papers in various and diverse journals.

The direction in which de Certeau's thought was later to move is indicated in an early theological article titled "Is There a Language of Unity?" (1970). This is an important article because it contains, in embryonic form, some of the themes and ideas that would come to obsess de Certeau in later years. Written in the wake

of the Second Vatican Council, it addresses the fact of plurality and its implications for a Christianity that appeared to be fragmenting as a result. In particular,
he identifies a discrepancy between the official ecclesiastical formulations of faith,
on the one hand, and the multiplicity of particular experiences of the Christian
life, on the other. He says that historical, sociological, and ethnological studies
"are bringing to light what for long has remained concealed by theological or pas-
toral teaching, or has been forgotten on account of the privileged position of the
history of ideas or the formulations drawn up by the 'clerisy', namely the great
variety to be found in *different*, puzzling, and often elusive forms of Christian
life."[48] He says (and here the context of Vatican II comes to the fore) that the state
of absolute certainty, whereby all that is not in accordance with the *magisterium*
is classed as "heresy," is now wavering; an "unknown world" stands before us,
"another country" that is "huge and many-sided beneath the forms of expression
(whether missionary or theological) which concealed it."[49]

De Certeau wants to claim that the relationship between official formulations
of faith and the actual experience of faith is akin to the analogical character of all
theological language. Such language must admit that although it is true that God
is "good" or "personal," in another respect it is untrue. He says, "The weight of
[God's] transcendence makes any proposition relative, even to the point that the
statement 'God exists' has to be followed by a denial. Perhaps the puzzling relationship between official formulations and actual experiences belongs to the same
order. Perhaps the fact that pronouncements of the *magisterium* are made relative by the immense extent of popular piety belongs to the mystery of the experience of God. This mystery, of course, must be expressed, but it goes far beyond
and negates, by disputing it, any statement."[50] So church doctrines are negated
by actual experience, and this experience is negated by church doctrines, in a
movement of mutual negation and unsettlement in the name of the God who
transcends both.

In this article, therefore, one may detect the beginnings of certain themes and
ideas that de Certeau would explicitly develop and expand in his later works.
There is, for instance, an awareness of the fragmentation of Christianity and the
shattering of metanarratives generally; a suspicion of all claims to universality; an
awareness and an explication of the voices of the marginalized and the oppressed
and those whose voices have been silenced by the clerical, cultural, and political
elite and holders of power; a recognition of the need to "take leave" of all systems
in the name of "another country" or an "unknown world"—that which is "other."
In the last of these, one may see the beginnings of a movement of perpetual
departure. Although at this stage it was a movement of departure that took place
within Christian theology, in only a few years it would become evident that, for
de Certeau, Christian theology itself would have to be left behind or "moved
through" in the name of the "other."

Frederick Bauerschmidt has summarized the major preoccupations of Michel
de Certeau's work as follows: "an awareness of the inescapableness of linguistic
representation, an overturning of traditional hierarchies of presence and absence,

a recognition of the shattering of meta-narratives, and, perhaps above all, a concern with otherness."[51] This concern with otherness was what motivated all his writing and induced his movement of perpetual departure. Luce Giard says that "it constituted a horizon of intelligibility toward which his work addressed itself in its entirety. This could not be otherwise, for his thought resisted all systematization and equally rejected the pious consolation of all global hypotheses."[52]

As one may expect, de Certeau's conception of the "other" resists systematization. Although he always seeks out the "other" wherever he wanders, this "other" has no unity of content; it is not an identifiable "something" that lies hidden and repressed beneath the present. Indeed, what is "other" in one discourse may be completely different to what is "other" in a second discourse. As Ward says of this heterological project, it "issues from a certain deconstruction, a stripping away, a peeling back, to find in the plethora of discourses the trace of the Other, an elusive difference. To confound any intellectual grasp of this spatiality—and obfuscate any epistemology—ocular metaphors blend into other metaphorical descriptions drawn from smell and hearing. The heterological space cannot become an object of knowledge, its shape and identity is far too Protean."[53] Thus, he says that de Certeau's heterological project is a practice rather than a theory, and that it will "result in retellings, new fables."

One such fable to which de Certeau repeatedly returned during his career was the "mystic fable." He makes clear that what attracted him to *mystics* was a passion for an unfettered ab-solute "other" that could be referred to in a language that could speak only by effacing itself.[54] Consequently, the "other" was the object of mystical discourse, and yet it was an object that resisted definition. De Certeau suggests that this is why the science of *mystics* was a short-lived one that lasted for no more than two centuries at most. After it had been substantivized as a noun, a science, it had to "determine its procedures and define its object." And yet, the latter task proved to be impossible precisely because its object is infinite. He says that its object "is never anything but the unstable metaphor for what is inaccessible. Every 'object' of mystical discourse becomes inverted into the trace of an ever-passing Subject."[55] Thus, he says that the practices of *mystics* are assembled and ordered in the name of something that cannot be made into an object in that it always escapes definition. It simultaneously judges and eludes the practice of *mystics*: "Mysticism vanished at its point of origin. Its birth pledges it to the impossible, as if, stricken by the absolute from the very beginning, it finally died of the question from which it was formed."[56] In this sense, *mystics* is rather like the metaphysical nihilism we considered in the previous chapter, for both seek the impossible, and both must die of their own respective questions. Both seek an other—whether divine or Nietzschean—that must always remain "other."

But what is the status of this impossible other? It stands as the object or referent of mystic discourse, and yet it is an impossible object or referent. De Certeau recognizes that all Western mystic discourse tells of a passion for what *is*, or for the thing itself (*das Ding*). In short, he says, it is a passion for that which is "self-authorised and depends on no exogenous guarantee." It is an absolute that "owes nothing to the language it haunts," and yet it cannot be considered independently of the work that is its vehicle. The Other that organizes the text is not outside the text: "To locate it apart, to isolate it from the texts that exhaust themselves trying to express it, would be tantamount to exorcising it by providing it with its own place and name, to identifying it with a remnant not assimilated by constituted rationalities, or to transforming the question that appears in the guise of a limit into a particular religious representation (in turn excluded from the scientific fields and fetishized as the substitute for what is lacking). It is to postulate behind the documents a something or other, a malleable ineffable that could be fashioned to fit any end, a 'night in which all cows are black'."[57]

It can be seen, therefore, that de Certeau wants to resist domesticating "the question that appears in the guise of a limit"; he wants to resist transforming this question into "a particular religious representation." This, however, leads us to consider the question of the relationship between the discourse of *mystics,* on the one hand, and religious or theological discourse, on the other. The object of *mystics* could not be defined, identified, and named, whereas the object of theological discourse is defined, identified, and named (however analogously and hesitatingly) as "God." Thus, although mystic discourse presupposed theological discourse and did not stand in opposition to it, this presupposition also gave rise to a radical questioning.

De Certeau says that mystical discourse presupposed the theological tradition but used its statements in order to "make them say the absence of what they designate. It is by taking words seriously, a life and death game in the body of language, that the secret of what they give is torn from them—and, as St John of the Cross says in relation to the 'holy *doctors*', to do that is to make them confess the secret of their 'impotence', of what they cannot 'give'."[58] In other words, mystic writing simultaneously presupposed and negated the theological tradition within which it was situated. It replied with an infinite "not that" to all theological statements and induced a movement of departure.

This movement of departure is central to de Certeau's reading of the mystics. He maintains that mystical writings are themselves "other" in that there is a distance between us and them, a recognition that they belong to a past apart from us; we should follow the movements of the mystics, though at a distance. This is another instance of how de Certeau's movement of departure does not *pass over* locations and traditions but *moves through* them. We must "follow" the movements of the mystics but "at a distance"; we must "commit" ourselves to them but also "leave them behind." In this process, he says that these writings "soon teach the way to get lost (even if it is only the way to lose a form of knowledge); following them may lead us, by the sound of its streets, to the city transformed into sea. A genre of literature would thus have revealed a part of what constructs it: the power to induce a departure."[59] This departure is an endless taking leave of all settlement of knowledge. It calls into question all systems and all metanarratives.

He says that for St. John of the Cross, the name of God is itself a "principle of travel." It sends all systems of knowledge on an endless voyage, by the force of "something else again." God, he says, is "a tool of dissuasion in every place, a *password*. It makes things pass. It dis-places; it is a 'short word . . . of one syllable', 'the shortest possible word' (*God* or *Love*, 'choose which you like, or perhaps some other'); it is an operative signifier, a part functioning as the *lapsus* or *raptus* the *Cloud of Unknowing* recommends for use."[60] This "operative signifier" is that in the name of which one departs. Expressing this movement of departure in formulaic terms, de Certeau designates this "operative siginifer" as Ω, while the stages of loss he designates as A_1, A_2 . . . A_i, and so forth. Each stage of movement is then expressed by the following formula: A_i = not Ω. There is no possibility of finding a resting point at any stage because each stage is confronted by a "this is not it." So this means that A_{i+1} = not A_{i+2}. Thus, every substantive or absolute term is negated or becomes adjectival by virtue of its relation to an "absolute." Of this absolute, de Certeau says that it "does not 'subsist by itself', it is off-stage. It is a name. It is not something that 'remains' (like a substance) or 'holds together' (like a symbol), but something that induces a departure. Mystic writing is this adjectivisation of language. It narrativizes an endless exodus of discourse."[61]

This "endless exodus of discourse" is explored by de Certeau in his much-discussed narrative of Labadie the Nomad, which appears at the end of *The Mystic Fable*. The centrality of the figure of Labadie for de Certeau's project cannot be denied. Dominique Julia and Luce Giard have both suggested that the figure of Labadie is an emblem for a question at the heart of de Certeau's project.[62] Bauerschmidt, too, has commented, "Like Jean de Labadie, the seventeenth century Jesuit turned Jansenist turned Calvinist turned 'Labadist', de Certeau wanders, always true to his vocation, his 'calling', toward the Other."[63] His friend and fellow Jesuit Joseph Moingt also understands de Certeau's wanderings as "Labadist" in character. He says that de Certeau was both literally and figuratively a traveler: "He moved rapidly, sometimes a little feverishly, from one place to another, always departing and in transit, as if he guessed that his days were already numbered."[64] Let us therefore turn to de Certeau's narrative of Labadie, a narrative in which the distinction between subject and object, between narrator and narratee, between de Certeau and Labadie, is repeatedly and constantly destabilized.

Jean de Labadie was born in 1610 in Bourg-en-Guyenne, and at the age of fifteen, he entered the Jesuit novitiate of Bordeaux. After fourteen years, however, he left the community, destined to become a wanderer and a traveler, physically, intellectually, and spiritually. After he left the Jesuits, he became successively Jansenist, Calvinist, pietist, chiliast, or millenarian, and finally what de Certeau terms "Labadist"—a mortal stage. He says that this inner journey was transformed into a geographical one as Labadie traveled ever northward from Guyenne in the South of France until he finally reached Altona in Denmark, where he died.[65] In almost every place, he was received and subsequently rejected, affirmed and subsequently negated. De Certeau says that "Labadie's story is that of indefinite space created by the impossibility of a place. . . . He passes on. He cannot stop."[66] But although Labadie keeps moving and cannot stop, he does not *pass over* the traditions of Jansenism, Calvinism, pietism, and so forth; neither does he *bypass* locations, whether Guyenne, Geneva, or Altona. On the contrary, he *moves through* them. Labadie's wanderings do not take place in the desert, in the nonplace of nowhere. Rather, he moves through embodied particularities, *through* traditions and *through* locations.

There is no goal to these wanderings, no destination, no final resting place. "The wanderer has no certain destination, goal, aim, purpose, or end."[67] In the absence of an "end," each movement cannot be regarded as an advance, merely as another movement. De Certeau says that the world in which Labadie traveled no longer really respected the medieval cosmic and spiritual hierarchy, so that a step forward was no longer perceived as an "ascent," a movement *higher*, but rather as a move *further*. From step to step, it was discovered that an order of grace and creation was being replaced by a space of "extension." He says that this "was probably the 'major' discovery to which Labadie bore witness in his travels."[68] This is also something to which de Certeau bears witness in his writings, where every movement is neither an ascent nor a descent but a movement *further on*, without a teleology, without a goal.

Michel de Certeau:
A Return to Theology?

Thus far, I have followed Luce Giard and others in presenting the narrative of Labadie's endless exile as paradigmatic for de Certeau's own project. At this point, however, it should be noted that such an interpretation has been called into question. Graham Ward, for instance, wants to redeem de Certeau's work from what he perceives to be the nihilistic drift of his wandering into ever deepening exile. He thus seeks to resituate de Certeau's project within its Jesuit context by putting him in conversation with the other Jesuit theologians of his generation. In particular, he argues that de Certeau's work can be "saved" from nihilism by its being supplemented by the neo-Patristic Trinitarian theology of Hans Urs von Balthasar.[69] Ward seems to be making two claims here: first, that de Certeau's project can be redeemed from nihilism only by a more explicitly theological supplement; and second, that de Certeau was himself "pushing towards a new space, a rewriting of the traditional space that is not the denial but the affirmation of tradition."[70] So, in this second claim, Ward is suggesting that there is something more going on in de Certeau's work than Labadie's endless exile. He admits that this "something more" is not explicit; but he nevertheless perceives a eucharistic siting that "haunts" de Certeau's work and "evokes" a theological space. In particular, Ward appeals to the latter part of the Labadie narrative and the following "Overture to a Poetics of the Body" and reads them as an attempt to reinstall the sacramental worldview. In what follows, however, I suggest that we should resist such a theological "domestication" of de Certeau's heterological project. It seems to me that the profound concern with the "other" and the displacements it affects pervades *The Mystic Fable* as a whole and ultimately precludes de Certeau from making the sort of theological move that Ward wants him to make. In other words, to "name" de Certeau's "other" theologically compromises its essential otherness and therefore necessarily entails a certain betrayal. My aim, therefore, is to guard de Certeau's work against an appropriation by radical orthodoxy.[71]

Ward quotes de Certeau at the end of the chapter on Labadie the Nomad, where he says, "We must return to the 'finite' place, the body . . . and let Labadie pass by."[72] For Ward, this suggests that de Certeau wishes to take leave of Labadie's endless exile in favor of something else, something more traditional, more theological. But what does it mean to let Labadie pass by? How are we to interpret this? For it seems to me that there are two possible ways of letting Labadie pass by, one that is true to his nomadic spirit and another that repudiates it.

The first way to let Labadie pass by is to do so affirmatively. Indeed, it may well be said that to be true to Labadie's spirit, one must *necessarily* let him pass by, take leave of him and go beyond him. One must keep moving, keep going *further on*. To be true to Labadie, one must let him pass by. The thinking here is rather like that of Nietzsche's Zarathustra, who "*orders* his disciples *not* to obey him."[73] To be true to Zarathustra, one must (dis)obey him. The second way of letting Labadie pass by, however, is to be *un*true to his spirit. This way would be to take leave of the nomadic spirit itself, to repudiate the endless exile and the necessary loss that it entails. There are thus both an affirmative and a pejorative sense in which we can let Labadie pass by. Ward wants to let Labadie pass by in the pejorative sense, in that he wants theologically to redeem de Certeau's wanderings from their nihilistic drift. But is this the sense in which de Certeau wants to let Labadie pass by? For he seems to want to let Labadie to continue wandering. Immediately after his injunction to let Labadie pass by, de Certeau says of him that he is "a man whose wanderings *continue* to elude the learned, who only see him cross the narrow field of their competency, and who, like Empedocles, leaves us nothing but his sandals."[74] It seems that to let Labadie pass by is to allow him to *continue* wandering, in which case de Certeau wants to let him pass by in an affirmative sense.

Indeed, such an interpretation is consistent with his other uses of the phrase "pass by" and its variants. For instance, he refers affirmatively to the spoken word (*logion*) preserved in the Gospel according to Thomas: "Jesus said: Be passerby."[75] Indeed, for de Certeau, Jesus himself is a "significant passerby" (*passant considérable*).[76] Further, *passerby* is a term de Certeau uses to describe all sorts of wanderers, "from the little passersby (like those Jesuits who became Protestants, or the other way around, and those about which numerous documents lie dormant in the Roman archives) to the great itinerants (such as Quirinius Kuhlmann, who went from Silesia to Constantinople, from there to Switzerland, then to Moscow, where he was eventually burned alive in 1689), not to mention the often even more radical, but more silent 'conversions' that took place in large numbers among the conquerors captivated by the New World, Africa, or Asia."[77] Labadie, de Certeau says, was "only one among all those passersby."[78] So Labadie *is* a passerby, in which case to let Labadie pass by is simply to let Labadie be himself, to allow him to do what he does best. In other words, to 'let Labadie pass by' is not to repudiate his wanderings but to affirm them.

The Mystic Fable concludes with the prose poem "Overture to a Poetics of the Body." Of this Ward says that the "final contrast of the book is between the walking with God, voiced by the thirteenth century writer Hadewijch of Anvers, and the walking in a contemporary culture unable to believe in God (which rehearses the silence and nihilism of Labadie, only now 'more solitary and lost than before')."[79] This "final contrast," however, is not as absolute as Ward seems to suggest. It appears that Ward reads the distinction between Hadewijch and Labadie in terms of a binary opposition between theology and nihilism that we have seen to frame John Milbank's project. But it is precisely such an opposition that de Certeau wants to resist. Writing of the space of the "other," he asks, "Is this space divine or Nietzschean?"[80] He leaves this question rhetorically unanswered, saying only that the essence "has no opposite."[81]

I suspect that, for de Certeau, this question must necessarily remain rhetorical and unanswered. But for Ward, an answer, a resolution, is essential, because without faith, this space must, necessarily, be nihilistic.[82] So we are presented with an either/or, theology or nihilism, and Ward reads the contrast between Hadewijch and Labadie in terms of this opposition. But if this is an opposition that de Certeau does not share, then his contrast between Hadewijch and Labadie likewise is not as oppositional as Ward reads it. It seems that for de Certeau, there is as much continuity as discontinuity;.for Hadewijch is also a "mystic and poet," and de Certeau says that her thirteenth-century experiences reappear everywhere in a thousand-year-old tradition and in the most varied historical settings, right down to the poems of Catherine Pozzi in the twentieth century, one of which de Certeau reproduces in his "Overture." So it seems that the experiences of Hadewijch are *repeated* (albeit differently) in the experiences of Labadie.

Furthermore, having described Hadewijch as "mystic," de Certeau says, "He or she is mystic who cannot stop walking and, with the certainty of what is lacking, knows of every place and object that it is *not that*; one cannot stay *there* nor be content with *that*. Desire creates an excess. Places are exceeded, passed, lost behind it. It makes one go further, elsewhere."[83] He then goes on to quote Hadewijch, who said that the desire is inhabited by "a noble *je ne sais quois*, neither this nor that, that leads us, introduces us to and absorbs us in our Origin."[84] So, in describing Hadewijch as a mystic, in defining a mystic in terms that allude to Labadie, and in quoting Hadewijch in the course of that description, de Certeau appears to blur and destabilize the distinction between Hadewijch and Labadie. It seems that he is concerned to emphasize more the continuity and the repetition than the difference and the opposition. Hadewijch, he seems to be suggesting, is also a wanderer, a passerby.

In asserting the "contrast" between Hadewijch and Labadie, however, Ward emphasizes in the latter the absence of God that de Certeau identifies as characteristic of contemporary culture. Although God is absent (hidden or dead) in contemporary culture, de Certeau says that the movement of perpetual departure remains: "as if, unable to ground itself in belief in God any longer, the experience only kept the form and not the content of traditional *mystics*. . . . Unmoored from the 'origin' of which Hadewijch spoke, the traveler no longer has foundation or goal."[85] It is not clear here whether the continuity or *discontinuity* is more important for de Certeau. Does he want to emphasise the continuity—the movement of perpetual departure that continues and is still being repeated—or is he concerned to emphasize the rupture—the unmooring from the origin? What is clear is that he does not think it possible to return to being "moored to the origin," for he repudiates any teleology and cannot develop a theology of history, and without either of these, he can have no foundation or goal.[86] Without foundation and goal, then, he gives himself over, with Labadie, to a nameless desire. Ward highlights de Certeau's characterization of this desire as "more solitary and lost than before," but he represses the following, less pejorative characterization of it as "less protected and more radical." De Certeau says that it is "ever seeking a body or poetic locus." But in finding such a body, it must always leave it behind again; it must pass it by. "It goes on walking, then, tracing itself out in silence, in writing."[87]

It can be seen, therefore, that if de Certeau does return to theology, it is not and cannot be a return to theology as metanarrative. Indeed, on my reading, and contrary to Ward, it even seems unlikely that de Certeau was moving, or was about to move, in a more theological and eucharistic direction. I have tried to show that any apparent suggestions in de Certeau's later writings that this was the case are too weak to justify so contentious a reading. Also, I have suggested that such a movement would entail such a betrayal of de Certeau's most deeply held heterological concerns that it renders Ward's suggestion "too extreme an hypothesis." I have argued that these concerns motivate his writings to the very end. And yet, there *is* a sense in which de Certeau does return to theology; for if "heterology" is what motivates all of his many and diverse writings, then it has to be said that theology is a heterological project par excellence.[88] So, if the theological body must ultimately be left behind, it is also a body that must be *moved through*. Theology returns to haunt the heterological movement of perpetual departure. As Luce Giard says, "It is altogether evident that the search for God is a journey toward the Other; de Certeau had pointed out, without dwelling on the matter, that all types of voyages are the same."[89] Indeed, his journey through *The Mystic Fable* may be regarded as an extended instance of the way in which he moves through theology, only in order to leave it behind.

So, if theology "returns" for de Certeau, it does not return in a "strong" sense as it does for John Milbank, where theology as metanarrative "positions" all other narratives and discourses. Rather, theology returns in a "weak" sense that may be described as *la faiblesse de croire*. It both returns and departs; it returns and does not return. This gives rise to an "endless exodus of discourse" in which opposites collapse and become destabilized. This is why Giard claimed that de Certeau occupied a "tertiary" position that was neither inside nor outside the church.[90] So, whereas Milbank's "strong" return of theology gives rise to an absolute and binary opposition between theology and nihilism, de Certeau insists that the "other" cannot be "named" as either divine or Nietzschean; it is "without an opposite."

This is perhaps most evident in the prose poem "White Ecstasy" (Extase Blanche), which stages an encounter between Simeon the monk and his visitor from Panoptie. Simeon speaks of the "exorbitant goal" of the travelers who have set out to see God. "Our authors" claim that the vision of God coincides with the disappearance of things seen: "To see God is, in the end, to see *nothing*; it is to see nothing in particular; it is to participate in a universal visibility that no longer is comprised of the cutting out of the individual, multiple, fragmentary, and mobile scenes which make up our perceptions."[91] Simeon says that the things we see are not so much the emblems of the victory of our seeing as the marks of the limits of its expansion. Seeing must expand until we see everything, or, which is the same thing, until we see nothing. Thus, seeing is devouring. "It is a leveling of history, a white eschatology that suppresses and 'confuses' all secrets."[92] He says that *to see* is a domineering verb that inhales the subject and object. They become "interchangeable and unstable" as they "pivot around the verb." Thus, the final bedazzlement would be "an absorption of objects and subjects in the act of seeing. No violence, only the unfolding of presence. Neither fold nor hole. Nothing hidden and thus nothing visible."[93]

This bedazzlement is not something of which we can speak or write, for as soon as we speak or write about it, we thereby distance ourselves from it. As Simeon says of "our authors," in writing of it, they protect themselves and put us on our guard: "Thus the inveigling of that which *is* without us creeps in, the whiteness that is beyond all division, the ecstasy that kills consciousness and extinguishes all spectacles, an illuminated death—a 'fortunate shipwreck,' as the Ancients said."[94] Bauerschmidt points out that Simeon's monologue finds its confirmation in the voice of the other, as the visitor from Panoptie finally speaks to confirm that the experience of which Simeon speaks is commonplace in his own country: "The universality of the absolute gaze which obliterates particular objects paradoxically can be registered only in the particular other of the visitor whom we encounter, who speaks to us of his own country."[95]

This essay is another instance of how theology both returns and departs for de Certeau. Although theology must be moved through, it is also something that must be left behind; although this essay is concerned with questions of God and the infinite, it also continues de Certeau's wanderings into an ever-deepening exile. He moves further on toward an unknown end, motivated by the thought of the (perhaps unattainable?) infinite gaze of white ecstasy. We have seen, then, that for de Certeau, to see God is to see *nothing*. The infinite and the *nihil* are conflated. Just as the infinite gaze of white ecstasy destabilizes the distinction between subject and object, so the distinction between God and the *nihil* is overcome in an infinite bedazzlement. God and nihilism become a thought of the "One"; they become as "one."[96]

Interlude

Fictional nihilism is not a "system" or a "position" but is rather a process of dispositioning (a disposition). If this is the case, then it must mean that the disposition of fictional nihilism may be written in any number of ways. What these many and diverse ways have in common, however, is the sense that they are all haunted by an "other" that eludes all attempts to contain it but that induces and motivates the process of writing or movement of departure. We saw that the nihilist textualism of Don Cupitt represses this "other," with the result that Cupitt's "system" becomes closed, static, and insufficiently fictionalist. Reflexivity is something to be "conquered" and "overcome" rather than something that continually returns to rupture all closure and stability. In contrast, we saw that Mark C. Taylor's awareness of the inescapability of the "other" induced him to embark on a movement of departure that results in an endless exile—the exile of the desert. In the desert, however, all shadows depart and the different becomes the same. Taylor's movement of departure seems to *pass over* all locations rather than *move through* them. Passing over and refusing all locations, he appears to be exiled to the nonplace of nowhere which is, in effect, the desert.

I have suggested that we would do better to move out of the white light of the desert and into the "land of shadows" where, paradoxically, we see more. As we turn into the shadows, distinctions, and ambiguities of the finite, we thereby move from antinarrative to narrative. Although these finite narratives must ultimately be left behind, they are nevertheless passed through rather than merely passed over. I have suggested that such a movement, such a disposition, is best exemplified in the writings of Michel de Certeau, who *moves through* locations, returns to the finite, and invents bodies. Although, as for Taylor, all locations, narratives, traditions, and habitations must ultimately be left behind in the name of the "other," for de Certeau they can properly be left behind only if they are also simultaneously inhabited. Thus, there is here the logic of the neither/nor.

More particularly, it is an alogic that is *neither* theological *nor* nihilistic. We have seen that although theology "returns" for de Certeau, it also departs. As a heterological project par excellence, theology must be moved through, but it must also be exceeded and left behind. Similarly, nihilism itself repeatedly returns, even though it must also be reduced, weakened, and ultimately left behind. I have maintained that this process of "reduction, diminution, weakening" of nihilism itself is characteristic of the movement from metaphysical to fictional nihilism, a movement that is accomplished and embodied in de Certeau's writings. The alogic of his wanderings says of every place and every object that it is *not that*. Places are exceeded, passed, and left behind. Neither properly inside nor properly outside (meta)narratives, de Certeau wanders through them. This alogic of the neither/nor, therefore, is also the alogic of fictional nihilism. Neither ontologically theological nor ontologically nihilistic, fictional nihilism both moves through and refuses both. Refusing the either/or of both Milbank's radical orthodoxy and Cupitt's nihilist textualism, Michel de Certeau, I suggest, shows us the way to get lost. Echoing the words of a noncanonical Jesus, Michel de Certeau repeatedly exhorts us: Be passerby.

Conclusion

If we no longer know where or how to begin, then conversely, we no longer know where or how to end. Now that we have reached the (temporary) end of these (particular) wanderings, we find that we are now confronted with the question of the "end," the question of a "conclusion." But the question of the "end" is, of course, the obverse side of the question of the "beginning" and, as such, is equally problematic. For in the course of our wanderings in this work, we have discovered that our wanderings are precisely end-*less*. Any end that we apparently reach can be nothing more than a temporary "travelers' rest": an *interlude*.

Radical orthodoxy and nihilist textualism share this sense of the impossibility of an "ending," though for each, this impossibility has quite different resonances. For nihilist textualism, the end is forever postponed or infinitely deferred. The paradigm for life is no longer the novel but the soap opera.[1] The story is told endlessly, world without end. For radical orthodoxy, we are also in the middle and without an end, but only because the divine kingdom for which these thinkers wait has not yet arrived; it is "the world to come," to which this world and this story are but a *prelude*. For them, therefore, the end is deferred, but not infinitely. There is no end and there can be no conclusion, but only for the time being. So there are two narratives of the "end," two faiths in a(n) (in)conclusion.

So, to write a conclusion is to attempt the impossible. But perhaps the impossible has to be attempted. Perhaps all writing is an attempt to write the impossible. Perhaps we are compelled to write this impossible writing. In which case, perhaps a conclusion *can* be written, even if it is an impossible conclusion, a conclusion that is not. For a conclusion no longer merely looks back to the text that precedes it but also looks forward to the text that is (necessarily) to come. In which case, to *conclude* is the same as to *prelude*, and both may be regarded as a form of *interlude*.

> . . . conclude
> . . . interlude . . .
> prelude . . .

When to conclude is the same as to prelude, both become an interlude; and an interlude is intrinsically temporary; it is something that cannot last. In which case, there is nothing left to do but move on, write on, even if to write on is to attempt to write the impossible.

At the (temporary) end of these (particular) wanderings, I undertake a twofold task. If a conclusion no longer merely looks back but also looks forward, my aim here is both to summarize our path up to this "interlude" and also to look forward to consider where this path may further lead us. The wandering route we have followed has erred back and forth between radical orthodoxy on the one hand and nihilist textualism on the other. But, of course, this path is an impossible path, and one repeatedly falls into the interstices, gaps, and fissures that rupture every path. Committed to the impossible, however, one keeps walking, keeps moving, never resting, without end. In this commitment, we thereby move and keep moving away from radical orthodoxy, even if radical orthodoxy continues to caution us against taking refuge in nihilist textualism.

Against radical orthodoxy, we have questioned the possibility of theology as metanarrative. In the course of our wanderings, we found that positions are constantly dis-positioned and consequently become dispositions. This very process is articulated or performed in the disposition of fictional nihilism, which is simultaneously the accomplishment and overcoming of nihilism. We saw that it is the accomplishment of nihilism insofar as metaphysics is now overcome, and that it is the overcoming of nihilism insofar as this entails the weakening and self-dissolution of the priority of nihilism itself. As nihilism weakens itself ontologically, it becomes a process, a movement, an operation. This operation is induced and motivated by the "other" of "pure" nihilism, which metaphysical nihilism impossibly tried to represent and which continues to haunt and make possible (or unavoidable) the movement of fictional nihilism (chapter 5).

But if this is the case, then there must also be a narrative body on which fictional nihilism operates and through which it induces us to move. This has to be the case because the commitment to some historical tradition, some narrative order, is unavoidable. To this extent, we can concur with Milbank. The idea that we can live without some form of narrative tradition is illusory. As long as we are formed by language and negotiate with our world and with one another through language, some form of linguistic ordering will always determine how we envisage and act in our world. Radical orthodoxy, of course, makes the further claim that it is not only the narrative but the *meta*-narrative that is unavoidable. We need not only some form of linguistic ordering but also some form of *ultimate* linguistic ordering, an organizing logic that weaves together the various narratives within which we dwell and orders the relationships among them. Again, we can concur with radical orthodoxy, at least to some extent. We have seen that every attempt to do without a metanarrative always ends up by unwittingly reinstating one. An ultimate, overarching, organizing logic always reinstalls itself, in spite of our attempts to repress it.

We have seen, however, that although there is a sense in which metanarratives are unavoidable, there is also simultaneously a sense in which they are impossible; for this ultimate metanarrative is always also inherently unstable. It is never as ultimate and self-sustaining as it appears. It is as much organized and positioned by other (meta)narratives as it seeks to organize and position them. Thus, an uncontaminated metanarrative that "founds" other narratives but is itself "unfounded" is revealed as being an illusion, an impossibility. Indeed, we have seen this to be the case with Milbank's own metanarrative. And yet, Milbank seeks to avoid this unavoidable paradox by insisting on the absolute necessity and presence of the metanarrative. Against radical orthodoxy, I have suggested that, on the contrary, we must dwell within this paradox, where the metanarrative is as unavoidable as it is impossible, and where all settlement and finality are deferred (chapter 4).

I have suggested that the best way to negotiate this paradox is by adopting a "fictional nihilist" disposition, which calls us to commit ourselves to particular narratives and traditions even though the disposition of fictional nihilism itself will preclude us from committing ourselves to them in any absolute or final way. Thus, the "fictional nihilist" disposition is constituted by a *dual movement*: by a "commitment to" narratives and a "taking leave" of them.[2] Following de Certeau, I have characterized this ambivalent disposition toward narratives as a call to *move through them* (chapter 6). But this raises the question of *which* narratives we are called to move through. To which traditions are we called? Whose invitation are we no longer able to avoid?

Increasingly, and perhaps unavoidably, the narratives through which we are called to move are *theological*. Why is this? There are numerous answers to this question, and it is not at all clear that they can be exhaustively displayed, but we

can at least identify some of the most significant, particularly as they have manifested themselves in this book. Perhaps one of the most significant is the preoccupation with "otherness," which we have seen to be a defining characteristic of
our contemporary condition. We have seen that it is this haunting sense of "otherness" that induces the movement of fictional nihilism. As this "other" is, by its
very nature, unrepresentable and unspecifiable, one is forced to look for various
forms of strategies and tactics whereby it may be indirectly communicated.

One of the most obvious resources in this respect is the language of theology.
Indeed, it may well be said that theology is itself a constant attempt to negotiate
radical alterity. Over two millennia, theology has developed a rich fund of
"traces" in its attempt to do the impossible—to speak of a God who is fundamentally and irreducibly "other." We have seen that the language of metaphysics,
which is, in many ways, coterminous with the language of modernity, is fundamentally inadequate for such a task, for the language of modernity is marked
above all else by a desire for presence and its consequent denial or repression of
the "other" (chapters 1 and 2). And so one finds oneself being called back again
and again to theology as the only discourse adequate to our task. In attempting
to articulate otherwise impossible heterological concerns, one finds that theology
becomes unavoidable.

Indeed, this unavoidable call back to theology is embodied in the writings of
many ostensibly secular postmodern thinkers. As Graham Ward has pointed out,
the works of Jacques Derrida, Luce Irigaray, Julia Kristeva, and Jean-François
Lyotard all bear witness to this unavoidable call of theology. He says that their "fundamental concern with what is exterior and other has led these thinkers to articulate this 'beyond' in a theological idiom. . . . Their evident interest in theological
texts and their employment of explicit theological language (incarnation, resurrec-
tion, parousia, for example), indicates that they are themselves aware of the theological horizons their thinking opens upon."[3] This invitation, therefore, can be
avoided no longer. We are called to dwell within and upon a theological host.

Second, theology also becomes unavoidable as a resource and foundation for
ethical resistance. Although the ethical concern has not been the primary preoccupation of this particular study, we have nevertheless noted the indispensable
significance of theology for ethical reflection and action. If it is the case that the
logic of modernity necessarily culminates in a metaphysical nihilism (chapters 2
and 5), we have seen that the ethical corollary of this development is ultimately
a totalizing fascism (chapter 5). To negotiate a way out of this nightmare, it is
necessary to return to the "other" and the "others" that modernity excludes. This
is why, for de Certeau as for other poststructural thinkers (most notably
Emmanuel Levinas), the heterological project is fundamentally an ethical one. As
we have seen, it is also inextricably linked with the movement from a metaphysical to a fictional nihilism. With this movement, a malign ethics of fascism gives
way to an ethical vacuum that demands to be filled.

Once again, it is at this point that theology rushes in to fill this vacuum. With
the ethics of modernity discredited and in disarray, and with the ethics of fascism

precluded by the overcoming of metaphysical nihilism, ethical reflection and action can now be effected only through commitment to particular narrative traditions. For we have seen that fictional nihilism precisely opens the way for, and indeed demands, commitment to such traditions. Confronted by the fragmentation, consumerism, and individualism of late modernity and late capitalism, theology returns to resist this social and cultural dissolution.[4] As Milbank points out, theology provides an alternative vision, an alternative *polis* of peace, harmony, and love, with which the present spirit may be challenged. Thus, as our terminal condition turns sour, theology returns to bear witness to that which has been lost. In the wake of secular modernity's failure to provide a coherent ethical framework, it seems that ethical concerns can only be expressed theologically, and that the only grounds and foundations for ethical resistance are to be found in theology itself.

In these ways, therefore (and doubtless in many others), our present condition appears to render theology unavoidable. If commitment to some form of narrative tradition is inescapable, and if the movement of "fictional nihilism" requires particular narrative traditions through which it can move, it seems that theology, above all others, will emerge as precisely such a tradition. To this extent, one can concur with John Milbank and radical orthodoxy. Contrary to Milbank, however, I have argued that the possibility, indeed the unavoidability, of theology is itself conditioned by a certain impossibility. The very conditions that allow for the return of theology simultaneously preclude a return to theology. In particular, the preoccupation with the "other," which renders theology inescapable, simultaneously renders it impossible. If heterological concerns repeatedly call us back to the theological narrative, those very concerns also call us to leave theology behind. This is because the haunting (non)presence of the "other" constantly disrupts theological commitment in two main ways.

First, we have seen that what is distinctive about the "otherness" of postmodernism (particularly, but not exclusively, in de Certeau) is that it ruptures all systems, metanarratives, and totalizing explanations. Insofar as theology is itself a totalizing metanarrative, it, too, is interrogated. It is destabilized both by the "other" that is found lurking in its own texts and by the "other" that it deliberately excludes. Its absoluteness is questioned, and its claims to universality are deconstructed. All settlement of knowledge, even if theological, is resisted. So the "other" that calls us back to theology also simultaneously precludes us from "settling" within or being "content" with theology. We are both called back and called to move on, which is to say that we are being called to "move through."

Second, however, the ever-circulating horizon of the "other" also renders theology impossible insofar as the "other" itself resists being "named," "captured," or "determined." We have seen that de Certeau wants to resist domesticating "the question that appears in the guise of a limit"; he wants to resist transforming this question into "a particular religious representation." The "other" must necessarily always remain other and eludes all attempts to "name" it. In speaking or writing about the "other," one only thereby distances oneself from it, "for when all is said and done, in writing of this sublime and terrible thing, [we] protect [ourselves] and . . . put us on our guard."[5] To "name" the "other" is only to betray it. The "other," it seems, is always destined to remain name-*less*. It is this that precludes a full return of theology, for theology "names" or "identifies" the other as "God," a naming that takes place on the basis of faith.

Perhaps the most influential account of how the wholly other may be named as God is articulated by Thomas Aquinas, who famously wrestled with the question of how one may name a God who is wholly other. We have seen that Aquinas's answer is that God may be named, but only analogically. This is because God is ontologically transcendent; God's being is "other" than our own. But if God is indeed wholly other, then how is an analogical rather than an equivocal naming of God possible at all? The answer, we have seen, is the theological notion of "participation": it is because the human participates in the Divine that the radical otherness of God is negotiated, however partially and inadequately (chapter 2).

The doctrine of "analogical participation" is derived from revelation, for Aquinas is quite clear that reason is not a sufficient basis on which to name the "other." That naming can take place only on the basis of God's self-revelation. It is only through God's initiative that humanity is able to name the other as God.[6] And yet, God's initiative becomes revelation *for us* only through an act of *faith*. So God is named by means of *revelation* and *faith*. It should be said that there is no foundationalism here, for both revelation and faith are mutually constitutive. One holds to revelation on the basis of faith, and yet one has faith on the basis of revelation. Without one or the other, this faithful circle collapses. Without revelation, there is a lack of faith, and without faith, there is a lack of revelation. When this happens, God can no longer be named, and the "other" once again becomes unnamed, wholly other.

But what if a lack of faith is alternatively viewed as faith in a lack? In this case, faith itself would be viewed as a lack of faith in a lack. What we have here, then, is two faiths in an/other. In one case, there is faith in an other that is named, while in the other case, there is a faith in an other that is unnnamed. For each faith, the other faith constitutes a betrayal. For the first, the named other constitutes a betrayal of the "otherness" of the other. For the second, the unnamed other constitutes a betrayal of the divine godliness of the other. What we have, therefore, are two faiths and two betrayals. We have seen these two faiths to have been embodied in the writings of radical orthodoxy on the one hand and of Michel de Certeau on the other. In particular, we have seen a confrontation between these two faiths in Graham Ward's engagement with de Certeau. The faith of Ward (and of radical orthodoxy) is in a named other. To refuse to name this other is to betray God and embrace nihilism. In contrast, I have suggested that de Certeau's other must necessarily lack a name, a lack that guards against betrayal. De Certeau's other is one that cannot be equated with any particular religious representation (chapter 6).

At this point, one could object that my distinction between a named and an unnamed other is overstated to the detriment of theology; for it may be said that theology recognizes that "God" is not a proper name.[7] To "name" God is not to "identify" or "capture" some "thing," and such an identification or capture is precluded by the recognition that God is wholly other. As we have already observed, the task of theology may be regarded as an attempt to negotiate this radical otherness. If God is indeed wholly other, may it not also be said that the wholly other is God? Need this necessarily be a betrayal of the "other"? Is it really the case that a full return to theology is precluded? Before answering this objection, I must first concede that there is indeed a close proximity between the "otherness" of God (and the ways in which that "otherness" is expressed linguistically) and our own heterological concerns. Indeed, it is partly this proximity that causes us to be called back to theology. At the same time, however, a full return to theology is ruled out because, I suggest, when the other is "named" as God, a necessary undecidability is precluded. This undecidability is expressed by the otherness of the "other" that cannot be named as either divine or Nietzschean. This distinction must, I think, be maintained.

It is a distinction that has been expressed by John D. Caputo in his use of the terms *hypernym* and *anonym*. Theologically, to say that God is "wholly other" is to utilize a hypernym, as opposed to the mysterious anonymity of the anonym. Theology demands the use of the hypernym: "Otherwise, the praise may go astray, the unchained predication may slip or misfire, and saying 'God is wholly other' may end up being overtaken by another Wholly Other. This high hypernym *wholly other* may get drawn into an ominous anonymity that will undo all the good it does and means to do. The anonym will saturate the hypernym, overtaking it, undermining it."[8] Theologically, it is important to contain and restrain the anonym in order to protect the hypernym. Otherwise, the "named" God will dissolve into a nameless other. But Caputo asks, "What if [the anonym] cannot be contained? What if it is impossible to control this confusion that the Wholly Other has become, to keep it in place, to hold it in check? . . . What if there is an uncontrollable slippage between the hypernym and the anonym; and what if the latter, more anonymous operation keeps seeping into and saturating the high hymnal praise and predicative excess that we mean to extend to the Most High?"[9] So, when the anonym "seeps into" the hypernym, the latter is destroyed and the anonym prevails. Are we to contain the anonym in order to protect the hypernym, or are we to allow the anonym to flood into the hypernym?

There is here, then, an unavoidable decision: to conceive of the other as God, so that the other becomes a divine hypernym (as with radical orthodoxy), or to conceive of the other as being beyond every name, so that the other becomes an unnamed anonym (as with de Certeau, for instance). And yet, to make this unavoidable decision in favor of the anonym opens up a radical *un*-decidability that de Certeau expressed when he asked whether the other is divine or Nietzschean.[10] We have seen that the other that so preoccupies and haunts our contemporary condition is an anonym. It resists every attempt to name it, every attempt to draw near to it, and every attempt to stabilize it. The more one attempts to do any of these things, the more the other eludes us. So the other that constantly calls us back to theology also simultaneously precludes us from dwelling within theology.

Thus it is that a "full" return to theology, in the manner of radical orthodoxy, is ruled out. And yet we find that the operation of fictional nihilism is constantly being drawn back to the theological. If theology (including, we have seen, Milbank's theology) is now always haunted by a certain nihilism, so, too, the movement of fictional nihilism finds itself compelled to undertake its journey by "moving through" the theological body. If this is the case, however, then where are we to dwell? If, unlike radical orthodoxy, we are unable to dwell in the city of God; and if, unlike Don Cupitt, we are unable to dwell in a fully present and realized eschaton; and if, unlike Mark C. Taylor, we are unable to wander in the desert, then where are we to call home? Neither city dwellers nor desert nomads, we are exiled to an intermediate zone.

Carl Raschke has characterized such a zone as an "Indian Territory." Following Caputo, he says that we are "outlaws": "The outlaw moves routinely and undetected, within the 'territory' from which he or she is a fugitive. Whereas the nomad has no 'home', no territory to signify as place, the outlaw knows his, or her, 'site'. The terrain is familiar. The postmodernist is like the *habiru* of ancient Egypt, an outlaw that 'displaces' the *topos* of imperial signification to the desert. Yet the desert is always a place from which to stage raids on the empire, to wander in and wander out, to settle and rule, then return."[11] So the outlaw "wanders in and wanders out" of (or "moves through") theology. Theology is the "familiar terrain" from which we are fugitives. It is a terrain that can be "accessed, disrupted, and called to the bar."[12] But if theology is the terrain through which we move, it is not our territory: "as a house is not a home, a terrain is not a territory." Raschke says that our territory is "native"; it is "telluric" and connotes what de Certeau calls "the space of the other." So he concludes, "We no longer have to say, as Taylor says, that we 'are in a time between times and a place between which is no place.' We are in the place from which we are free to raid and return. We are in Indian Territory."[13]

To dwell within Indian Territory is to dwell in a condition of suspension, as we find ourselves suspended in and between opposites—between theology and nihilism, between theism and atheism, between radical orthodoxy and nihilist textualism. Faced with these opposites, we are confronted with a decision that must necessarily be left unmade. Deprived of a place where this undecidability may be unproblematically expressed, we must necessarily resort to *tactics*—the tactics of the "outlaw," of the "native," tactics that are enacted through the movement of fictional nihilism.

But what will it mean to enact such tactics? We have seen that we cannot avoid the terrain of theology, and yet it is a terrain from which we are simultaneously exiled. Consequently, our tactics will be to *move through* theology, intellectually, ethically, and ecclesiastically. Intellectually, we are required to think theologically, even if that thinking is not circumscribed by theology as metanarrative. It will be necessary "to reread the theological tradition against the grain to discern the points at which thought is constructed by excluding or repressing alterity."[14] Ethically, it will require our moral reflection to be informed by and rooted in theology, even though this will be with a "critical reserve." In the absence of theology as metanarrative, we need to recognize that theology *alone* may not always be adequate to address the unique ethical challenges posed by our contemporary network culture, just as we also need to recognize that, at times, theology may itself stand in need of an ethical interrogation. Ecclesiastically, we are called to participate in liturgical faith communities, even if this participation is enacted "at a distance." Indeed, this may be the most performative instance of a "moving through" the theological body. Like de Certeau, we are called to attempt a "tertiary" position that is not quite within, but neither is it outside, the church.

This sketch of our tactics gives some indication of what it would mean to "move through" theology. Precisely because it is a sketch, it is inevitably inadequate, but it does at least "look forward" in the way that this conclusion promised to do. It "looks forward" to tasks to be performed and work to be done. These tactics, then, are constituted by a "movement of perpetual departure," a movement "without foundation or goal," a movement "ever seeking (and moving through) a body or poetic locus." Is this our postmodern condition? Or a response to it? Or a symptom of it? Or an answer to it? Or a defiance of it? Or a *writing* of it? Perhaps all of them. Perhaps none of them.

When to conclude is the same as to prelude, both become an interlude; and an interlude is intrinsically temporary; it is something that cannot last. In which case, there is nothing left to do but move on, write on, even if to write on is to attempt to write the impossible . . . world without end . . . Amen. . . .

Notes

Introduction

1. See, for instance, Fredric Jameson, *Postmodernism, or, the Cultural Logic of Late Capitalism* (Durham, N.C.: Duke University Press, 1991), p. 1; and Gerard Loughlin, "Christianity at the End of the Story or the Return of the Master-Narrative," *Modern Theology* 8 (1992): 365.
2. See Mark C. Taylor, *Erring: A Postmodern A/Theology* (Chicago: University of Chicago Press, 1984).
3. See Don Cupitt, *After God: The Future of Religion.* (London: Weidenfeld & Nicolson, 1997), p. 100.
4. I am here borrowing the title of David Harvey's book *The Condition of Postmodernity* (Oxford: Basil Blackwell, 1990). It should also be noted that not all scholars would want to characterize our contemporary cultural condition as "postmodern." There is a debate to be had with them, but that would belong to another book. In this book, I locate myself within the description of our condition narrated by Jameson and Harvey and assumed by the two major forms of postmodern theology I consider in the following pages.
5. I am aware that the terms *religion* and *theology* are highly political. For a discussion

of the distinction between the two and the politics it involves, see Graham Ward, "Review Essay: Religionists and Theologians: Toward a Politics of Difference," *Modern Theology* 16 (2000): 541–47. In an attempt to disrupt this opposition, I use both terms in this book. My choice is usually determined by the particular writers under discussion and the terms they have adopted.

6. Gianni Vattimo, "The Trace of the Trace," in Jacques Derrida and Gianni Vattimo, eds., *Religion* (Cambridge: Polity Press, 1998), p. 79.

7. Ibid., p. 80.

8. Ibid., p. 81.

9. This is a distinction that has been made by numerous commentators. See, for instance, Gerard Loughlin, *Telling God's Story: Bible, Church and Narrative Theology* (Cambridge: Cambridge University Press, 1996), pp. 3–26; and Graham Ward, "Postmodern Theology," in David F. Ford, ed., *The Modern Theologians*, 2d ed. (Oxford: Basil Blackwell, 1997), pp. 585–601.

10. Mark C. Taylor, *About Religion: Economies of Faith in Virtual Culture* (Chicago: University of Chicago Press, 1999), p. 11.

11. Mark C. Taylor, "Introduction," in Mark C. Taylor, ed., *Critical Terms for Religious Studies* (Chicago: University of Chicago Press, 1998), p. 4.

12. See especially Cupitt, *After God*, part 3.

13. Loughlin, *Telling God's Story*, p. 10.

14. Cupitt says, "They call me a nihilist: but I'm beginning to feel at ease, *at home* in nihilism" (*After God*, p. 99). Mark C. Taylor says that "to love the world is, in a certain sense, *radically* nihilistic" (*Nots* [Chicago: University of Chicago Press, 1993], p. 60).

15. See, for instance, Ward, "Postmodern Theology."

16. See, for instance, Catherine Pickstock, "Necrophilia: The Middle of Modernity. A Study of Death, Signs and the Eucharist," *Modern Theology* 12 (1996): 405–31.

17. See, for instance, John Milbank, *Theology and Social Theory: Beyond Secular Reason* (Oxford: Basil Blackwell, 1990), pp. 5, 343.

18. See John Milbank, Catherine Pickstock, and Graham Ward, eds., *Radical Orthodoxy: A New Theology* (London: Routledge, 1999). It should be noted that "radical orthodoxy" is by no means an homogenous school of theology. Although the various radical orthodox writers share the conviction that the end of modernity creates the space for the return of an authentic theological metanarrative, the ways in which this conviction is performed in practice and the particular forms of theology that result are various. This diversity is well manifested in the *Radical Orthodoxy* collection itself. Throughout this book, I take the work of John Milbank as a paradigm of radical orthodoxy, but it will become evident that many aspects of his project are challenged by a number of writers from within the radical orthodox project itself.

Chapter 1. (A/)Theology and the Postmodern Condition

1. See, for instance, the work of Francis Fukuyama, *The End of History and the Last Man* (London: Hamish Hamilton, 1992).

2. On the Buddhist doctrine of dependent co-origination, especially as expounded by the second-century Madhyamika philosopher Nagarjuna, see Jay L. Garfield, *The Fundamental Wisdom of the Middle Way* (Oxford: Oxford University Press, 1995). For a discussion of divergent interpretations of this doctrine by Western scholars and their respective relationships to postmodern theology, see Newman Robert Glass, "Splits and Gaps in Buddhism and Postmodern Theology," *Journal of the American Academy of Religion* 63 (1995): 303–19.

3. See Jean-François Lyotard, *The Differend: Phrases in Dispute*, trans. Georges Van Den Abbeele (Manchester: Manchester University Press, 1988), p. 136.

4. Ludwig Wittgenstein, *On Certainty*, ed. G. E. M. Anscombe and G. H. von Wright, trans. Denis Paul and G. E. M. Anscombe (Oxford: Basil Blackwell, 1969), §471, p. 62.

5. Gerard Loughlin, "Prefacing Pluralism: John Hick and the Mastery of Religions," *Modern Theology* 7 (1990): 29.

6. Jacques Derrida, *Margins of Philosophy*, trans. Alan Bass (Chicago: University of Chicago Press, 1984), p. 6.

7. Jacques Derrida, *Of Grammatology*, trans. Gayatri Chakravorty Spivak (Baltimore: Johns Hopkins University Press, 1976), p. 162. Both of these passages are referred to by Geoffrey Bennington, "Derridabase" in Geoffrey Bennington and Jacques Derrida, *Jacques Derrida*, trans. Geoffrey Bennington (Chicago: University of Chicago Press: 1993), p. 15.

8. In this account, I concentrate on the emergence of postmodernism as a cultural and philosophical (and therefore "secular") phenomenon in order to situate the postmodern theology debate in a wider cultural context and to show how the projects of Cupitt and Milbank are antithetically related to it. An alternative, "theological" account of postmodernism is provided by Graham Ward in "Introduction, or, A Guide to Theological Thinking in Cyberspace," in Graham Ward, ed., *The Postmodern God: A Theological Reader* (Oxford: Blackwell, 1997), pp. xv–xlvii.

9. Margaret Atwood, *Cat's Eye* (London: Virago Press, 1990), p. 86. I am grateful to Thomas Evans of St. John's College, Cambridge, for referring me to this novel.

10. Fredric Jameson, *The Cultural Turn: Selected Writings on the Postmodern, 1983–1998* (London: Verso, 1998), pp. 1–2.

11. Ibid., p. 2.

12. Ben Quash, "Drama and the Ends of Modernity," in Lucy Gardner, David Moss, Ben Quash, and Graham Ward, *Balthasar at the End of Modernity* (Edinburgh: T. & T. Clark, 1999), p. 145. Quash recognizes, however, the ambivalent character of Hegel's thought, saying that he was also "a most nuanced student of embodied particulars, and the dramatic interchange of human beings in their shared existence." Neither was Hegel a "pedlar of illusions about an asocial autonomy of the self."

13. Mark C. Taylor, *Altarity* (Chicago: University of Chicago Press, 1987), p. xxiv.

14. The psychological notion of the "repressed" recurs throughout Freud's writings. Its first appearance was in the 1893 paper "On the Psychical Mechanism of Hysterical Phenomena," which was reprinted in Josef Breuer and Sigmund Freud, *Studies on Hysteria*, trans. James Strachey, *The Standard Edition of the Complete Psychological Works of Sigmund Freud*, vol. 2 (London: Hogarth Press, 1955), p. 10. See also Strachey's comments on p. 10, n. 1. In *Moses and Monotheism*, Freud says, "What is forgotten is not extinguished but only 'repressed'; its memory traces are present in all their freshness, but isolated by 'anticathexes.' They cannot enter into communication with other intellectual processes; they are unconscious—inaccessible to consciousness" (see *Moses and Monotheism* in *The Standard Edition of The Complete Psychological Works*, vol. 23 [London: Hogarth Press, 1964], p. 94).

15. Jean-François Lyotard, "Universal History and Cultural Differences," in Andrew Benjamin, ed., *The Lyotard Reader* (Oxford: Basil Blackwell, 1989), p. 314.

16. Derrida, *Of Grammatology*, pp. 13–14.

17. Perry Anderson, *The Origins of Postmodernity* (London: Verso, 1998).

18. David Bromwich, "What We Have," *London Review of Books* 21, 3 (1999): 16.

19. See Anderson, *Origins*, p. 4.

20. Ihab Hassan, *The Dismemberment of Orpheus: Toward a Postmodern Literature*, 2d ed. (Madison: University of Wisconsin Press, 1982), p. 4. This new line is referred to by Hassan as a "literature of silence" and runs through the works of Sade, Mallarmé, Valéry, Kafka, Genet, and Beckett (p. 7). Hassan says that silence is his "metaphor of

a language that expresses, with harsh and subtle cadences, the stress in art, culture and consciousness. The crisis is modern and postmodern, current and continuous, though discontinuity and apocalypse are also images of it. Thus the language of silence conjoins the need both of autodestruction and self-transcendence" (p. 12).

21. Ihab Hassan, "POSTmodernISM: A Paracritical Bibliography," *New Literary History* 3 (autumn 1971): 22–23.
22. See ibid., pp. 24–28.
23. Ibid., p. 30.
24. Anderson, *Origins*, p. 20.
25. Mark C. Taylor, *Disfiguring: Art, Architecture, Religion* (Chicago: University of Chicago Press, 1992), p. 189. Taylor says that since Venturi's critique of modernism "defines the terms of what comes to be known as postmodern architecture . . . I shall use this term to describe Venturi's own position" (p. 336, n. 3).
26. Robert Venturi, Denise Scott Brown, and Stephen Izenour, *Learning from Las Vegas* (Cambridge, Mass.: MIT Press, 1972), p. 2.
27. Ibid.
28. Ibid., p. 58.
29. Charles Jencks, *The Language of Post-Modern Architecture*, rev. ed. (New York: Rizzoli, 1978), p. 7.
30. Ibid.
31. Ibid., p. 8.
32. Ibid., p. 6. A visual definition of this double-coding was a Classical Greek temple, "a geometric architecture of elegantly fluted columns below, and a riotous billboard of struggling giants above, a pediment painted in deep reds and blues."
33. Anderson, *Origins*, p. 22.
34. See ibid., pp. 30 and 24.
35. Jean-François Lyotard, *The Postmodern Condition: A Report on Knowledge*, trans. Geoff Bennington and Brian Massumi (Manchester: Manchester University Press, 1984), p. 23.
36. On foundationalism as the dominant philosophical framework of modernity, see Michael Allen Gillespie, *Nihilism before Nietzsche* (Chicago: University of Chicago Press, 1995), chaps. 1 and 2. On the end of foundationalism, see Richard Rorty, *Philosophy and the Mirror of Nature* (Oxford: Basil Blackwell, 1980); and D. Z. Phillips, *Faith after Foundationalism* (London: Routledge, 1988).
37. Lyotard, *Postmodern Condition*, p. 27.
38. Ibid., p. 39.
39. Jean-François Lyotard, *The Postmodern Explained: Correspondence 1982–1985*, trans. Don Barry et al., ed. Julian Pefanis and Morgan Thomas (Minneapolis: University of Minnesota Press, 1992), p. 19.
40. See John Milbank, *Theology and Social Theory: Beyond Secular Reason* (Oxford: Basil Blackwell, 1990), p. 1.
41. Lyotard, *Postmodern Explained*, pp. 17–18.
42. Lyotard, *Postmodern Condition*, p. 37.
43. Ibid., p. 60.
44. See the inteview with Lyotard in *Lotta Poetica*, 1, 1, 3d series (1987): 82. The relevant passage is quoted by Anderson, *Origins*, p. 26, n. 25.
45. Anderson, *Origins*, p. 26.
46. See, for instance, Jürgen Habermas, "Modernity versus Postmodernity," *New German Critique* 22 (winter 1981): 3–14. He says, "I fear that the ideas of antimodernity, together with an additional touch of premodernity, are becoming popular in the circles of alternative culture. When one observes the transformations of consciousness within political parties in Germany, a new ideological shift (*Tenden-*

zwende) becomes visible. And this is the alliance of postmodernists with pre-modernists" (p. 14).

47. Anderson, *Origins*, p. 36. Anderson points out that although Habermas's address was widely regarded as a response to Lyotard's work, it was, in fact, probably written in ignorance of it. He says that Habermas was rather reacting to the Venice Biennale exhibition of 1980, a showcase for Jencks's version of postmodernism, about which Lyotard had himself been ignorant (p. 37).

48. Frederic Jameson, *Postmodernism, or, the Cultural Logic of Late Capitalism* (Durham, N.C.: Duke University Press, 1991), p. 9.

49. Ibid., p. 18.

50. Ibid., pp. 19, 25.

51. Ibid., p. 25.

52. Ibid., p. 34.

53. Ibid., pp. 37–38.

54. The logic of this link has been explicated more fully by David Harvey in his book *The Condition of Postmodernity* (Oxford: Basil Blackwell, 1990).

55. Jameson, *Cultural Turn*, p. 50.

56. Jameson, *Postmodernism*, p. 47.

57. Ibid., p. 54.

58. Bromwich, "What We Have," p. 16.

59. This goes some way toward explaining Jameson's unifying and encyclopedic account of postmodernism. It has been pointed out that such an account is profoundly *un*postmodern, and that there is something improper about an attempt to unify and master a postmodernism that itself resists all unity and mastery in favor of heteronomy and difference. Jameson addresses this criticism in his essay "Marxism and Postmodernism" (1989), reprinted in *Cultural Turn*, pp. 33–49. He claims that a "mastery" of history is inescapable for any narrative of liberation that wants to overcome the otherwise blind forces of history that threaten to "master" us. In other words, Jameson's unifying account is situated "above" postmodernism at a metalevel, rather than merely "within" it.

60. See, for instance, Jameson, *Cultural Turn*, p. 33.

61. Ibid., p. 73.

62. I use the term *genealogy*, here and throughout, not in the stronger Nietzschean or Foucauldian sense of a process committed to unmasking structures of power. Rather, I use it in the weaker sense of a mere tracing of historical and intellectual lineages.

63. See Amos Funkenstein, *Theology and the Scientific Imagination: From the Middle Ages to the Seventeenth Century* (Princeton, N.J.: Princeton University Press, 1986). Funkenstein says that the modern framework was one "in which theological concerns were expressed in terms of secular knowledge, and scientific concerns were expressed in theological terms. Theology and other sciences became almost one" (p. 346).

64. On the protests of these thinkers, see John Milbank, *The Word Made Strange: Theology, Language, Culture* (Oxford: Blackwell, 1997), chaps. 3 and 4.

65. I owe this succinct characterization of Nietzsche's fictionalism to Mark C. Taylor, "Introduction: System . . . Structure . . . Difference . . . Other," in Mark C. Taylor, ed. *Deconstruction in Context: Literature and Philosophy* (Chicago: University of Chicago Press, 1986), pp. 15–16.

66. Friedrich Nietzsche, *The Will to Power*, trans. Walter Kaufmann and R. J. Hollingdale, ed. Walter Kaufmann (London: Weidenfeld & Nicolson, 1968), §481, p. 267.

67. It should be noted that, contrary to the reading I am providing here, Freud has often been read as the epitome of the "scientific" mode of knowledge. There are undoubtedly aspects of Freud's texts that are open to such an interpretation, but there is also

an "other" Freud who repeatedly calls the presuppositions of the "scientific" Freud into question. Writers such as Jacques Lacan and Michel de Certeau have labored to bring this "other" Freud to light. A contemporary reading of this sort may be found in James J. DiCenso, *The Other Freud: Religion, Culture and Psychoanalysis* (London: Routledge, 1999).

68. I am particularly indebted at this point to Michel de Certeau, *The Writing of History*, trans. Tom Conley (New York: Columbia University Press, 1988), p. 348, n. 3, for isolating the key German terms in *Moses and Monotheism*.

69. See Freud, *Studies on Hysteria*, p. 160.

70. See, for instance, Sigmund Freud, *The Interpretation of Dreams*, trans. Joyce Crick (Oxford: Oxford University Press, 1999), pp. 394, 398.

71. DiCenso, *Other Freud*, p. 68.

72. Michel Foucault, *Power, Truth and Strategy*, trans. W. Suchting, p. 75, quoted in Graham Ward, *Theology and Contemporary Critical Theory*, 2d ed. (London: Macmillan, 2000), p. 60.

73. de Certeau, *Writing of History*, p. 11.

74. Michel de Certeau, *The Mystic Fable,* vol. 1: *The Sixteenth and Seventeenth Centuries*, trans. Michael B. Smith (Chicago: University of Chicago Press, 1992), pp. 58–59.

75. See ibid., p. 58.

76. Michel de Certeau, *The Practice of Everyday Life*, trans. Steven Rendall (Berkeley: University of California Press, 1984), p. 186.

77. On this, see Jean-Luc Marion, *God without Being*, trans. Thomas A. Carlson (Chicago: University of Chicago Press, 1991). This theme is further developed in Laurence Paul Hemming, "Nihilism: Heidegger and the Grounds of Redemption," in John Milbank, Catherine Pickstock, and Graham Ward, eds., *Radical Orthodoxy: A New Theology* (London: Routledge, 1999), pp. 91–108.

78. In his book *Varieties of Postmodern Theology* (Albany: State University of New York Press, 1989), David Ray Griffin identifies four types of postmodern theology: constructive (or revisionary), deconstructive (or eliminative), liberationist, and restorationist (or conservative). We may loosely understand the deconstructive variety as that represented by Mark C. Taylor and Don Cupitt and the restorationist as the equivalent of that represented by John Milbank. Here, I follow Gerard Loughlin in regarding the other versions as "fashionable" but still "modernist liberal theology." See Gerard Loughlin, *Telling God's Story: Bible, Church and Narrative Theology* (Cambridge: Cambridge University Press, 1996), p. 10, n. 15.

79. I do, however, discuss Taylor's work and the differences between the respective projects of Cupitt and Taylor in chapter 6.

80. See the "Preface to the Second Edition" of Don Cupitt, *Christ and the Hiddenness of God,* 2d ed. (London: SCM Press, 1985), p. 5.

81. These are complex themes with long histories. We have already identified the connection between Nietzsche's proclamation of the "death of God" and late-twentieth-century postmodernism. For a classic account of a "death of God" theology, see Thomas J. J. Altizer, *The Gospel of Christian Atheism* (Philadelphia: Westminster Press, 1966); and, more recently, Thomas J. J. Altizer, *The Contemporary Jesus* (London: SCM Press, 1998). In the latter, however, Altizer eschews "postmodernism" in favor of "full modernity." See Gavin Hyman's review of *The Contemporary Jesus* in *Theology* 101 (1998): 447–48. On the end of foundationalism, see note 42, above.

82. Don Cupitt, *The Long-Legged Fly* (London: SCM Press, 1987), p. 18.

83. Don Cupitt, *The Last Philosophy* (London: SCM Press, 1995), p. 51.

84. Geoffrey Bennington, *Lyotard: Writing the Event* (Manchester: Manchester University Press, 1988), p. 123; quoted in Loughlin, *Telling God's Story*, p. 182.

85. Cupitt, *Last Philosophy*, p. 23.

86. Ibid., p. 24.

87. Don Cupitt, *Mysticism after Modernity* (Oxford: Blackwell, 1998), pp. 7–8.

88. Cupitt, *Last Philosophy,* p. 47.

89. See Don Cupitt, *After God: The Future of Religion* (London: Weidenfeld & Nicolson, 1997), p. 91. The parallels I have identified between Cupitt's philosophy and those of Descartes and Spinoza have led some theologians to call Cupitt's "postmodern" credentials into question, as we see in chapter 6. Although Cupitt insists that he has subverted the modernist tradition into a subsequent postmodernism, he nevertheless acknowledges that this subversion is continuous with a certain philosophical tradition of modernity. For instance, he says that "a humanistic philosophy of the future is in one way or another proposed by Hegel, Marx, Feuerbach, Nietzsche and many others; and the 'non-realist cosmic humanism' of this present essay may be seen as indebted to that tradition" (*Last Philosophy*, p. 116). So Cupitt's subversion of modernity is simultaneously a logical extension of it. I discuss this in more detail in chapter 2.

90. Don Cupitt, *After All: Religion without Alienation* (London: SCM Press, 1994), p. 16.

91. Don Cupitt, *What Is a Story?* (London: SCM Press, 1991, p. 81).

92. See ibid., p. 139. Cf. Paul Ricoeur, "Life in Quest of Narrative," in David Wood, ed., *On Paul Ricoeur: Narrative and Interpretation* (London: Routledge, 1991), pp. 20–33.

93. See Cupitt, *What Is a Story?* p. 6.

94. Ibid., p. 139.

95. Ibid., p. 61.

96. Ibid., p. 130.

97. See ibid., p. 96.

98. Ibid., p. 153.

99. See Lyotard, "Universal History," p. 318.

100. Cupitt, *What is a Story?* p. 154.

101. Don Cupitt, "A Reply to Rowan Williams," *Modern Theology* 1 (1984): 25. See also Don Cupitt, *The Leap of Reason*, 2d ed. (London: SCM Press, 1985), p. 78.

102. Cupitt says that "the late-capitalist economy promises the most perfect synthesis of total social organization and total personal fulfilment yet achieved on earth" (*The Time Being* [London: SCM Press, 1992], p. 78). This defense of late capitalism is developed on pp. 72–82.

103. Bromwich, "What We Have," p. 18.

104. See Gavin Hyman, Review of *Radical Orthodoxy: A New Theology*, ed., John Milbank, Catherine Pickstock, and Graham Ward, *New Blackfriars* 80 (1999): 425–28.

105. Gerard Loughlin, "Rains for a Famished Land," *Times Literary Supplement*, 10 April 1998, p. 13.

106. Compare Catherine Pickstock, *After Writing: The Liturgical Consummation of Philosophy* (Oxford: Basil Blackwell, 1997), pp. 1–118, with Graham Ward, *Barth, Derrida and the Language of Theology* (Cambridge: Cambridge University Press, 1995).

107. This is how Loughlin characterizes the difference between Ward and Pickstock in "Rains for a Famished Land," pp. 12–13.

108. See, for instance, John Milbank, "Problematizing the Secular: The Post-Postmodern Agenda," in Philippa Berry and Andrew Wernick, eds., *Shadow of Spirit: Postmodernism and Religion* (London: Routledge, 1992), pp. 30–44; and John Milbank, "The End of Enlightenment: Post-Modern or Post-Secular," in C. Geffré and J.-P. Jossua, eds., *The Debate on Modernity* (London: SCM Press, 1992), pp. 39–48.

109. John Milbank, "'Postmodern Critical Augustinianism': A Short *Summa* in Forty Two Responses to Unasked Questions," *Modern Theology* 7 (1991): 225.

110. Milbank, *Theology and Social Theory*, p. 242.
111. Milbank, "Postmodern Critical Augustinianism," p. 225.
112. Milbank, *Theology and Social Theory*, p. 267.
113. Ibid.
114. Ibid.
115. Milbank, "Postmodern Critical Augustinianism," p. 225.
116. Ibid., p. 227.
117. Ibid. For more detailed accounts of the ways in which theology has itself promoted a "postmodern" understanding of language that is suspicious of "essences" and "substance," see Milbank, *Word Made Strange*, chap. 4; and John Milbank, "Man as Creative and Historical Being in Nicholas of Cusa," *Downside Review* 97 (1979): 245–57.
118. Milbank, "Postmodern Critical Augustinianism," p. 226.
119. See John Milbank, "Knowledge: The Theological Critique of Philosophy in Hamann and Jacobi," in Milbank, Pickstock, and Ward, eds., *Radical Orthodoxy*, pp. 21–37.
120. See, for instance, Cupitt in his more Deleuzian moments. He says that the diversity of the world is "the product of the interplay of opposed forces. Life struggles against the non-living, every living organism must experience some conflict of force within itself, we human beings have produced our fabulously complex cultures because of our extreme need to find catharsis through symbolic expression, and so on. At every stage of the argument I have stressed the interplay of opposed forces both in nature and culture" (Cupitt, *After All*, pp. 116–17).
121. Milbank, "Postmodern Critical Augustinianism," p. 227.
122. Ibid., p. 228.
123. See note 88, above.

Chapter 2. (A/)Theology and Modernity

1. Peter Drucker was one of the first to point out that the economic, social, and political conditions associated with "modernity" no longer exist, and so we would do best to see modernity as a period that has now come to an end. In *The Landmarks of Tomorrow* (London: Heinemann, 1959), he says that his task is to show how "the old view of the world, the old tasks and the old centre, calling themselves 'modern' and 'up to date' only a few years ago just make no sense any more" (p. ix).
2. See Stephen Toulmin, *Cosmopolis: The Hidden Agenda of Modernity* (Chicago: University of Chicago Press, 1990), p. 5.
3. See Richard Rorty, *Philosophy and the Mirror of Nature* (Oxford: Basil Blackwell, 1980), pp. 133–34.
4. See Toulmin, *Cosmopolis*, pp. 22f.
5. It should be noted that in the present context, my account of this shift is necessarily a brief and somewhat rapid survey of what is a detailed analysis of a long period of intellectual thought. Nevertheless, such a survey must be conducted, however briefly, to facilitate a proper understanding of the respective relationships of our two versions of postmodern theology to the philosophical sensibility of modernity.
6. Graham Ward, "Karl Barth's Postmodernism," *Zeitschrift für dialektische Theologie* 14 (1998): 34.
7. As Ward points out (see note 6, above), Michel de Certeau provides a theological genealogy of modernity that centers on William of Ockham's linguistic innovations. See Michel de Certeau, *The Mystic Fable*, vol. 1: *The Sixteenth and Seventeenth Centuries*, trans. Michael B. Smith (Chicago: University of Chicago Press, 1992), pp. 79–94. It should also be pointed out that Balthasar and de Certeau diverge radically in their *evaluations* of their respective genealogies. Whereas Balthasar is committed to exposing the genesis of an "error," de Certeau is concerned merely to locate the contingent rupture that gave rise to a whole new mode of thought. The relationship

between Balthasar and de Certeau is an interesting one that is composed of both con-vergences and divergences. Both Graham Ward and Rowan Williams have suggested that it would be fruitful to read them against and through each other. See Graham Ward, "The Voice of the Other," *New Blackfriars* 77 (1996): 518–28; and Rowan Williams, "Afterword: Making Differences," in Lucy Gardner, David Moss, Ben Quash, and Graham Ward, *Balthasar at the End of Modernity* (Edinburgh: T. & T. Clark, 1999), p. 179.

8. Hans Urs von Balthasar, *The Glory of the Lord: A Theological Aesthetics,* vol. 5: *The Realm of Metaphysics in the Modern Age,* trans. Oliver Davies et al. (Edinburgh: T. & T. Clark, 1991), p. 12.

9. Thomas Aquinas, *Summa Theologiae,* vol. 3, trans. Herbert McCabe (London: Blackfriars, 1964), p. 67.

10. Ibid.

11. See Balthasar, *Glory of the Lord,* vol. 5, p. 10.

12. John Duns Scotus, *Philosophical Writings,* ed. and trans. Allan Wolter (Edinburgh: Nelson, 1962), p. 5.

13. Balthasar, *Glory of the Lord,* vol. 5, p. 16. My emphasis.

14. Duns Scotus, *Philosophical Writings,* p. 2.

15. Gerard Loughlin makes this distinction in the context of a discussion of John Hick's conception of God. See Gerard Loughlin, "Prefacing Pluralism: John Hick and the Mastery of Religions," *Modern Theology* 7 (1990): 39.

16. Éric Alliez, *Capital Times: Tales from the Conquest of Time,* trans. Georges Van Den Abbeele (Minneapolis: University of Minnesota Press, 1996), p. 200.

17. Catherine Pickstock, *After Writing: The Liturgical Consummation of Philosophy* (Oxford: Basil Blackwell, 1997), p. 123.

18. See William C. Placher, *The Domestication of Transcendence: How Modern Thinking about God Went Wrong* (Louisville, Ky.: Westminster John Knox Press, 1996), pp. 71–74. I am particularly indebted to Placher's reading of Cajetan.

19. See Bushinski's introduction to Thomas de Vio, Cardinal Cajetan, *The Analogy of Names and the Concept of Being,* trans. Edward A. Bushinski, 2d ed. (Pittsburgh: Duquesne University Press, 1959), p. 7.

20. For instance, David B. Burrell says that "Aquinas is perhaps best known for his the-ory of analogy. On closer inspection it turns out that he never had one. Rather he made do with a few vague remarks and that grammatical astuteness which I have sug-gested as a replacement for intuition. Others, of course [especially Cajetan], orga-nized those remarks of his into a theory, and that is what Aquinas has become famous for" (*Aquinas: God and Action* [London: Routledge & Kegan Paul, 1979], p. 55). Fol-lowing Burrell, Placher says, "More than anyone else, Thomas de Vio, Cardinal Caje-tan, systematized Aquinas' varied references into a 'theory of analogy'." This was another stage in what Placher calls the modern "domestication" of God's transcen-dence. See Placher, *Domestication of Transcendence,* p. 72.

21. De Vio, *Analogy of Names,* p. 11.

22. See ibid., pp. 14, 22–23.

23. Ibid., p. 15.

24. Ibid.

25. Ibid., p. 20.

26. Ibid., pp. 24, 25.

27. Ibid., p. 26.

28. Ibid., pp. 27, 28.

29. See ibid., p. 28.

30. Ibid., p. 54.

31. Placher, *Domestication of Transcendence,* p. 74.

32. This is Jean-Luc Marion's phrase in his "The Essential Incoherence of Descartes' Definition of Divinity," in Amélie Oksenberg Rorty, ed., *Essays in Descartes' Meditations* (Berkeley: University of California Press, 1986), p. 306: "When one is aware of the univocist drift that analogy undergoes with Suarez and others, there can be no doubt that this cautious style conceals an actual univocity." This is also referred to by Placher, *Domestication of Transendence*, p. 76.

33. Balthasar, *Glory of the Lord*, vol. 5, pp. 23–24.

34. Francisco Suárez, *Disputationes metaphysicae*, disp. 2, sec. 2, no. 9, quoted in Balthasar, *Glory of the Lord*, vol. 5, p. 24. My emphasis.

35. Suárez, *Disputationes metaphysicae*, disp. 1, sec. 1, no. 19, quoted in Balthasar, *Glory of the Lord*, vol. 5, p. 24.

36. See Balthasar, *Glory of the Lord*, vol. 5, p. 24.

37. Ibid., p. 25.

38. See Pickstock, *After Writing*, p. 123.

39. Alliez, *Capital Times*, p. 218.

40. See ibid., p. 201.

41. See Pickstock, *After Writing*, pp. 135–58.

42. I am here following Balthasar, Alliez, Pickstock, and others in my characterization of Duns Scotus as the "founder" of modernity. It should be noted, however, that other scholars provide a less rhetorical account of Scotus's thought and its relationship to that of Aquinas. See, for instance, Richard Cross, *Duns Scotus* (Oxford: Oxford University Press, 1999).

43. Alliez, *Capital Times*, p. 226.

44. Ibid., p. 231.

45. Ibid., p. 225.

46. Ibid.

47. Bernard M. G. Reardon, *Kant as Philosophical Theologian* (Basingstoke: Macmillan, 1988), p. 177.

48. See the following by Gerard Loughlin: "Mirroring God's World: A Critique of John Hick's Speculative Theology" (unpublished diss., University of Cambridge, 1986); "On Telling the Story of Jesus," *Theology* 87 (1984): 323–29; "Paradox and Paradigms," *New Blackfriars* 66 (1985): 127–35; "Persons and Replicas," *Modern Theology* 1 (1985): 303–19; "Myths, Signs and Significations," *Theology* 89 (1986): 268–75; "Noumenon and Phenomena," *Religious Studies* 23 (1987): 493–508; "See-Saying/Say-Seeing," *Theology* 91 (1988): 201–9; "Prefacing Pluralism," pp. 29–55; and "Squares and Circles: John Hick and the Doctrine of the Incarnation," in Harold Hewitt Jr., ed., *Problems in the Philosophy of Religion: Critical Studies of the Work of John Hick* (Basingstoke: Macmillan, 1991), pp. 181–205. I am particularly indebted to Loughlin's insights in this section of the chapter, but I further want to show how Hick's work is related to the specifically Scotist and Kantian moves I have been discussing.

49. Don Cupitt, "Thin-Line Theism," *Times Literary Supplement*, 8 August 1980, p. 902.

50. Adrian Hastings, *A History of English Christianity, 1920–1990* (London: SCM Press, 1991), p. 499. A concise account of the theological and cultural climate of the 1950s may be found in chap. 32, pp. 491–504.

51. A. G. N. Flew and A. C. MacIntyre, eds., *New Essays in Philosophical Theology* (London: Macmillan, 1955).

52. Hastings, *History of English Christianity*, p. 499.

53. R. B. Braithwaite, "An Empiricist's View of the Nature of Religious Belief," in Basil Mitchell, ed., *The Philosophy of Religion* (Oxford: Oxford University Press, 1971), pp. 72–91.

54. John Hick, *Faith and Knowledge*, 2d ed. (London: Macmillan, 1988), p. 169.
55. Ibid., p. 177.
56. See R. M. Hare, "Theology and Falsification," in Flew and MacIntyre, eds., *New Essays*, pp. 99–103.
57. Hick, *Faith and Knowledge*, p. 194.
58. See also Loughlin, "Prefacing Pluralism," pp. 31–34.
59. John Hick, "Preface" (1988), in *Faith and Knowledge*, p. ix.
60. Loughlin says, "Hick's Real does appear to be an extremely 'thingy' sort of thing; a sort of divine transmitter 'out there' or 'behind' the scenes" ("Prefacing Pluralism," p. 39).
61. Hick, *Faith and Knowledge*, p. 97.
62. Ibid., p. 119.
63. Ibid., p. 281.
64. Ibid.
65. See also Loughlin, "Prefacing Pluralism," p. 39.
66. I discuss Hick's conception of "metaphor" in more detail in Gavin Hyman, "Hick and Loughlin on Disputes and Frameworks," *New Blackfriars* 79 (1998): 391–405; see especially pp. 396–98.
67. John Hick, *God and the Universe of Faiths* (London: Macmillan, 1973), p. 186.
68. An early attempt at such a linguistic theory of metaphor that transcends this antinomy is Janet Martin Soskice, *Metaphor and Religious Language* (Oxford: Oxford University Press, 1985).
69. John Hick, *Death and Eternal Life*, 2d ed. (London: Macmillan, 1985), p. 24.
70. See ibid., particularly pp. 408–10.
71. Loughlin, "Mirroring God's World," p. 14. On the links between Hick's project and a Kantian epistemology, see also Loughlin, "Noumenon and Phenomena."
72. John Hick, *An Interpretation of Religion* (Basingstoke: Macmillan, 1989), p. 240.
73. John Hick, in Michael Goulder and John Hick, *Why Believe in God?* (London: SCM Press, 1983), p. 44.
74. Hick, *Interpretation*, p. 242.
75. Immanuel Kant, *Critique of Pure Reason*, trans. Norman Kemp Smith (London: Macmillan: 1933), p. 88. Quoted by Hick in *Interpretation*, p. 241. Kant's emphasis.
76. Hick, *Interpretation*, p. 241.
77. Kant, *Critique of Pure Reason*, p. 268. Quoted by Hick, *Interpretaion*, p. 241. Kant's emphasis. It should be pointed out, however, that Kant does use the term *noumenon* in a positive sense, insofar as it is that which makes possible everything else.
78. Hick, *Interpretation*, p. 244.
79. Ibid.
80. Immanuel Kant, *Prolegomena to Any Future Metaphysics*, trans. Paul Carus, rev. James W. Ellington (Indianapolis: Hackett, 1977), p. 66.
81. Paul Eddy, "Religious Pluralism and the Divine: Another Look at John Hick's Neo-Kantian Proposal," *Religious Studies* 30 (1994): 475.
82. Ibid. The article Eddy is drawing on here is J. William Forgie, "Hyper-Kantianism in Recent Discussions of Mystical Experience," *Religious Studies* 21 (1985): 205–18. It should be said that Forgie's "hyper-Kantian" label is a more apposite one for Hick's project than Eddy's preferred "neo-Kantian."
83. John Hick replies to Eddy's criticism by claiming that his appeal to Kantian epistemology does not entail that the entirety of religious experience is supplied by the experiencer. He says that the Real is affecting us all the time, and that when we allow this to come to consciousness, it does so in the various forms of what we call religious experience: "The 'givenness'" of the experience is thus the impact upon the human spirit of the Divine, whilst the 'form' that the experience takes is supplied

by our own religious concepts and imagery" ("Religious Pluralism and the Divine: A Response to Paul Eddy," *Religious Studies* 31 [1995]: 419). The difficulty with this is that Hick's affirmation of the "impact upon the human spirit of the Divine" seems contentless as well as arbitrary and groundless. If the images and even the concepts in the experience originate from the experiencer, one is left wondering what exactly it is that "impacts upon the human spirit."

84. Hick, *Interpretation*, p. 350.
85. In this chapter, I again concentrate on Cupitt's transition, but one could also trace a related transition in the work of Mark C.Taylor, from *Journeys to Selfhood: Hegel and Kierkegaard* (Berkeley: University of California Press, 1980), through *Deconstructing Theology* (Atlanta: Scholars Press, 1982), to *Erring: A Postmodern A/Theology* (Chicago: University of Chicago Press, 1984). In Taylor's case, however, the modernist pressures that tipped him into postmodernism are more Hegelian than Kantian. For a discussion of this transition, see Mark C. Taylor, "Retracings," in Jon R. Stone, ed., *The Craft of Religious Studies* (Basingstoke: Macmillan, 1998), pp. 258–76.
86. Don Cupitt, "Preface to the Second Edition" in *Christ and the Hiddenness of God*, 2d ed. (London: SCM Press, 1985), p. 5.
87. See Don Cupitt, "Mansel's Theory of Regulative Truth," *Journal of Theological Studies* 18 (1967): 104–26.
88. Reardon, *Kant as Philosophical Theologian*, p. 180.
89. Ibid., p. 181.
90. Cupitt, *Christ and the Hiddenness of God*, p. 43.
91. Don Cupitt, *The Leap of Reason*, 2d ed. (London: SCM Press, 1985), pp. 75–76.
92. Ibid., p. 76.
93. Ibid., p. 78.
94. See Rowan Williams, "'Religious Realism': On Not Quite Agreeing with Don Cupitt," *Modern Theology* 1 (1984): pp. 3, 22 n. 3.
95. Cupitt, *Leap of Reason*, p. 55.
96. Ibid., p. 65.
97. Cupitt, "Thin-Line Theism," p. 902.
98. Ibid.
99. Stephen Ross White, *Don Cupitt and the Future of Christian Doctrine* (London: SCM Press, 1994), p. 71.
100. Don Cupitt, *Taking Leave of God* (London: SCM Press, 1980), p. 13.
101. See Denys Turner, "Cupitt, the Mystics and the 'Objectivity' of God," in Colin Crowder, ed., *God and Reality: Essays on Christian Non-Realism* (London: Mowbray, 1997), pp. 114–27.
102. Don Cupitt, "Kant and the Negative Theology," in Brian Hebblethwaite and Stewart Sutherland, eds., *The Philosophical Frontiers of Christian Theology* (Cambridge: Cambridge University Press, 1982), p. 60.
103. Ibid.
104. Ibid., p. 58.
105. Ibid., p. 59.
106. Cupitt, *Taking Leave of God*, p. 76.
107. Ibid., p. 77.
108. Ibid.
109. Immanuel Kant, *Religion within the Limits of Reason Alone*, trans. Theodore M. Greene and Hoyt H. Hudson (New York: Harper & Row, 1960), p. 3.
110. Ibid., pp. 3–4.
111. Balthasar, *Glory of the Lord*, vol. 5, p. 497.
112. See John Milbank, "Sublimity: The Modern Transcendent," in Paul Heelas, ed., *Religion, Modernity and Postmodernity* (Oxford: Basil Blackwell, 1998), p. 265.

113. See Kenneth E. Kirk, *The Vision of God: The Christian Doctrine of the Summum Bonum* (London: Longmans, 1931), pp. 415–72.
114. Milbank, "Sublimity," p. 265.
115. John Milbank, "Can a Gift Be Given? Prolegomena to a Future Trinitarian Metaphysic," *Modern Theology* 11 (1995): 132.
116. See Don Cupitt, "After Liberalism," in D. W. Hardy and P. H. Sedgwick, eds., *The Weight of Glory* (Edinburgh: T. & T. Clark, 1991), p. 255.
117. Ibid., p. 254. My emphasis.
118. Graham Ward, "Postmodern Theology," in David F. Ford, ed., *The Modern Theologians*, 2d ed. (Oxford: Blackwell, 1997), p. 590.
119. John Milbank, "History of the One God," *Heythrop Journal* 38 (1997): 396.
120. See John Milbank, *The Word Made Strange: Theology, Language, Culture* (Oxford: Blackwell, 1997), chap. 2.
121. Ibid., p. 9.
122. Ibid.
123. See ibid., pp. 9–10. See also Kant, *Prolegomena*, p. 93. Kant says that boundaries (in extended beings) "always presuppose a space existing outside a certain definite space and inclosing it; limits do not require this, but are mere negations which affect a quantity so far as it is not absolutely complete. But our reason, as it were, sees in its surroundings a space for the cognition of things in themselves, though we can never have determinate concepts of them and are limited to appearances only."
124. Milbank, *Word Made Strange*, p. 11.
125. Ibid.
126. John Milbank, "Knowledge: The Theological Critique of Philosophy in Hamann and Jacobi," in John Milbank, Catherine Pickstock, and Graham Ward, eds., *Radical Orthodoxy: A New Theology* (London: Routledge, 1999), p. 26.
127. Ibid., p. 27.
128. See ibid., p. 32.
129. Ibid.
130. Ibid.
131. Milbank, *Word Made Strange*, p. 112.

Chapter 3. Disputes and Frameworks

1. Ludwig Wittgenstein, *On Certainty*, ed. G. E. M. Anscombe and G. H. von Wright, trans. Denis Paul and G. E. M. Anscombe (Oxford: Basil Blackwell, 1969), §609, p. 80.
2. Ibid., §611, p. 81.
3. Ibid., §612, p. 81.
4. Ibid., §617, p. 82.
5. Ludwig Wittgenstein, *Lectures and Conversations on Aesthetics, Psychology and Religious Belief*, ed. Cyril Barrett (Oxford: Basil Blackwell, 1969), p. 27.
6. Ibid., p. 28.
7. Ibid.
8. John Hick, "Preface to Reissue," in John Hick, ed., *The Myth of God Incarnate*, 2d ed. (London: SCM Press, 1993), p. xii.
9. Don Cupitt, "Preface to the Second Edition," in *Crisis of Moral Authority*, 2d ed. (London: SCM Press, 1985), p. 9.
10. Michael Dummett, "Realism" (1963), in *Truth and Other Enigmas* (London: Duckworth, 1978), p. 146.
11. Don Cupitt, *The Last Philosophy* (London: SCM Press, 1995), p. 148. It should be noted that Cupitt prefers to describe his own position as "*non*-realist." He says, "Because non-realism does not give rise to such sudden and disconcerting paradoxes as anti-realism, it is more suitable for popularization" (p. 149).

12. "The name, the definition, and the referent for atheism are set by the going theism. The *meaning* of atheism, then, is always dialectical, that is, it merges from its contradiction" (Michael J. Buckley, *At the Origins of Modern Atheism* [New Haven, Conn.: Yale University Press, 1987], p. 338).

13. Ludwig Wittgenstein, *Philosophical Remarks*, trans. Raymond Hargreaves and Roger White (Oxford: Basil Blackwell, 1975), p. 86.

14. See Fergus Kerr, "What's Wrong with Realism Anyway?" in Colin Crowder, ed., *God and Reality: Essays on Christian Non-Realism* (London: Mowbray, 1997), p. 131.

15. Fergus Kerr, *Theology after Wittgenstein*, 2d ed. (London: SPCK, 1997), p. 123.

16. Martin Heidegger, *Basic Questions of Philosophy: Selected 'Problems' of 'Logic'*, trans. Richard Rojcewicz and André Schuwer (Bloomington: Indiana University Press, 1994), p. 11.

17. Ibid., p. 14.

18. Ibid.

19. Ibid., pp. 16–17.

20. Ibid., p. 17.

21. I am grateful to Laurence Hemming for discussions on Heidegger's evaluation of the realist/anti-realist framework.

22. Thomas S. Kuhn, *The Structure of Scientific Revolutions* (Chicago: University of Chicago Press, 1962), p. 110.

23. Ibid., pp. 118, 120, 125.

24. It should be noted that Kuhn's account has been subject to numerous criticisms, one of the most prominent of which is that articulated by Donald Davidson in his *Inquiries into Truth and Interpretation* (Oxford: Clarendon, 1984), essays 9 and 13. Davidson's main criticism is that Kuhn's "metaphor" of "different worlds" entails "a dualism of total scheme (or language) and uninterpreted content" (p. 187). He dismisses the concept of incommensurate conceptual schemes as incoherent. In Malcolm Bull's words, Davidson's argument against relativism "involves totalising relativity so that it is no longer meaningful to speak of it" (*Seeing Things Hidden: Apocalypse, Vision and Totality* [London: Verso, 1999], p. 180). For a defense of the idea of "incommensurate conceptual schemes," however, see John Milbank's convincing reply to Davidson in *Theology and Social Theory: Beyond Secular Reason* (Oxford: Basil Blackwell, 1990), chap. 11.

25. If I am right in my suggestion that Hick and Cupitt stand at opposite ends of a common framework, it may be expected that Hick (mis)responds to radical orthodoxy in essentially the same way as Cupitt does. I have elsewhere demonstrated that this is indeed the case. See Gavin Hyman, "Hick and Loughlin on Disputes and Frameworks," *New Blackfriars* 79 (1998): 391–405.

26. See Rowan Williams, "'Religious Realism': On Not Quite Agreeing with Don Cupitt," *Modern Theology* 1 (1984): 3–24; and Graham Ward, "Postmodern Theology," in David F. Ford, ed., *The Modern Theologians*, 2d ed. (Oxford: Blackwell, 1997), pp. 585–601.

27. I have already suggested that what unites the many and diverse theologians of radical orthodoxy is the shared conviction that the end of modernity creates a space for the return of an authentic theological metanarrative. Furthermore, they would all agree that the realist/anti-realist framework is a fundamentally inappropriate one within which to discuss theological questions. Insofar as Rowan Williams shares these convictions, we may broadly place him in a radical orthodox framework. In his article "Postmodern Theology" (p. 593), Graham Ward has connected Williams's work with that of John Milbank, Edith Wyschogrod, and Ward himself and suggests that they share a common methodological approach, which he describes as "conservative postmodern theology." In the context of this chapter, it seems apposite to fol-

low Ward in placing Williams in a framework common with Milbank and other radical orthodox theologians. At the same time, however, it should be recognized that there are very substantial divergences in the respective projects of Milbank and Williams.

28. See Don Cupitt, "A Reply to Rowan Williams," *Modern Theology* 1 (1984): 25–31; and Don Cupitt, "My Postmodern Witch," *Modern Believing* 39, 4 (1998): 5–10.
29. Williams, "Religious Realism," p. 4.
30. Ibid.
31. This task of "persuasion" is one shared by all radically orthodox theologians. As John Milbank has said, his task is to "*persuade* people—for reasons of 'literary taste'—that Christianity offers a much better story" (*Theology and Social Theory*, p. 330).
32. Williams, "Religious Realism," p. 5.
33. Williams criticized points of view that Cupitt no longer holds and made his own points against Cupitt that the latter later came to accept. For instance: "The language we learn already encodes for us certain ways of perceiving, of 'arranging' the world. It is strictly unimaginable what it would be like to arrive at a way of seeing free from linguistic conditioning (langauge is not a *hindrance* to understanding, a veil between mind and truth)" (Williams, "'Religious Realism,'" p. 8). This is something that Cupitt himself would come to accept in a few years time and, indeed, was to become the central insight of his philosophy, so that he later abandoned the "contextless creation of moral values" that Williams is here criticizing.
34. Williams, "Religious Realism," p. 13.
35. Ibid., p. 17.
36. Ibid., p. 19.
37. See Rowan Williams, "Foreword," in Crowder, ed., *God and Reality*, p. vi.
38. Cupitt, "Reply to Rowan Williams," p. 26.
39. Williams, "Religious Realism," p. 3.
40. Cupitt, "Reply to Rowan Williams," p. 26. My emphasis.
41. This point has been made by Graham Ward in conversation.
42. Cupitt, "Reply to Rowan Williams," p. 26.
43. Ludwig Wittgenstein, *Remarks on the Foundations of Mathematics*, ed. G. H. von Wright, R. Rhees, and G. E. M. Anscombe, trans. G. E. M. Anscombe (Oxford: Basil Blackwell, 1978), 6. 23, p. 325. Quoted in Kerr, *Theology after Wittgenstein*, p. 131.
44. Cupitt, "My Postmodern Witch," p. 8.
45. Ibid., p. 9.
46. It should be noted that Cupitt has also been criticized for reading John of the Cross, Meister Eckhart, and certain strands of Buddhist thought in terms of his essentially alien realist/anti-realist framework. On John of the Cross, see Williams, "Religious Realism," p. 18; on Eckhart, see Denys Turner, "Cupitt, the Mystics and the 'Objectivity' of God," in Crowder, ed., *God and Reality*, pp. 122–24; and on Buddhism, see Gavin Hyman, "Towards a New Religious Dialogue: Buddhism and Postmodern Theology," *Heythrop Journal* 39 (1998): 394–412.
47. Janet Martin Soskice makes the point that Cupitt has not taken account of this paradigm shift when she says that Cupitt's greatest but unspoken debt is to Locke, Hobbes, and Hume, being in the mainstream of empiricist assessments of religious language. See her *Metaphor and Religious Language* (Oxford: Oxford University Press, 1985), p. 142.

Chapter 4. Narrative, Metanarrative, and Theology

1. Aidan Nichols, "'Non tali auxilio': John Milbank's Suasion to Orthodoxy," *New Blackfriars* 73 (1992): 326–27.
2. Jean-François Lyotard, *The Postmodern Condition: A Report on Knowledge,* trans.

Geoff Bennington and Brian Massumi (Manchester: Manchester University Press, 1984), p. 27.

3. Graham Ward, "John Milbank's Divina Commedia," *New Blackfriars* 73 (1992): 315.

4. See John Milbank, *The Religious Dimension in the Thought of Giambattista Vico, 1688–1744*, 2 vols. (Lampeter: Edwin Mellen Press, 1991–1992).

5. John Milbank, *Theology and Social Theory: Beyond Secular Reason* (Oxford: Basil Blackwell, 1990), p. 147. Milbank is "for" Hegel, however, in his theological critique of Enlightenment, his historical narration of the interconnection between politics and religion, his self-critique of Christian historical practice, and the transformation of the philosophical by the theological, so that thought itself becomes inescapably Christian. These four "Hegelian tasks" are taken up and developed by Milbank in chapter 6.

6. Ibid., p. 177. Again, however, Milbank is "for" Marx in that he may be read as a deconstructor of the secular, and that "certain elements of the Marxist critique of capitalism and the state need to be retained and re-elaborated."

7. Gerard Loughlin, "Christianity at the End of the Story, or the Return of the Master-Narrative," *Modern Theology* 8 (1992): 380–81.

8. Paul Julian Smith, *The Body Hispanic: Gender and Sexuality in Spanish and Spanish American Literature* (Oxford: Clarendon Press, 1989), pp. 179–80.

9. Jean-François Lyotard, "Universal History and Cultural Differences," in Andrew Benjamin, ed., *The Lyotard Reader* (Oxford: Basil Blackwell, 1989), p. 318.

10. John Milbank, Catherine Pickstock, and Graham Ward, "Introduction," in John Milbank, Catherine Pickstock, and Graham Ward, eds., *Radical Orthodoxy: A New Theology* (London: Routledge, 1999), p. 3.

11. Ibid.

12. Ibid., p. 4.

13. Milbank, *Theology and Social Theory*, p. 1.

14. Steven Shakespeare, "The New Romantics: A Critique of Radical Orthodoxy," *Theology* 103 (2000): 167.

15. Michel de Certeau, *The Mystic Fable*, vol. 1: *The Sixteenth and Seventeenth Centuries*, trans. Michael B. Smith (Chicago: University of Chicago Press, 1992), p. 123.

16. Ibid., pp. 89–90. See also Graham Ward, "Karl Barth's Postmodernism," *Zeitschrift für dialektische Theologie* 14 (1998): 34.

17. de Certeau, *Mystic Fable*, vol. 1, p. 88.

18. See Stephen Toulmin, *Cosmopolis: The Hidden Agenda of Modernity* (Chicago: University of Chicago Press, 1990), pp. 107–8.

19. Ibid., p. 107.

20. On this, see Gerard Loughlin, "See-Saying/Say-Seeing," *Theology* 91 (1988): 201–9.

21. John Milbank, "Postmodern Critical Augustinianism: A Short *Summa* in Forty Two Responses to Unasked Questions," *Modern Theology* 7 (1991): 225.

22. Ibid., p. 226.

23. John D. Caputo, "Post-Secular, Para-Secular" (unpublished paper delivered at the Annual Meeting of the American Academy of Religion in Nashville, Tennessee, 19 November 2000), p. 2.

24. Catherine Pickstock similarly argues that this doctrine exonerates Plato of the charges of dualism and otherworldliness. See her *After Writing: The Liturgical Consummation of Philosophy* (Oxford: Blackwell, 1997), chap. 1.

25. Ward, "John Milbank's Divina Commedia," pp. 311–12.

26. Milbank, *Theology and Social Theory*, p. 2.

27. John Milbank, *The Word Made Strange: Theology, Language, Culture* (Oxford: Blackwell, 1997), p. 85.

28. John Milbank, "The Sublime in Kierkegaard," in Phillip Blond, ed., *Post-Secular Philosophy: Between Philosophy and Theology* (London: Routledge, 1998), p. 132. Catherine Pickstock makes a similar point in reply to those who would accuse radical orthodoxy of "nostalgia." She says that "the past only existed as part of the forward flow of time, so to cleave lacrimally to it as if it were some lost locus of magnificence is not to be true to the past in its own emergence." "Radical Orthodoxy and the Mediations of Time," in Laurence Paul Hemming, ed., *Radical Orthodoxy?—A Catholic Enquiry* (Aldershot: Ashgate, 2000), pp. 63–64.

29. Milbank, "Sublime in Kierkegaard," p. 140.

30. Don Cupitt, "My Postmodern Witch," *Modern Believing* 39, 4 (1998): 5.

31. Augustine, *The Trinity*, trans. Edmund Hill (New York: New City Press, 1991), p. 437. Quoted in Gerard Loughlin, *Telling God's Story: Bible, Church and Narrative Theology* (Cambridge: Cambridge University Press, 1996), p. 102.

32. Milbank, "Postmodern Critical Augustinianism," p. 229.

33. Ibid.

34. Wayne John Hankey, "Re-Christianizing Augustine Postmodern Style: Readings by Jacques Derrida, Robert Dodaro, Jean-Luc Marion, Rowan Williams, Lewis Ayres and John Milbank," *Animus* 2 (1997), an electronic journal at http://www.mun.ca/animus, para. 69. A similar point has been made by Steven Shakespeare, who refers to radical orthodoxy's "patron saint," Augustine, "who happily recommended the violent persecution of schismatics. 'Compel them to come in': after all, it was for their own good, and you couldn't expect their poor corrupted wills to do anything about it. Only God's grace could save—and that grace found embodiment in the unsheathed sword of an empire driven by the Church" ("New Romantics," p. 174).

35. Milbank, *Theology and Social Theory*, p. 403.

36. Ibid.

37. Robert Dodaro, "Loose Canons: Augustine and Derrida on Themselves," in John D. Caputo and Michael J. Scanlon, eds., *God, the Gift and Postmodernism* (Bloomington: Indiana University Press, 1999), p. 89.

38. Milbank, *Theology and Social Theory*, p. 402.

39. Dodaro, "Loose Canons," p. 89.

40. Ibid.

41. Augustine, *Sermo* 13.7. Quoted in Dodaro, "Loose Canons," p. 91.

42. Dodaro, "Loose Canons," p. 91.

43. Ibid., p. 92.

44. Hankey, "Re-Christianizing Augustine," para. 73.

45. See Romand Coles, "Storied Others and Possibilities of *caritas*: Milbank and Neo-Nietzschean Ethics," *Modern Theology* 8 (1992): 349.

46. G. W. F. Hegel, *The Phenomenology of Spirit*, trans. A. V. Miller (Oxford: Clarendon Press, 1977), 808, p. 493.

47. Ibid., 77, p. 49.

48. Ibid., 89, p. 57.

49. On the "mastery" of reality, see Gerard Loughlin, "Prefacing Pluralism: John Hick and the Mastery of Religions," *Modern Theology* 7 (1990): 29–55.

50. Milbank, *Theology and Social Theory*, p. 6.

51. Ward, "John Milbank's Divina Commedia," p. 312.

52. Milbank, *Theology and Social Theory*, p. 298.

53. Ibid., p. 6. My emphasis.

54. As Graham Ward asks, "What enables Milbank to know? What authorizes John Milbank to assert that differences can remain different in an ontology of peace; what enables him to write this Christian metanarrative from God's perspective?" ("John Milbank's Divina Commedia," p. 317).

55. Loughlin, "Christianity at the End of the Story," p. 374.
56. Milbank, *The Word Made Strange*, p. 1. This passage is quoted by Steven Shakespeare in "New Romantics," pp. 172–73, and is referred to by Gareth Jones in his review of *The Word Made Strange* by John Milbank, *Reviews in Religion and Theology* 2 (1997): 6. Jones mischievously paraphrases this passage as follows: "In the beginning was God. And God spoke God's Word, Jesus Christ: revelation. The church worshipped the Word, in truth. Then came theologians: they messed everything up, because they persisted in trying to accommodate God's Word to society's words—'the most puerile form of betrayal' (p. 1). But fear not: now there is John Milbank, and everything will be fine again."
57. Shakespeare, "New Romantics," p. 173. Graham Ward makes a similar point when he says: "If all differences are to be accorded a place within the unfolding creativity of the Godhead, then there can only be *one* metanarrative; for there is only one meta-narrator. But how does the Christian story relate to this one metanarrative? Does John Milbank not too readily assume that they are the same?" ("John Milbank's Divina Commedia," p. 316).
58. Oliver Davies, "Revelation and the Politics of Culture: A Critical Assessment of the Theology of John Milbank," in Hemming, ed., *Radical Orthodoxy?* p. 123.
59. Ibid., pp. 123–24.
60. I am, however, only too well aware that I have had to resort to a similar philosophical and writing style in order to "out-narrate" Milbank.
61. Gillian Rose, *The Broken Middle: Out of Our Ancient Society* (Oxford: Blackwell, 1992), p. 279.
62. S. W. Sykes, "Theology through History," in David F. Ford, ed., *The Modern Theologians*, 2d ed. (Oxford: Blackwell, 1997), p. 231.
63. Milbank, *Theology and Social Theory*, p. 1.
64. Ibid., p. 347.
65. Milbank reports that a similar point has been made by Michael Banner. See John Milbank, "The Programme of Radical Orthodoxy," in Hemming, ed., *Radical Orthodoxy?* p. 37.
66. Ibid.
67. Ibid.
68. Loughlin, "Christianity at the End of the Story," p. 381.
69. Ibid. My emphasis of "content."
70. Milbank, *Theology and Social Theory*, p. 424.
71. Ibid., pp. 429–30.
72. For an alternative contemporary reading, see David Brown, *The Divine Trinity* (London: Duckworth, 1985). For Brown, it is important that the doctrine of the Trinity and incarnation can be "substantiated" by examination of the "evidence" (p. 105). He also claims that "the doctrine of the Trinity depend[s] for its justification on certain key experiences" (p. xi). For Brown, it is important to provide "justification" of the doctrine (chaps. 3 and 4) and also to prove its "coherence" (chap. 7). Such an approach to the doctrine is clearly antithetical to that of Milbank.
73. Milbank, "Postmodern Critical Augustinianism," p. 227. My emphases.
74. Graham Ward, *Theology and Contemporary Critical Theory*, 2d ed. (London: MacMillan, 2000), p. 4.
75. See Milbank, *Theology and Social Theory*, pp. 382–88.
76. Milbank, "Postmodern Critical Augustinianism," p. 231.
77. Ibid., p. 232.
78. Another example of this would be Milbank's adoption of Balthasar's narrative that "positions" premodernity and modernity, as we considered in chapter 2.
79. Milbank, *Theology and Social Theory*, p. 381.

80. Ibid., p. 417. My emphasis.
81. Ibid., p. 347.
82. Gerard Loughlin, for instance, argues that John Hick and Maurice Wiles employ this method of "translation," particularly when they mistreat theological "myths" as "allegories." He quotes Paul Ricoeur as saying that allegories "can always be translated into a text that can be understood by itself; once this better text has been made out, the allegory falls away like a useless garment; what the allegory showed, while concealing it, can be said in a direct discourse that replaces the allegory" (Paul Ricouer, *The Symbolism of Evil* [Boston: Beacon Press, 1969], p. 163; quoted by Gerard Loughlin in "Myths, Signs and Significations," *Theology* 89 [1986]: 271–72). For a discussion on how this method is applied by liberal theologians to the Jesus narratives, see also Gerard Loughlin, "On Telling the Story of Jesus," *Theology* 87 (1984): 323–29.
83. R. R. Reno, "The Radical Orthodoxy Project," *First Things* 100 (2000): 40. My emphasis.
84. Ibid.
85. Ibid.
86. Milbank, *Theology and Social Theory*, p. 397.
87. Reno, "The Radical Orthodoxy Project," p. 40.
88. Ibid., p. 41.
89. Ibid., p. 42.
90. Ibid., p. 43.
91. Lyotard, "Universal History," p. 318.
92. Jean-François Lyotard, *The Differend: Phrases in Dispute*, trans. Georges Van Den Abbeele (Manchester: Manchester University Press, 1988), p. 136.
93. Wayne J. Hankey, "*Theoria versus Poesis*: Neoplatonism and Trinitarian Difference in Aquinas, John Milbank, Jean-Luc Marion and John Zizioulas," *Modern Theology* 15 (1999): 393.
94. See ibid. More broadly, Graham Ward acknowledges the extent to which radical orthodoxy is itself a product of a certain cultural politics. He says that radical orthodoxy "is also historically and culturally embedded, and contingent. It is not a view from nowhere. It is not free of ideologies itself" ("Radical Orthodoxy and/as Cultural Politics" in Hemming, ed., *Radical Orthodoxy?* p. 108).
95. Frederick Christian Bauerschmidt, "The Word Made Speculative? John Milbank's Christological Poetics," *Modern Theology* 15 (1999): 429.
96. Ibid., p. 417.
97. See ibid., p. 429.
98. Coles, "Storied Others and Possibilities of *Caritas*," p. 349.
99. Milbank, *Theology and Social Theory*, p. 335.
100. Milbank, "Postmodern Critical Augustinianism," p. 225.
101. Milbank, *Theology and Social Theory*, p. 279.
102. Ibid., p. 347.
103. Ibid., p. 330.
104. Ibid.
105. Ibid.
106. Davies, "Revelation and the Politics of Culture," p. 116.
107. Shakespeare, "New Romantics," p. 168.

Chapter 5. (A/)Theology and Nihilism

1. For a rendering of Milbank's project as a "narrative drama," see Gerard Loughlin, "Christianity at the End of the Story or the Return of the Master-Narraative," *Modern Theology* 8 (1992): 365–84.

2. See Michael Allen Gillespie, *Nihilism before Nietzsche* (Chicago: University of Chicago Press, 1995), p. 255.
3. Ibid., p. 256.
4. See John Milbank, "Knowledge: The Theological Critique of Philosophy in Hamann and Jacobi," in John Milbank, Catherine Pickstock, and Graham Ward, eds., *Radical Orthodoxy: A New Theology* (London: Routledge, 1999), p. 24.
5. Richard Freeborn says that this is evident from Turgenev's sketches for his novel: see the "Introduction" to Ivan Turgenev, *Fathers and Sons*, trans. Richard Freeborn (Oxford: Oxford University Press, 1991), p. viii. I am indebted to Freeborn for the background information that follows.
6. Ibid., p. xii.
7. Turgenev, quoted in ibid., p. xiii.
8. Freeborn, "Introduction," p. xiv.
9. Turgenev, *Fathers and Sons*, p. 27.
10. René Descartes, *Meditations on First Philosophy*, trans. and ed. John Cottingham (Cambridge: Cambridge University Press, 1996), p. 12.
11. Karl Barth suggests that René Descartes may have been led to these conclusions if only he had "seriously doubted and not just pretended to do so": see *Church Dogmatics* III/1, ed. G. W. Bromiley and T. F. Torrance, trans. J. W. Edwards, O. Bussey, and Harold Knight (Edinburgh: T. & T. Clark, 1958), p. 362. See also Graham Ward, "Karl Barth's Postmodernism," *Zeitschrift für dialektische Theologie* 14 (1998): 40.
12. Turgenev, *Fathers and Sons*, p. 27.
13. Arthur C. Danto, *Nietzsche as Philosopher*, 2d ed. (New York: Columbia University Press, 1980), p. 29.
14. Friedrich Nietzsche, *The Gay Science*, §347. Quoted in Danto, *Nietzche as Philosopher*, p. 29.
15. Friedrich Nietzsche, *The Gay Science,* §125, in *The Portable Nietzsche*, ed. and trans. Walter Kaufmann (London: Penguin, 1976), p. 95.
16. Friedrich Nietzsche, *Human, All Too Human*, §515, in *The Nietzsche Reader*, ed. and trans. R. J. Hollingdale (London: Penguin, 1977), p. 198.
17. Nietzsche, *The Gay Science*, §109, in *The Nietzsche Reader*, p. 201.
18. Alexander Nehemas, *Nietzsche: Life as Literature* (Cambridge, Mass.: Harvard University Press, 1985), p. 2.
19. Michel Haar, "Nietzsche and Metaphysical Language," in David B. Allison, ed., *The New Nietzsche* (Cambridge, Mass.: MIT Press, 1985), p. 6.
20. Martin Heidegger, *Nietzsche*, vol. 1, trans. David Farrell Krell (London: Routledge & Kegan Paul, 1981), p. 149.
21. Ibid., pp. 152–53.
22. Martin Heidegger, *Schellings Abhandlung über das Wesen der menschlichen Freiheit* (1809), p. 61, trans. and quoted by Laurence Paul Hemming, "Nihilism: Heidegger and the Grounds of Redemption," in Milbank, Pickstock, and Ward, eds., *Radical Orthodoxy*, p. 95.
23. Heidegger, *Nietzsche*, p. 161.
24. Ibid., pp. 209–10.
25. Michael Allen Gillespie, "Heidegger's Nietzsche," *Political Theory* 15 (1987): 431.
26. See Gillespie, *Nihilism before Nietzsche*, pp. 175–76.
27. Walter Kaufmann, *Nietzsche: Philosopher, Psychologist, Antichrist* (Princeton, N.J.: Princeton University Press, 1968), p. 74.
28. Danto, *Nietzsche as Philosopher*, p. 22.
29. Gianni Vattimo, "Nietzsche and Contemporary Hermeneutics," in Yirmiyahu Yovel, ed., *Nietzsche as Affirmative Thinker* (Dordrecht: Martinus Nijhoff, 1986), p. 61.
30. Gillespie, *Nihilism before Nietzsche*, p. 178.

31. See Gillespie, "Heidegger's Nietzsche," pp. 428–29.
32. Jacques Derrida, "Interpreting Signatures (Nietzsche/Heidegger): Two Questions," in Laurence A. Rickels, ed., *Looking after Nietzsche* (Albany: State University of New York Press, 1990), p. 12.
33. Gillespie, "Heidegger's Nietzsche," p. 429.
34. Ibid., p. 431.
35. See ibid., pp. 431–32.
36. Friedrich Nietzsche, *Beyond Good and Evil*, trans. Helen Zimmern (London: George Allen & Unwin, 1967), §232, p. 183.
37. Jacques Derrida, *Spurs: Nietzsche's Styles*, trans. Barbara Harlow (Chicago: University of Chicago Press, 1978), p. 85.
38. Vattimo, "Nietzsche and Contemporary Hermeneutics," p. 61.
39. Ibid., p. 66.
40. Ibid.
41. See ibid., pp. 67–68.
42. Gianni Vattimo, *The End of Modernity: Nihilism and Hermeneutics in Post-Modern Culture*, trans. Jon R. Snyder (Cambridge: Polity Press, 1988), p. 29.
43. Derrida, *Spurs*, p. 103.
44. Ibid., p. 107.
45. See ibid., p. 135.
46. Gianni Vattimo, "The Trace of the Trace," in Jacques Derrida and Gianni Vattimo, eds., *Religion* (Cambridge: Polity Press, 1998), p. 93.
47. See Vattimo, *End of Modernity*, p. 103.
48. Catherine Pickstock, *After Writing: The Liturgical Consummation of Philosophy* (Oxford: Blackwell, 1987), p. 94.
49. Mark C. Taylor, *Altarity* (Chicago: University of Chicago Press, 1987), p. 144.
50. See Jean-François Lyotard, *The Differend: Phrases in Dispute*, trans. Georges Van Der Abbeele (Manchester: Manchester University Press, 1988), passim.
51. As I shall show, Milbank conceives of nihilism on several different "levels" of interpretation. On the one hand, he follows Augustine in reading nihilism *theologically*, as that which falls outside God's creative and "conservative" activity. On the other hand, he conceives of nihilism as a rival metanarrative to theology, a secular heresy to be out-narrated. In this chapter, I am concerned more with the latter conception. At the same time, it has to be said that the two conceptions are not unrelated.
52. See John Milbank, *Theology and Social Theory: Beyond Secular Reason* (Oxford: Basil Blackwell, 1990), p. 252.
53. See ibid., p. 260.
54. Ibid., p. 261.
55. Ibid., p. 279.
56. See ibid., p. 288.
57. See ibid., p. 282.
58. See ibid., p. 279.
59. Ibid., pp. 281–82.
60. Ibid., p. 288.
61. Derrida, "Interpreting Signatures," p. 12.
62. Eric Blondel, "Nietzsche's Style of Affirmation: The Metaphors of Genealogy," in Yovel, ed., *Nietzsche as Affirmative Thinker*, p. 134.
63. Friedrich Nietzsche, *On the Genealogy of Morality*, trans. Carol Dieth, ed. Keith Ansell-Pearson (Cambridge: Cambridge University Press, 1994), preface, pp. 9–10.
64. See David C. Hoy, "Nietzsche, Hume and the Genealogical Method," in Yovel, ed., *Nietzsche as Affirmative Thinker*, p. 23.
65. Ibid., p. 24.

66. Nietzsche, *On the Genealogy of Morality*, preface, pp. 8–9.
67. Blondel, "Nietzsche's Style of Affirmation," p. 136.
68. In Milbank's discussion of Nietzsche's *Genealogy* in *Theology and Social Theory*, he refers to essay three but once (p. 322, n. 19) and does not refer to the preface at all. In contrast, he refers repeatedly to essays one and two (see pp. 321–22, nn. 5–20).
69. On the significance of the "preface," see Jacques Derrida, *Dissemination*, trans. Barbara Johnson (London: Athone Press, 1981), pp. 3–59. See also Gerard Loughlin, "Prefacing Pluralism: John Hick and the Mastery of Religions," *Modern Theology* 7 (1990): 29–55, but especially 29–31, to which I am particularly indebted at this point.
70. Nietzsche, *On the Genealogy of Morality*, preface, p. 6.
71. Ibid., pp. 8–9.
72. Ibid., p. 10.
73. Ibid., essay three, pp. 91–92.
74. Ibid., p. 92.
75. Ibid., p. 119.
76. Ibid., p. 120.
77. Hoy, "Nietzsche, Hume and the Genealogical Method," p. 31.
78. Milbank, *Theology and Social Theory*, p. 294.
79. John Milbank, "Postmodern Critical Augustinianism: A Short *Summa* in Forty Two Responses to Unasked Questions," *Modern Theology* 7 (1991): 226.
80. As Loughlin points out, "If all master-narratives are rhetorically established, though some are blind to their own rhetoricity, one cannot distinguish the stories one wants from those one does not by reference to the *form* of the story (stories *as* stories are stories are stories), but only by the *content* of the story" ("Christianity at the End of the Story," p. 381).
81. Catherine Pickstock, for instance, concurs with Milbank when she says that "the sceptical postmodern subject still speaks in the face of what is present to it, even though what it announces is the flux of the nothing. Indeed, to announce the flux at all is to *represent* reality, and so the postmodern subject is the modern subject, self-present, contemplative, and distinct from the flux it observes" (*After Writing*, p. 110).
82. Milbank, *Theology and Social Theory*, p. 298.
83. Phillip Blond, "Introduction," in Phillip Blond, ed., *Post-Secular Philosophy: Between Philosophy and Theology* (London: Routledge, 1998), pp. 61–62, n. 38.
84. Loughlin, "Christianity at the End of the Story," p. 378.
85. Vattimo, *End of Modernity*, p. 25.
86. Milbank, *Theology and Social Theory*, pp. 313–14.
87. Ibid., p. 314.
88. Ibid., p. 279.
89. Vattimo, "Nietzsche and Contemporary Hermeneutics," p. 66.
90. Milbank, *Theology and Social Theory*, p. 305.
91. Vattimo, "Trace of the Trace," p. 93.
92. Milbank, Pickstock, and Ward, "Introduction," in *Radical Orthodoxy*, p. 1.
93. Jean-Luc Marion, *God without Being*, trans. Thomas A. Carlson (Chicago: University of Chicago Press, 1991), pp. 37–38.
94. Hemming, "Nihilism," p. 97.
95. Ibid., p. 102.
96. Ibid., p. 105.
97. It should be pointed out that both Marion and Hemming seek a "stronger" return of theology than I am calling for here. Both Marion and Hemming would accord an ultimate priority to theology. But they do at least point to a more nuanced understanding of the relationship between theology and nihilism than is allowed for by Milbank's rhetoric.

98. See Nick Land, *The Thirst for Annihilation: Georges Bataille and Virulent Nihilism* (London: Routledge, 1992), pp. 101f.

99. Augustine, *De genesi contra Manichaeos* 1, 6 (10). Quoted in N. Joseph Torchia, *Creatio ex nihilo and the Theology of St Augustine: The Anti-Manichaean Polemic and Beyond* (New York: Peter Lang, 1999), p. 98.

100. Augustine, "Of True Religion," 17.33–18.35, in *Augustine: Earlier Writings*, trans. John H. S. Burleigh (London: SCM Press, 1953), p. 241.

101. Torchia, *Creatio ex nihilo*, p. 258.

102. Land, *Thirst for Annihilation*, pp. 101–2. It should be said that for both Augustine and Aquinas, of course, such ambiguity of ontological priority would have been anathema.

103. Mark C. Taylor, "Introduction," in Mark C. Taylor, ed., *Critical Terms for Religious Studies* (Chicago: University of Chicago Press, 1998), p. 7.

Chapter 6. (A/)Theology and the "Other"

1. Michel de Certeau, *The Mystic Fable*, vol. 1: *The Sixteenth and Seventeenth Centuries*, trans. Michael B. Smith (Chicago: University of Chicago Press, 1992), p. 299. Phrases such as "movement of perpetual departure," "move through," "pass by," which I use in this chapter, are derived from de Certeau, particularly *The Mystic Fable*.

2. Don Cupitt, *After God: The Future of Religion* (London: Weidenfeld & Nicholson, 1997), p. 91.

3. Ibid.

4. Graham Ward, "Postmodern Theology," in David F. Ford, ed., *The Modern Theologian*, 2d ed. (Oxford: Blackwell, 1997), p. 591.

5. Don Cupitt, *The Last Philosophy* (London: SCM Press, 1995), p. 63.

6. Ward, "Postmodern Theology," p. 591.

7. Ibid., p. 592.

8. Gerard Loughlin, *Telling God's Story: Bible, Church and Narrative Theology* (Cambridge: Cambridge University Press, 1996), p. 17.

9. Don Cupitt, *What Is a Story?* (London: SCM Press, 1991), p. 80. Quoted by Loughlin, *Telling God's Story*, p. 17.

10. Loughlin, *Telling God's Story*, p. 17.

11. Roland Barthes, *Roland Barthes by Roland Barthes*, trans. Richard Howard (New York: Hill & Wang, 1977), p. 172. Quoted in Gerard Loughlin, "Prefacing Pluralism: John Hick and the Mastery of Religions," *Modern Theology* 7 (1990): 29.

12. Quoted in Loughlin, "Prefacing Pluralism," p. 49.

13. Loughlin, "Prefacing Pluralism," p. 49.

14. For a discussion of reflexivity, particularly in relation to Nietzsche, Heidegger, and Derrida, see Hilary Lawson, *Reflexivity: The Post-Modern Predicament* (London: Hutchinson, 1985).

15. Don Cupitt, "Post-Christianity," in Paul Heelas, ed., *Religion, Modernity and Postmodernity* (Oxford: Blackwell, 1998), p. 221.

16. Ibid., p. 222.

17. Cupitt, *Last Philosophy*, p. 121.

18. Ibid.

19. Ibid., p. 25. My emphasis on "sidestep."

20. Cupitt, "Post-Christianity," p. 222. My emphases.

21. Jacques Derrida, *Writing and Difference*, trans. Alan Bass (Chicago: University of Chicago Press, 1978), p. 3.

22. Jean-François Lyotard, *The Differend: Phrases in Dispute*, trans. Georges Van Den Abbeele (Manchester: Manchester University Press, 1988), p. 77.

23. Cupitt, *After God*, p. 100.
24. Graham Ward, "Michel de Certeau's 'Spiritual Spaces,'" *New Blackfriars* 79 (1998): 429.
25. There is often a tendency to "equate" the thought of Taylor and Cupitt. See, for instance, Loughlin, *Telling God's Story*, pp. 10–17; and Ward, "Postmodern Theology," pp. 588–92. But in this chapter, I am suggesting that in many respects their projects are antithetical, particularly with regard to their respective attitudes to the "other." Like the relationship between the radical orthodox writers, the relationship between Taylor and Cupitt should be regarded more as a "family resemblance."
26. Mark C. Taylor, *Disfiguring: Art, Architecture, Religion* (Chicago: University of Chicago Press, 1992), p. 50.
27. Mark C. Taylor, "Introduction," in Mark C. Taylor, ed., *Deconstruction in Context: Literature and Philosophy* (Chicago: University of Chicago Press, 1986), p. 26.
28. Ibid., p. 31.
29. On the distinction between logocentrism and logo centrism, see Taylor, *Disfiguring*, pp. 188–89.
30. Ibid., pp. 222–23.
31. Ibid., p. 230.
32. Ibid., p. 231.
33. Ibid., p. 267.
34. Ibid.
35. Graham Ward has made a similar point in his review essay on Taylor's *About Religion*, "Religionists and Theologians: Toward a Politics of Difference," *Modern Theology* 16 (2000): 541–47.
36. This is the title of a collection of essays of literary criticism by Clive James. In it he says, "In the land of shadows, there are only local patches, instead of a universal incidence, of that remorseless, enervating white light. . . . The land of shadows is where we should be proud to live" (*From the Land of Shadows* [London: Picador, 1983], pp. 11, 9).
37. Mark C. Taylor, *Nots* (Chicago: University of Chicago Press, 1993), p. 152.
38. Ibid., pp. 152–53.
39. Michel de Certeau, "White Ecstasy," in Graham Ward, ed., *The Postmodern God: A Theological Reader* (Oxford: Basil Blackwell, 1997), pp. 155–56, 157–58.
40. Taylor, *Nots*, p. 153.
41. See Ward, "Michel de Certeau's 'Spiritual Spaces,'" p. 440. Speaking of de Certeau's desire for "white ecstasy," Ward says: "This is a denial of incarnation and community, and an appeal to death."
42. de Certeau, *Mystic Fable*, p. 199.
43. See ibid., p. 293.
44. Ibid., p. 299.
45. Luce Giard, "Michel de Certeau's Heterology and the New World," *Representations* 33 (winter 1991): 217.
46. Frederick Christian Bauerschmidt, "Michel de Certeau (1925–1986): Introduction," in Ward, ed., *Postmodern God*, p. 137.
47. Ibid., p. 139.
48. Michel de Certeau, "Is There a Language of Unity?" *Concilium* 6 (1970): 90.
49. Ibid., p. 91.
50. Ibid.
51. Bauerschmidt, "Michel de Certeau," p. 135.
52. Giard, "Michel de Certeau's Heterology," p. 217.
53. Graham Ward, "The Voice of the Other," *New Blackfriars* 77 (1996): 523.
54. See de Certeau, *Mystic Fable*, p. 15. The term *mystics*, appearing here in italics is a translation of de Certeau's term *la mystique*. Of this, Michael B. Smith says that it

"cannot be rendered accurately by the English word 'mysticism', which would correspond rather to the French *la mysticisme*, and be far too generic and essentialist a term to convey the historical specificity of the subject of this study." He goes on to say that this "grammatical promotion has its parallel in English, in the development of such terms as 'Mathematics' or 'physics', fields of inquiry of increasing autonomy, also taking their names from an adjectival forerunner. I have, therefore, *in extremis*, adopted the bold solution of introducing a made-up English term, *mystics* (always in italics, to distinguish it from the plural of 'a mystic'), to render *la mystique*, a field that might have won (but never did, in English) a name alongside metaphysics, say, or optics" ("Translator's Note," in de Certeau, *Mystic Fable*, pp. ix–x).

55. de Certeau, *Mystic Fable*, p. 77.
56. Ibid.
57. Ibid., p. 15.
58. Michel de Certeau, "Mystic Speech," in *Heterologies: Discourse on the Other*, trans. Brian Massumi (Manchester: Manchester University Press, 1986), pp. 99–100.
59. Ibid., p. 83.
60. de Certeau, "Surin's Melancholy," in *Heterologies*, p. 111.
61. Ibid., p. 113.
62. See Ward, "Michel de Certeau's 'Spiritual Spaces,'" p. 438. He cites "'Feux persistants': Entretiens sur Michel de Certeau," *Esprit* (May 1996): 151.
63. F. C. Bauerschmidt, "The Abrahamic Voyage: Michel de Certeau and Theology," *Modern Theology* 12 (1996): 8.
64. Joseph Moingt, "Traveller of Culture: Michel de Certeau," *New Blackfriars* 77 (1996): 479.
65. This is a brief summary of de Certeau's detailed account of Labadie's nomadic life in *Mystic Fable*, pp. 274–88.
66. de Certeau, *Mystic Fable*, p. 271.
67. Mark C. Taylor, *Erring: a Postmodern A/Theology* (Chicago: University of Chicago Press, 1984), p. 157.
68. de Certeau, *Mystic Fable*, pp. 289–90.
69. See Ward, "Voice of the Other."
70. Ward, "Michel de Certeau's 'Spiritual Spaces,'" p. 439.
71. I am not, however, calling into question the *legitimacy* of Ward's theological interpretation, for de Certeau's texts are open to any number of readings, including the theological. Indeed, I concur with Ward when he says that in the end, the mystery of how de Certeau is to be interpreted remains: "For Certeau himself remains other than himself, because he is now what he has written and excessive to all the ways we try to catalogue him" (Graham Ward, "Introduction," in Graham Ward, ed., *The Certeau Reader* [Oxford: Blackwell, 2000], p. 12).
72. de Certeau, *Mystic Fable*, p. 293. Quoted by Ward, "Michel de Certeau's 'Spiritual Spaces,'" p. 438.
73. I owe this neat way of paraphrasing Zarathustra's command to Don Cupitt, *Solar Ethics* (London: SCM Press, 1995), p. 64. Nietzsche's own words are "Now I bid you lose me and find yourselves; and only when you have all denied me will I return to you" (Friedrich Nietzsche, *Thus Spoke Zarathustra: A Book for All and None*, in *The Portable Nietzsche*, ed. and trans. Walter Kaufmann [London: Penguin, 1976], p. 190).
74. de Certeau, *Mystic Fable*, p. 293. My emphasis.
75. *The Gospel according to Thomas*, logion 42. Quoted in de Certeau, *Mystic Fable*, p. 177.
76. See Michel de Certeau, "The Weakness of Believing: From the Body to Writing, a Christian Transit," in Ward, ed., *Certeau Reader*, p. 237.

77. de Certeau, *Mystic Fable*, p. 292.
78. Ibid.
79. Ward, "Michel de Certeau's 'Spiritual Spaces,'" p. 439.
80. de Certeau, *Mystic Fable*, p. 175.
81. Ibid. He is here quoting Evagrius, *Centuries* 1.1.
82. It is not always clear whether or not Ward thinks de Certeau can avoid this nihilism without the theo-logic provided by, for instance, von Balthasar's trinitarianism. On the one hand, he says that "Certeau avoids this nihilism" through his announcement of an exteriority, an excess, an unnameable that is demanded by his work. But on the other hand, without this theo-logic, Ward asks, "does Certeau's work not leave itself open to a nihilism: an endless dissemination, a multiplicity of Christian languages minus the living God, a wandering without direction or promise into ever deepening exile? Without the theological horizon his project simply continues modernity's secularization of reason" ("Voice of the Other," pp. 527–28).
83. de Certeau, *Mystic Fable*, p. 299.
84. Hadeweijch d'Anvers, *Écrits mystiques* (Paris: Seuil, 1954), p. 134. Quoted in de Certeau, *Mystic Fable*, p. 299.
85. de Certeau, *Mystic Fable*, p. 299.
86. Ward himself acknowledges that de Certeau has no theology of history; see "Michel de Certeau's 'Spiritual Spaces,'" p. 437.
87. de Certeau, *Mystic Fable*, p. 299.
88. See Ward, "Voice of the Other," p. 526.
89. Giard, "Michel de Certeau's Heterology," p. 213.
90. See the reference to Giard's comment in Bauerschmidt, "The Abrahamic Voyage," p. 2. The reference is specifically to de Certeau's membership of the Society of Jesus.
91. de Certeau, "White Ecstasy," pp. 155–56.
92. Ibid., p. 157.
93. Ibid.
94. Ibid., pp. 157–58.
95. Bauerschmidt, "Michel de Certeau," p. 140.
96. When the respective (in)conclusions of *The Mystic Fable* and "White Ecstasy" are viewed in light of each other, they appear to be paradoxically contradictory. Interpreted in terms of my nihilistic typology in chapter 5, it seems that whereas *The Mystic Fable* embodies a form of "fictional nihilism," "White Ecstasy" yearns for a "pure nihilism." Like much else in de Certeau's work, this paradox remains tantalizingly unresolved.

Conclusion

1. Paul S. Fiddes, however, has argued that the contemporary novel is becoming more like the soap opera in the sense that "many modern novelists find it difficult to bring their books to an end." Discussing John Fowles's novel *The French Lieutenant's Woman*, he discusses "the alternative endings provided, though we immediately become aware that the options are not exhausted. There could have been others as well; as Fowles himself points out, life is not to be shrunk to one riddle." And of *Flaubert's Parrot*, by Julian Barnes, he says, "Though the book purports to have one semi-realist ending, it implies several ways of closure. . . . The reluctance to close a novel has been magnified in recent writing" (*The Promised End: Eschatology in Theology and Literature* [Oxford: Basil Blackwell, 2000], pp. 1, 2, 4). For a classic discussion of texts and their "endings," see Frank Kermode, *The Sense of an Ending: Studies in the Theory of Fiction* (Oxford: Oxford University Press, 1967).
2. In his unpublished paper "Post-Secular, Para-Secular" (delivered at the Annual Meeting of the American Academy of Religion in Nashville, Tennessee, 19 November

2000), John D. Caputo made reference to what I perceived to be a similar sort of dual movement which he characterized as a "historical association" and a "messianic dissociation."

3. Graham Ward, "Theology and Postmodernism," *Theology* 100 (1997): 436.

4. For a portrayal of this contemporary "spirit," see Mark C. Taylor's essay "Christianity and the Capitalism of Spirit," in *About Religion: Economics of Faith in Virtual Culture* (Chicago: University of Chicago Press, 1999), pp. 140–67.

5. Michel de Certeau, "White Ecstasy," in Graham Ward, ed., *The Postmodern God: A Theological Reader* (Oxford: Blackwell, 1997), p. 157.

6. See Thomas Aquinas, *Summa theologiae*, vol. 3, trans. Herbert McCabe (London: Blackfriars, 1964), where he says that although "reason can know *that* a simple form is, . . . it cannot attain to understanding *what* it is" (p. 41). "Although in this life revelation does not tell us what God is, and thus joins us to him as an unknown, nevertheless it helps us to know him better in that we are shown more and greater works of his and are taught certain things about him that we could never have known through natural reason" (p. 45).

7. See, for instance, Gerard Loughlin, *Telling God's Story: Bible, Church and Narrative Theology* (Cambridge: Cambridge University Press, 1996), p. 195.

8. John D. Caputo, "God Is Wholly Other—Almost: 'Différance' and the Hyperbolic Alterity of God," in Orrin F. Summerell, ed., *The Otherness of God* (Charlottesville: University Press of Virginia, 1998), p. 191.

9. Ibid., p. 192.

10. It seems that Caputo wants to maintain a radical undecidability with respect to the hypernym and the anonym. On my account, however, it is precisely the decision to conceive of the other in terms of an anonym that opens up this undecidability and brings the hypernym back into play.

11. Carl Raschke, "Indian Territory: Postmodernism under the Sign of the Body" (unpublished paper delivered at the Annual Meeting of the American Academy of Religion in Nashville, Tennessee, 19 November 2000), pp. 6–7.

12. Ibid., p. 12.

13. Ibid.

14. Mark C. Taylor, "Postmodern Times," in Summerell, ed., *Otherness of God*, p. 189.

Bibliography

Alliez, Éric. *Capital Times: Tales from the Conquest of Time.* Translated by Georges Van Den Abbeele. Minneapolis: University of Minnesota Press, 1996.

Altizer, Thomas J. J. *The Gospel of Christian Atheism.* Philadelphia: Westminster Press, 1966.

———. *The Contemporary Jesus.* London: SCM Press, 1998.

Anderson, Perry. *The Origins of Postmodernity.* London: Verso, 1998.

Aquinas, Thomas. *Summa Theologiae.* Vol. 3. Translated by Herbert McCabe. London: Blackfriars, 1964.

Atwood, Margaret. *Cat's Eye.* London: Virago Press, 1990.

Augustine. *Augustine: Earlier Writings.* Translated by John H. S. Burleigh. London: SCM Press, 1953.

Balthasar, Hans Urs von. *The Glory of the Lord: A Theological Aesthetics.* Vol. 5: *The Realm of Metaphysics in the Modern Age.* Translated by Oliver Davies, Andrew Louth, Brian McNeil, John Saward, and Rowan Williams. Edinburgh: T. & T. Clark, 1991.

Barth, Karl. *Church Dogmatics* III/1. Edited by G. W. Bromiley and T. F. Torrance. Translated by J. W. Edwards, O. Bussey, and Harold Knight. Edinburgh: T. & T. Clark, 1958.

Bauerschmidt, Frederick Christian. "The Abrahamic Voyage: Michel de Certeau and Theology." *Modern Theology* 12 (1996): 1–26.

———. "Michel de Certeau (1925–1986): Introduction." In Graham Ward, ed., *The Postmodern God: A Theological Reader,* pp. 135–42. Oxford: Blackwell, 1997.

———. "The Word Made Speculative? John Milbank's Christological Poetics." *Modern Theology* 15 (1999): 417–32.

Bennington, Geoffrey, and Jacques Derrida. *Jacques Derrida.* Translated by Geoffrey Bennington. Chicago: University of Chicago Press, 1993.

Blond, Phillip, ed. *Post-Secular Philosophy: Between Philosophy and Theology.* London: Routledge, 1998.

Blondel, Eric. "Nietzsche's Style of Affirmation: The Metaphors of Genealogy." In Yirmiyahu Yovel, ed., *Nietzsche as Affirmative Thinker,* pp. 132–46. Dordrecht: Martinus Nijhoff, 1986.

Braithwaite, R. B. "An Empiricist's View of the Nature of Religious Belief." In Basil Mitchell, ed., *The Philosophy of Religion,* pp. 72–91. Oxford: Oxford University Press, 1971.

Bromwich, David. "What We Have." *London Review of Books* 21, 3 (1999): 16–18.

Brown, David. *The Divine Trinity.* London: Duckworth, 1985.

Buckley, Michael J. *At the Origins of Modern Atheism.* New Haven, Conn.: Yale University Press, 1987.

Bull, Malcolm. *Seeing Things Hidden: Apocalypse, Vision and Totality.* London: Verso, 1999.

Burrell, David B. *Aquinas: God and Action.* London: Routledge & Kegan Paul, 1979.

Caputo, John D. "God is Wholly Other—Almost: 'Différance' and the Hyperbolic Alterity of God." In Orrin F. Summerell, ed., *The Otherness of God,* pp. 190–205. Charlottesville: University Press of Virginia, 1998.

———. "Post-Secular, Para-Secular." Unpublished paper delivered at the Annual Meeting of the American Academy of Religion in Nashville, Tennessee, 19 November 2000.

Coles, Romand. "Storied Others and Possibilities of *caritas*: Milbank and Neo-Nietzschean Ethics." *Modern Theology* 8 (1992): 319–29.

Cross, Richard. *Duns Scotus.* Oxford: Oxford University Press, 1999.

Cupitt, Don. "Mansel's Theory of Regulative Truth." *Journal of Theological Studies* 18 (1967): 104–26.

———. *Taking Leave of God.* London: SCM Press, 1980.

———. "Thin-Line Theism." *Times Literary Supplement,* 8 August 1980, p. 902.

———. "Kant and the Negative Theology." In Brian Hebblethwaite and Stewart Sutherland, eds., *The Philosophical Frontiers of Christian Theology,* pp. 55–67. Cambridge: Cambridge University Press, 1982.

———. "A Reply to Rowan Williams." *Modern Theology* 1 (1984): 25–31.

———. *Christ and the Hiddenness of God.* 2d ed. London: SCM Press, 1985.

———. *Crisis of Moral Authority.* 2d ed. London: SCM Press, 1985.

———. *The Leap of Reason.* 2d ed. London: SCM Press, 1985.

———. *The Long-Legged Fly.* London: SCM Press, 1987.

———. *What Is a Story?* London: SCM Press, 1991.

———. "After Liberalism." In D. W. Hardy and P. H. Sedgwick, eds., *The Weight of Glory,* pp. 251–56. Edinburgh: T. & T. Clark, 1991.

———. *The Time Being.* London: SCM Press, 1992.

———. *After All: Religion without Alienation.* London: SCM Press, 1994.

———. *The Last Philosophy.* London: SCM Press, 1995.

———. *Solar Ethics.* London: SCM Press, 1995.

———. *After God: The Future of Religion.* London: Weidenfeld and Nicolson, 1997.

———. *Mysticism after Modernity.* Oxford: Blackwell, 1998.

———. "My Postmodern Witch." *Modern Believing* 39, 4 (1998): 5–10.

———. "Post-Christianity." In Paul Heelas, ed., *Religion, Modernity and Postmodernity,* pp. 218–32. Oxford: Blackwell, 1998.

Danto, Arthur C. *Nietzsche as Philosopher.* 2d ed. New York: Columbia University Press, 1980.

Davidson, Donald. *Inquiries into Truth and Interpretation.* Oxford: Clarendon, 1984.

Davies, Oliver. "Revelation and the Politics of Culture: A Critical Assessment of the Theology of John Milbank." In Laurence Paul Hemming, ed., *Radical Orthodoxy?—A Catholic Enquiry,* pp. 112–25. Aldershot: Ashgate, 2000.

de Certeau, Michel. "Is There a Language of Unity?" *Concilium* 6 (1970): 79–93.

———. *The Practice of Everyday Life.* Translated by Steven Rendall. Berkeley: University of California Press, 1984.

———. *Heterologies: Discourse on the Other.* Translated by Brian Massumi. Manchester: Manchester University Press, 1986.

———. *The Writing of History.* Translated by Tom Conley. New York: Columbia University Press, 1988.

————. *The Mystic Fable.* Vol. 1: *The Sixteenth and Seventeenth Centuries.* Translated by Michael B. Smith. Chicago: University of Chicago Press, 1992.

————. "White Ecstasy." In Graham Ward, ed., *The Postmodern God: A Theological Reader*, pp. 155–58. Oxford: Blackwell, 1997.

————. "The Weakness of Believing: From the Body to Writing, a Christian Transit." In Graham Ward, ed., *The Certeau Reader*, pp. 214–43. Oxford: Blackwell, 2000.

Derrida, Jacques. *Of Grammatology.* Translated by Gayatri Chakravorty Spivak. Baltimore: Johns Hopkins University Press, 1976.

————. *Spurs: Nietzsche's Styles.* Translated by Barbara Harlow. Chicago: University of Chicago Press, 1978.

————. *Writing and Difference.* Translated by Alan Bass. Chicago: University of Chicago Press, 1978.

————. *Dissemination.* Translated by Barbara Johnson. London: Athone Press, 1981.

————. *Margins of Philosophy.* Translated by Alan Bass. Chicago: University of Chicago Press: 1984.

————. "Interpreting Signatures (Nietzsche/Heidegger): Two Questions." In Laurence A. Rickels, ed., *Looking after Nietzsche*, pp. 1–17. Albany: State University of New York Press, 1990.

Descartes, René. *Meditations on First Philosophy.* Translated and edited by John Cottingham. Cambridge: Cambridge University Press, 1996.

de Vio, Thomas, Cardinal Cajetan. *The Analogy of Names and the Concept of Being.* Translated by Edward A. Bushinski. 2d ed. Pittsburgh: Duquesne University Press, 1959.

DiCenso, James J. *The Other Freud: Religion, Culture and Psychoanalysis.* London: Routledge, 1999.

Dodaro, Robert. "Loose Canons: Augustine and Derrida on Themselves." In John D. Caputo and Michael J. Scanlon, eds., *God, the Gift and Postmodernism*, pp. 79–111. Bloomington: Indiana University Press, 1999.

Drucker, Peter. *The Landmarks of Tomorrow.* London: Heinemann, 1959.

Dummett, Michael. *Truth and Other Enigmas.* London: Duckworth, 1978.

Duns Scotus, John. *Philosophical Writings.* Edited and translated by Allan Wolter. Edinburgh: Nelson, 1962.

Eddy, Paul. "Religious Pluralism and the Divine: Another Look at John Hick's Neo-Kantian Proposal." *Religious Studies* 30 (1994): 467–78.

Fiddes, Paul S. *The Promised End: Eschatology in Theology and Literature.* Oxford: Blackwell, 2000.

Flew, A. G. N., and A. C. MacIntyre, eds. *New Essays in Philosophical Theology.* London: Macmillan, 1955.

Freud, Sigmund. *Studies on Hysteria.* Translated by James Strachey. In *The Standard Edition of the Complete Psychological Works of Sigmund Freud.* Vol. 2. London: Hogarth Press, 1955.

————. *Moses and Monotheism.* In *The Standard Edition of the Complete Psychological Works of Sigmund Freud.* Vol. 23. London: Hogarth Press, 1964.

————. *The Interpretation of Dreams.* Translated by Joyce Crick. Oxford: Oxford University Press, 1999.

Fukuyama, Francis. *The End of History and the Last Man.* London: Hamish Hamilton, 1992.

Funkenstein, Amos. *Theology and the Scientific Imagination: From the Middle Ages to the Seventeenth Century.* Princeton, N.J.: Princeton University Press, 1986.

Gardner, Lucy, David Moss, Ben Quash, and Graham Ward. *Balthasar at the End of Modernity.* Edinburgh: T. & T. Clark, 1999.

Garfield, Jay L. *The Fundamental Wisdom of the Middle Way.* Oxford: Oxford University Press, 1995.

Giard, Luce. "Michel de Certeau's Heterology and the New World." *Representations* 33 (winter 1991): 212–21.

Gillespie, Michael Allen. "Heidegger's Nietzsche." *Political Theory* 15 (1987): 424–35.

———. *Nihilism before Nietzsche.* Chicago: University of Chicago Press, 1995.

Glass, Newman Robert. "Splits and Gaps in Buddhism and Postmodern Theology." *Journal of the American Academy of Religion* 63 (1995): 303–19.

Goulder, Michael, and John Hick. *Why Believe in God?* London: SCM Press, 1983.

Griffin, David Ray. *Varieties of Postmodern Theology.* Albany: State University of New York Press, 1989.

Haar, Michel. "Nietzsche and Metaphysical Language." In David B. Allison, ed., *The New Nietzsche.* Cambridge, Mass.: MIT Press, 1985, pp. 5–36.

Habermas, Jürgen. "Modernity versus Postmodernity." *New German Critique* 22 (winter 1981): 3–14.

Hankey, Wayne John. "Re-Christianizing Augustine Postmodern Style: Readings by Jacques Derrida, Robert Dodaro, Jean-Luc Marion, Rowan Williams, Lewis Ayres and John Milbank." *Animus* 2 (1997), an electronic journal at http://www.mun.ca/animus.

———. "*Theoria versus Poesis*: Neoplatonism and Trinitarian Difference in Aquinas, John Milbank, Jean-Luc Marion and John Zizioulas," *Modern Theology* 15 (1999): 387–415.

Harvey, David. *The Condition of Postmodernity.* Oxford: Basil Blackwell, 1990.

Hassan, Ihab. *The Dismemberment of Orpheus: Toward a Postmodern Literature.* 2d ed. Madison: University of Wisconsin Press, 1982.

———. "POSTmodernISM: A Paracritical Bibliography." *New Literary History* 3 (autumn 1971): 5–30.

Hastings, Adrian. *A History of English Christianity, 1920–1990.* London: SCM Press, 1991.

Hegel, G. W. F. *The Phenomenology of Spirit.* Translated by A. V. Miller. Oxford: Clarendon Press, 1977.

Heidegger, Martin. *Nietzsche.* Vol. 1. Translated by David Farrell Krell. London: Routledge & Kegan Paul, 1981.

———. *Basic Questions of Philosophy: Selected 'Problems' of 'Logic'.* Translated by Richard Rojcewicz and André Schuwer. Bloomington: Indiana University Press, 1994.

Hemming, Laurence Paul. "Nihilism: Heidegger and the Grounds of Redemption." In John Milbank, Catherine Pickstock, and Graham Ward, eds., *Radical Orthodoxy: A New Theology,* pp. 91–108. London: Routledge, 1999.

Hick, John. *God and the Universe of Faiths.* London: Macmillan, 1973.

———. *Death and Eternal Life.* 2d ed. London: Macmillan, 1985.

———. *Faith and Knowledge.* 2d ed. London: Macmillan, 1988.

———. *An Interpretation of Religion.* Basingstoke: Macmillan, 1989.

———. "Religious Pluralism and the Divine: A Response to Paul Eddy." *Religious Studies* 31 (1995): 417–20.

———, ed. *The Myth of God Incarnate.* 2d ed. London: SCM Press, 1993.

Hoy, David C. "Nietzsche, Hume and the Genealogical Method." In Yirmiyahu Yovel, ed., *Nietzsche as Affirmative Thinker,* pp. 20–38. Dordrecht: Martinus Nijhoff, 1986.

Hyman, Gavin. "Hick and Loughlin on Disputes and Frameworks." *New Blackfriars* 79 (1998): 391–405.

———. Review of *The Contemporary Jesus* by Thomas J. J. Altizer. *Theology* 101 (1998): 447–48.

———. "Towards a New Religious Dialogue: Buddhism and Postmodern Theology." *Heythrop Journal* 39 (1998): 394–412.

————. Review of *Radical Orthodoxy: A New Theology*, ed. John Milbank, Catherine Pickstock, and Graham Ward. *New Blackfriars* 80 (1999): 425–28.

James, Clive. *From the Land of Shadows.* London: Picador, 1983.

Jameson, Fredric. *Postmodernism, or, the Cultural Logic of Late Capitalism.* Durham, N.C.: Duke University Press, 1991.

————. *The Cultural Turn: Selected Writings on the Postmodern, 1983–1998.* London: Verso, 1998.

Jencks, Charles. *The Language of Post-Modern Architecture.* Rev. ed. New York: Rizzoli, 1978.

Jones, Gareth. Review of *The Word Made Strange* by John Milbank. *Reviews in Religion and Theology* 2 (1997): 6.

Kant, Immanuel. *Critique of Pure Reason.* Translated by Norman Kemp Smith. London: Macmillan, 1933.

————. *Religion within the Limits of Reason Alone.* Translated by Theodore M. Greene and Hoyt H. Hudson. New York: Harper & Row, 1960.

————. *Prolegomena to any Future Metaphysics.* Translated by Paul Carus. Revised by James W. Ellington. Indianapolis: Hackett, 1977.

Kaufmann, Walter. *Nietzsche: Philosopher, Psychologist, Antichrist.* Princeton, N.J.: Princeton University Press, 1968.

Kermode, Frank. *The Sense of an Ending: Studies in the Theory of Fiction.* Oxford: Oxford University Press, 1967.

Kerr, Fergus. *Theology after Wittgenstein.* 2d ed. London: SPCK, 1997.

————. "What's Wrong with Realism Anyway?" In Colin Crowder, ed., *God and Reality: Essays on Christian Non-Realism*, pp. 128–43. London: Mowbray, 1997.

Kirk, Kenneth E. *The Vision of God: The Christian Doctrine of the Summum Bonum.* London: Longmans, 1931.

Kuhn, Thomas S. *The Structure of Scientific Revolutions.* Chicago: University of Chicago Press, 1962.

Land, Nick. *The Thirst for Annihilation: Georges Bataille and Virulent Nihilism.* London: Routledge, 1992.

Lawson, Hilary. *Reflexivity: The Post-Modern Predicament.* London: Hutchinson, 1985.

Loughlin, Gerard. "Mirroring God's World: A Critique of John Hick's Speculative Theology." Unpublished diss. University of Cambridge, 1986.

————. "On Telling the Story of Jesus," *Theology* 87 (1984): 323–29.

————. "Paradox and Paradigms." *New Blackfriars* 66 (1985): 127–35.

————. "Persons and Replicas." *Modern Theology* 1 (1985): 303–19.

————. "Myths, Signs and Significations." *Theology* 89 (1986): 268–75.

————. 'Noumenon and Phenomena." *Religious Studies* 23 (1987): 493–508.

————. "See-Saying/Say-Seeing." *Theology* 91 (1988): 201–9.

————. "Prefacing Pluralism: John Hick and the Mastery of Religions." *Modern Theology* 7 (1990): 29–55.

————. "Squares and Circles: John Hick and the Doctrine of the Incarnation." In Harold Hewitt Jr., ed., *Problems in the Philosophy of Religion: Critical Studies of the Work of John Hick*, pp. 181–205. Basingstoke: Macmillan, 1991.

————. "Christianity at the End of the Story or the Return of the Master-Narrative." *Modern Theology* 8 (1992): 365–84.

————. *Telling God's Story: Bible, Church and Narrative Theology.* Cambridge: Cambridge University Press, 1996.

————. "Rains for a Famished Land." *Times Literary Supplement*, 10 April 1998, pp. 12–13.

Lyotard, Jean-François. *The Postmodern Condition: A Report on Knowledge.* Translated by Geoff Bennington and Brian Massumi. Manchester: Manchester University Press, 1984.

————. *The Differend: Phrases in Dispute*. Translated by Georges Van Den Abbeele. Manchester: Manchester University Press, 1988.

————. *The Lyotard Reader*. Edited by Andrew Benjamin. Oxford: Basil Blackwell, 1989.

————. *The Postmodern Explained: Correspondence 1982–1985*. Translated by Don Barry, Bernadette Maher, Julian Pefanis, Virginia Spate, and Morgan Thomas. Edited by Julian Pefanis and Morgan Thomas. Minneapolis: University of Minnesota Press, 1992.

Marion, Jean-Luc. "The Essential Incoherence of Descartes' Definition of Divinity." In Amélie Oksenberg Rorty, ed., *Essays in Descartes' Meditations*, pp. 297–338. Berkeley: University of California Press, 1986.

————. *God without Being*. Translated by Thomas A. Carlson. Chicago: University of Chicago Press, 1991.

Milbank, John. "Man as Creative and Historical Being in Nicholas of Cusa." *Downside Review* 97 (1979): 245–57.

————. *Theology and Social Theory: Beyond Secular Reason*. Oxford: Basil Blackwell, 1990.

————. "'Postmodern Critical Augustinianism': A Short *Summa* in Forty Two Responses to Unasked Questions." *Modern Theology* 7 (1991): 225–37.

————. *The Religious Dimension in the Thought of Giambattista Vico, 1688–1744*. 2 vols. Lampeter: Edwin Mellen Press, 1991–1992.

————. "The End of Enlightenment: Post-Modern or Post-Secular.'" In C. Geffré and J.-P. Jossua, eds., *The Debate on Modernity*, pp. 39–48. London: SCM Press, 1992.

————. "Problematizing the Secular: The Post-Postmodern Agenda." In Philippa Berry and Andrew Wernick, eds., *Shadow of Spirit: Postmodernism and Religion*, pp. 30–44. London: Routledge, 1992.

————. "Can a Gift Be Given? Prolegomena to a Future Trinitarian Metaphysic." *Modern Theology* 11 (1995): 119–61.

————. "History of the One God." *Heythrop Journal* 38 (1997): 371–400.

————. *The Word Made Strange: Theology, Language, Culture*. Oxford: Blackwell, 1997.

————. "The Sublime in Kierkegaard." In Phillip Blond, ed., *Post-Secular Philosophy: Between Philosophy and Theology*, pp. 131–56. London: Routledge, 1998.

————. "Sublimity: The Modern Transcendent." In Paul Heelas, ed., *Religion, Modernity and Postmodernity*, pp. 258–84. Oxford: Blackwell, 1998.

————. "Knowledge: The Theological Critique of Philosophy in Hamann and Jacobi." In John Milbank, Catherine Pickstock, and Graham Ward, eds., *Radical Orthodoxy: A New Theology*, pp. 21–37. London: Routledge, 1999.

————. "The Programme of Radical Orthodoxy." In Laurence Paul Hemming, ed., *Radical Orthodoxy?—A Catholic Enquiry*, pp. 33–45. Aldershot: Ashgate, 2000.

Milbank, John, Catherine Pickstock. and Graham Ward, eds., *Radical Orthodoxy: A New Theology*. London: Routledge, 1999.

Moingt, Joseph. "Traveller of Culture: Michel de Certeau." *New Blackfriars* 77 (1996): 479–83.

Nehemas, Alexander. *Nietzsche: Life as Literature*. Cambridge, Mass: Harvard University Press, 1985.

Nichols, Aidan. "'Non tali auxilio': John Milbank's Suasion to Orthodoxy." *New Blackfriars* 73 (1992): 326–32.

Nietzsche, Friedrich. *Beyond Good and Evil*. Translated by Helen Zimmern. London: George Allen & Unwin, 1967.

————. *The Will to Power*. Translated by Walter Kaufmann and R. J. Hollingdale. Edited by Walter Kaufmann. London: Weidenfeld & Nicolson, 1968.

————. *The Portable Nietzsche*. Edited and translated by Walter Kaufmann. London: Penguin, 1976.

————. *The Nietzsche Reader*. Edited and translated by R. J. Hollingdale. London: Penguin, 1977.

————. *On the Genealogy of Morality*. Translated by Carol Dieth. Edited by Keith Ansell-Pearson. Cambridge: Cambridge University Press, 1994.

Phillips, D. Z. *Faith after Foundationalism*. London: Routledge, 1988.

Pickstock, Catherine. "Necrophilia: The Middle of Modernity. A Study of Death, Signs and the Eucharist." *Modern Theology* 12 (1996): 405–31.

————. *After Writing: The Liturgical Consummation of Philosophy*. Oxford: Blackwell, 1997.

————. "Radical Orthodoxy and the Mediations of Time." In Laurence Paul Hemming, ed., *Radical Orthodoxy?—A Catholic Enquiry*, pp. 63–75. Aldershot: Ashgate, 2000.

Placher, William C. *The Domestication of Transcendence: How Modern Thinking about God Went Wrong*. Louisville, Ky.: Westminster John Knox Press, 1996.

Raschke, Carl. "Indian Territory: Postmodernism under the Sign of the Body." Unpublished paper delivered at the Annual Meeting of the American Academy of Religion in Nashville, Tennessee, 19 November 2000.

Reardon, Bernard M. G. *Kant as Philosophical Theologian*. Basingstoke: Macmillan, 1988.

Reno, R. R. "The Radical Orthodoxy Project." *First Things* 100 (2000): 37–44.

Ricoeur, Paul. "Life in Quest of Narrative." In David Wood, ed., *On Paul Ricoeur: Narrative and Interpretation*, pp. 20–33. London: Routledge, 1991.

Rorty, Richard. *Philosophy and the Mirror of Nature*. Oxford: Basil Blackwell, 1980.

Rose, Gillian. *The Broken Middle: Out of Our Ancient Society*. Oxford: Blackwell, 1992.

Shakespeare, Steven. "The New Romantics: A Critique of Radical Orthodoxy." *Theology* 103 (2000): 163–77.

Smith, Paul Julian. *The Body Hispanic: Gender and Sexuality in Spanish and Spanish American Literature*. Oxford: Clarendon Press, 1989.

Soskice, Janet Martin. *Metaphor and Religious Language*. Oxford: Oxford University Press, 1985.

Sykes, S. W. "Theology through History." In David F. Ford, ed., *The Modern Theologians*, 2d ed., pp. 229–51. Oxford: Blackwell, 1997.

Taylor, Mark C. *Journeys to Selfhood: Hegel and Kierkegaard*. Berkeley: University of California Press, 1980.

————. *Deconstructing Theology*. Atlanta: Scholars Press, 1982.

————. *Erring: A Postmodern A/Theology*. Chicago: University of Chicago Press, 1984.

————. *Altarity*. Chicago: University of Chicago Press, 1987.

————. *Disfiguring: Art, Architecture, Religion*. Chicago: University of Chicago Press, 1992.

————. *Nots*. Chicago: University of Chicago Press, 1993.

————. "Postmodern Times." In Orrin F. Summerell, ed., *The Otherness of God*, pp. 173–89. Charlottesville: University Press of Virginia, 1998.

————. "Retracings." In Jon R. Stone, ed., *The Craft of Religious Studies*, pp. 258–76. Basingstoke: Macmillan, 1998.

————. *About Religion: Economies of Faith in Virtual Culture*. Chicago: University of Chicago Press, 1999.

————, ed. *Critical Terms for Religious Studies*. Chicago: University of Chicago Press, 1998.

————, ed. *Deconstruction in Context: Literature and Philosophy*. Chicago: University of Chicago Press, 1986.

Torchia, N. Joseph. *Creatio ex nihilo and the Theology of St. Augustine: The Anti-Manichaean Polemic and Beyond*. New York: Peter Lang, 1999.

Toulmin, Stephen. *Cosmopolis: The Hidden Agenda of Modernity*. Chicago: University of Chicago Press, 1990.

Turgenev, Ivan. *Fathers and Sons*. Translated by Richard Freeborn. Oxford: Oxford University Press, 1991.

Turner, Denys. "Cupitt, the Mystics and the 'Objectivity' of God." In Colin Crowder, ed., *God and Reality: Essays on Christian Non-Realism*, pp. 114–27. London: Mowbray, 1997.

Vattimo, Gianni. "Nietzsche and Contemporary Hermeneutics." In Yirmiyahu Yovel, ed., *Nietzsche as Affirmative Thinker*, pp. 58–68. Dordrecht: Martinus Nijhoff, 1986.

———. *The End of Modernity: Nihilism and Hermeneutics in Post-Modern Culture*. Translated by Jon R. Snyder. Cambridge: Polity Press, 1988.

———. "The Trace of the Trace." In Jacques Derrida and Gianni Vattimo, eds., *Religion*, pp. 79–94. Cambridge: Polity Press, 1998.

Venturi, Robert, Denise Scott Brown, and Stephen Izenour. *Learning from Las Vegas*. Cambridge, Mass.: MIT Press, 1972.

Ward, Graham. "John Milbank's Divina Commedia." *New Blackfriars* 73 (1992): 311–18.

———. *Barth, Derrida and the Language of Theology*. Cambridge: Cambridge University Press, 1995.

———. "The Voice of the Other." *New Blackfriars* 77 (1996): 518–28.

———. "Postmodern Theology." In David F. Ford, ed., *The Modern Theologians*, pp. 585–601. 2d ed. Oxford: Blackwell, 1997.

———. "Theology and Postmodernism." *Theology* 100 (1997): 435–40.

———. "Karl Barth's Postmodernism." *Zeitschrift für dialektische Theologie* 14 (1998): 32–51.

———. "Michel de Certeau's 'Spiritual Spaces.'" *New Blackfriars* 79 (1998): 428–42.

———. "Radical Orthodoxy and/as Cultural Politics." In Laurence Paul Hemming, ed., *Radical Orthodoxy?—A Catholic Enquiry*, pp. 97–111. Aldershot: Ashgate, 2000.

———. *Theology and Contemporary Critical Theory*. 2d ed. London: Macmillan, 2000.

———. "Review Essay: Religionists and Theologians: Toward a Politics of Difference." *Modern Theology* 16 (2000): 541–47.

———, ed. *The Postmodern God: A Theological Reader*. Oxford: Blackwell, 1997.

———, ed. *The Certeau Reader*. Oxford: Blackwell, 2000.

White, Stephen Ross. *Don Cupitt and the Future of Christian Doctrine*. London: SCM Press, 1994.

Williams, Rowan. "'Religious Realism': On Not Quite Agreeing with Don Cupitt." *Modern Theology* 1 (1984): 3–24.

———. "Foreword." In Colin Crowder, ed., *God and Reality: Essays on Christian Non-Realism*, pp. v–ix. London: Mowbray, 1997.

Wittgenstein, Ludwig. *On Certainty*. Edited by G. E. M. Anscombe and G. H. von Wright. Translated by Denis Paul and G. E. M. Anscombe. Oxford: Basil Blackwell, 1969.

———. *Lectures and Conversations on Aesthetics, Psychology and Religious Belief*. Edited by Cyril Barrett. Oxford: Basil Blackwell, 1969.

———. *Philosophical Remarks*. Translated by Raymond Hargreaves and Roger White. Oxford: Basil Blackwell, 1975.

———. *Remarks on the Foundations of Mathematics*. Edited by G. H. von Wright, R. Rhees, and G. E. M. Anscombe. Translated by G. E. M. Anscombe. Oxford: Basil Blackwell, 1978.

Index